Empowering Negotiators

Empowering Negotiators

Bargaining Successfully Using the TABLE Method

SECOND EDITION

Lynn A. Epstein
PROFESSOR EMERITA OF LAW
NOVA SOUTHEASTERN UNIVERSITY
COLLEGE OF LAW

Elena Maria Marty-Nelson
PROFESSOR OF LAW
NOVA SOUTHEASTERN UNIVERSITY
COLLEGE OF LAW

CAROLINA ACADEMIC PRESS
Durham, North Carolina

Library of Congress Cataloging-in-Publication Data is
available at https://www.loc.gov

ISBN 978-1-5310-2488-8
eISBN 978-1-5310-2489-5

CAROLINA ACADEMIC PRESS
700 Kent Street
Durham, North Carolina 27701
(919) 489-7486
www.cap-press.com

Printed in the United States of America

Contents

Preface and Acknowledgments **xi**

Chapter 1 | Introduction 3

New Developments in Negotiation Practice 3

Expanded Role-Playing Scenarios 4

Preparing Future Attorneys 4

The TABLE Method 5

Authors' Notes on the Exercises and Problems 6

PART I

The TABLE Method

Chapter 2 | Tactical Planning 11

Step 1: Identifying the Relationship 12

Arms-Length, Arms-Open 12

Balance of Power 14

Personality Styles 15

Step 2: Conducting Research 17

EXERCISE 2-1: Conducting Research 19

Step 3: Setting An Optimal Realistic Goal and Determining a Minimum Acceptable Level 19

EXERCISES 2-2 and 2-3: Setting Goals 22

Step 4: Formulating Alternative Options If Negotiations Fail 23

EXERCISE 2-4: Formulating Alternative Options 23

Step 5: Preparing Opening Offers, Concessions, and Counteroffers 24

EXERCISE 2-5: Preparing Opening Offers, Concessions, and Counteroffers Exercise 27

Step 6: Devising Questions and Preparing Responses to Anticipated Questions 28

EXERCISES 2-6, 2-7, 2-8, and 2-9: Devising Questions and Preparing Responses to Anticipated Questions 31

Chapter 3 | Arranging the Negotiation 33

Various Platforms for Negotiations 34

In-Person 34

Phone Negotiations 35

Email Negotiations 36

Videoconferencing 37

Text Messaging 39

EXERCISE 3-1: Text Message 41

Choosing the Initial Platform for Negotiating 42

EXERCISES 3-2, 3-3, and 3-4: Choosing the Initial Platform for Negotiating 42

Chapter 4 | Bargaining 45

Ice-Breaking 45

Offers, Counteroffers, and Concessions 47

Communicating Objective Criteria behind Offers and Counteroffers 49

EXERCISES 4-1 and 4-2: Offers, Counteroffers, and Concessions 52

Questions 53

Bargaining Tactics 56

Chapter 5 | Letting Go or Resolving 61

Letting Go or Resolving 61

Time Constraints 62

Assess Your Progress 62

Examining Your Alternative Options 64

Splitting the Difference to Reach Agreement 64

Scheduling Another Negotiating Session 66

Executing the Agreement 67

Drafting the Agreement 69

EXERCISE 5-1: Executing the Agreement 70

Chapter 6 | Ethics & Equity 71
Ethics 72
Why Do Negotiators Lie? 72
Types of Lies 73
Consequences of Lying 74
Uncovering Lies during Negotiations 75
Inconsistent Statements 76
Saying No 76
Changes in Behavior 76
Truth Emphasizers 77
Physical Signs 77
Responses to Lying 77
EXERCISES 6-1 and 6-2: Ethics 78
Equity 80
Awareness 83
Mindfulness Meditation 83
Preparation 83
Mentors and Social Networks 84
Activate Egalitarian Goals 84

PART II

Applying the TABLE Method

Chapter 7 | Negotiating Business Relationships 87
Instructions 88
Laws Relevant to Salary Offers 89
Federal Laws Relevant to Salary Offers 89
State and Local Laws Relevant to Salary Offers 90
Strategies for Employers Negotiations of Salary 92
Strategies for Employees Negotiations of Salary 95
PROBLEM 7-1: Salary 97
Laws Relevant to Non-Disclosure Agreements 101
Federal Laws Relevant to Trade Secrets 101
Enforceability of NDAs 102
PROBLEM 7-2: Non-Disclosure Agreement 103

Laws Relevant to Small Business Acquisitions 107

PROBLEM 7-3: Acquiring a Small Bakery Business 109

Laws Relevant to Homeowners' Associations 112

PROBLEM 7-4: Homeowners' Association 115

Chapter 8 | Negotiating Family Relationships 119

Instructions 120

Laws Relevant to Prenuptial Agreements 121

Overview of Different Default Legal Systems Absent a Prenup 122

Common Law States and Community Property States 122

Common Law States 123

Common Law States—Equitable Distribution upon Divorce 123

Common Law States—Surviving Spouse's Rights upon Death 125

Community Property States 126

Community Property States—Division of Property on Divorce 127

Death—Community Property States 127

Moving from Community Property States to Common Law States 127

Moving from Common Law States to Community Property States 128

Other Issues Involving Community Property 128

Alimony and Spousal Support in Common Law and Community Property States 130

Prenuptial Agreements 130

Enforceability of Prenuptial Agreements 130

Benefits of Prenuptial Agreements 131

Standard Coverage of a Prenup 134

Other Provisions in a Prenuptial Agreement 135

Lifestyle Provisions in Prenuptial Agreements 135

Caution on Lifestyle Provisions 138

Attorney's Fees in Prenuptial 138

Mediation or Arbitration Provisions 138

Sunset and Escalator Provisions 139

Companion Documents 140

Trust Created by Fiancé 140

Wills, Health Care Proxies, and Durable Powers of Attorney 141

PROBLEM 8-1: Prenuptial Agreements 142

PROBLEM 8-2 and 8-3: Prenuptial Agreements 146

Laws Relevant to Testamentary Capacity and Undue Influence 151
Testamentary Capacity 152
Undue Influence 152
Revocation 154
PROBLEM 8-4: Testamentary Capacity and Undue Influence 155
PROBLEM 8-5: Testamentary Capacity and Undue Influence, Multi-party 157
Exhibit 8-A: Fictional No-Prenup Martial Contract 160
Exhibit 8-B: Sample Prenuptial Agreement 162

Chapter 9 | Negotiating Additional Practice Problems **181**
Instructions 181
Laws Relevant to Dog Bites 182
PROBLEM 9-1: Dog Bite 184
Laws Relevant to Security Deposit Disputes 187
Maximum-Security Deposit Permitted by Law 187
Charges Landlord May Claim Against the Security Deposit 188
Time Frame for Landlord to Return Deposit or Provide Accounting to Tenant 188
Requirement of a Walk-through Inspection of Apartment Prior to Tenant Vacating 189
Landlord Placing Security Deposit in a Separate and/or Interest-Bearing Account 189
PROBLEM 9-2: Security Deposit 190
Laws Relevant to Plea Bargaining and Embezzlement 193
Plea Bargaining 194
Embezzlement 195
PROBLEM 9-3: Plea Bargaining in an Embezzlement Case 196

Chapter 10 | Conclusion 199

APPENDICES

Appendix A | Tactical Planning Worksheet **203**
Appendix A-1 | Multi-party Tactical Planning Worksheet **205**
Appendix B | Post-Negotiation Self-Reflection Worksheet **207**

Notes **209**
Index **223**

Preface and Acknowledgments

Our goals for this second edition of the book are described in Chapter 1, the Introduction. This preface is instead our opportunity to thank and acknowledge those who have contributed their wisdom, time, humor, and guidance to this project.

General Acknowledgments

We wish to acknowledge with appreciation the following authors and publishers, who have graciously granted us permission to reprint excerpts from their publication.

> Rutkin, Oldham, & Hogan, § 50:57. Sample Prenuptial Agreement 8A Conn. Prac., Family Law & Prac. § 50:57 (3d ed.) Westlaw, Reprinted by Permission of Thomson Reuters, all rights reserved.

We continue to be grateful to Samantha Gozlan for the excellent research assistance we received on the first edition of the book. We also continue to recognize the wonderful illustrations by Christopher J. Carter.

For this second edition we want to acknowledge with gratitude the professors who adopted our book and who have generously shared their thoughts with us. We are particularly grateful to Kamilah Clark, Dean of Students, Nova Southeastern University College of Law, for her invaluable insights from teaching from the book and her contributions to this second edition.

Our thanks also to our many students over the years not only in our negotiation courses, but also in courses as varied as evidence, professional responsibility, torts, federal securities regulations, income tax, property, international tax, wills, and trusts. Our students' insights, questions, and enthusiastic participation have greatly enhanced our teaching in this complex and fascinating world of negotiations.

Personal Acknowledgments

Lynn A. Epstein

To my husband, David Weiss, the best negotiator I know. Thank you for your guidance and optimism; my love and admiration always. To my son, Alex, thanks for your support and for being my millennial consultant. Love you lots.

Elena Maria Marty-Nelson

I appreciate and thank my brilliant husband, David Nelson, an exceptionally skilled attorney and negotiator. I am also grateful to my sons, Scott and Matt, for their encouragement and wit. Finally, I thank my inspiring mother, Judy Marty, who continues to teach, lead, and negotiate.

Empowering Negotiators

CHAPTER 1

Introduction

Negotiations are an integral part of our personal and professional lives. Parties engage in negotiations to resolve conflicts, reach compromises, and achieve objectives. These negotiations may involve couples, families, business associates, friends, or strangers. They could take place in various settings, including by text, phone, online, or in conference rooms, courtrooms, or living rooms. Due to their ubiquitous nature, negotiation skills are considered essential for both personal fulfillment and professional success. Negotiations can impact a person's professional life—including salary, working arrangements, and business opportunities—as well as their personal life, such as relationships with future spouses, friends, or family. They also play a pivotal role in major life events like buying or selling a home. Negotiations, on behalf of others, such as an attorney negotiating on behalf of her client, may encompass a range of personal and professional issues. For example, an attorney may negotiate the client's prenuptial agreement or the client's purchase of a business.

New Developments in Negotiation Practice

This second edition of the book builds upon the foundation of negotiation principles established in the first edition while addressing significant developments that have transformed the practice of negotiation including the prevalence of virtual negotiations and the use of generative artificial intelligence (AI) tools to assist in preparing for negotiations. The COVID-19 pandemic profoundly affected how attorneys conduct negotiations. With in-person meetings often impossible during lockdowns, platforms such as Zoom became prevalent for conducting negotiations remotely. This shift introduced both benefits and drawbacks to post-pandemic negotiation forums as discussed in Chapter 3. On the one hand, virtual negotiations offer convenience and accessibility; on the other hand, they may hinder rapport-building and nuanced communication that are often critical to successful outcomes.

Another emerging trend covered in this edition is the use of AI tools to assist attorneys in researching and planning for negotiations. AI tools can streamline preparation by analyzing legal precedents, business customs and practices, identifying negotiation strategies, and providing data-driven insights. While these technologies enhance efficiency and decision-making, they also raise ethical considerations and challenges that negotiators must address.

Expanded Role-Playing Scenarios

This second edition also expands on the previous edition by introducing new role-playing negotiation problems in additional subject areas including negotiations involving homeowners' associations, plea bargaining in criminal cases, and business acquisitions. It also includes numerous multi-party negotiations. The inclusion of plea bargaining simulations in criminal cases provides valuable insights into a crucial aspect of the legal system. Plea bargaining is the practice of negotiating an agreement between the prosecution and the defense in a criminal matter. Plea bargaining draws parallels to negotiations in civil contexts, as both involve strategic decision-making, risk assessment, and the balancing of competing interests.

The multi-party scenarios add complexity to the negotiation process, as they require participants to consider multiple perspectives, manage diverse interests, and find creative solutions that satisfy various parties. A multi-party negotiation involves three or more parties working to resolve conflicting interests, where each party has distinct goals and priorities. Unlike two-party negotiations, which focus on balancing two perspectives, multi-party scenarios require managing a multitude of relationships, information, and power dynamics. The biggest difference between a multi-party and a two-party negotiation lies in the formation of alliances. In two-party negotiations, you only need to respond to your opponent's demands, but with multiple parties, alliances between two or more parties will complicate and may shift bargaining power. For example, weaker parties might team up to counter a dominant party, but these alliances can shift suddenly, forcing constant strategy adjustments. Sharing information also becomes riskier as confidential details disclosed to one party might leak to others, especially if competitors are involved. With more voices at the table, simply tracking everyone's priorities, let alone reconciling them, becomes a major challenge. In a multi-party negotiation, to reach a settlement, multiple separate agreements may be required, which slows progress and risks unsatisfying compromises. In contrast, two-party negotiations can focus on mutual concessions, while multi-party negotiations often require multiple creative solutions that try and offer something valuable to each party, even if the outcome is below what was expected or desired for a party.

Preparing Future Attorneys

For law students learning negotiation skills, this second edition continues the goal of preparing them for real-world scenarios through class simulations and problem-solving exercises before they become practicing attorneys. This approach aligns with the Next Generation Bar Exam (Next Gen Bar), which now includes testing on negotiation concepts to ensure that future attorneys are equipped with these critical skills. By incorporating role-playing problems and addressing modern challenges in negotiation, this book offers readers a more comprehensive understanding of negotiation dynamics across different legal settings, preparing them for the various challenges they may encounter in their professional careers.

The TABLE Method

As in the first edition of this book, the TABLE method remains central to this book's framework for teaching negotiations. The TABLE method develops effective negotiation skills that will minimize conflicts and streamline resolutions. The TABLE method is a five-stage process:

> ***Tactical Planning:*** Planning for the negotiation is a critical, but often overlooked, pre-negotiation stage. Planning is facilitated through the use of a Tactical Planning Worksheet, which is included in the materials as Appendix A. The T serves as a reminder that without the T in tactical planning, one may be ABLE but not TABLE ready to negotiate.
>
> ***Arranging the Negotiation:*** Traditional negotiations usually occurred in person in an office conference room setting. However, with the ubiquity of technology and our on-the-run lifestyles, negotiations may take place at any time and location. For example, parties may be thousands of miles apart and choose to negotiate by Zoom or other videoconferencing platforms, by email, phone, or even by text messaging. The A in TABLE focuses on choosing from among the vast array of negotiation forums to begin or continue a negotiation session. Chapter 3 explores both the positive and negative aspects of the various settings that may be used for a negotiation.
>
> ***Bargaining:*** Bargaining is the meat of any negotiation and appropriately the B is centered in TABLE as the main course. As negotiators would say, "this is what we came for." Chapter 4 breaks down the bargaining process and focuses on offers, counteroffers, and concessions. It also provides insight into certain tricks and tactics negotiators should be aware of and includes suggestions for appropriate responses.
>
> ***Letting Go or Resolving:*** The bargaining phase ends in one of two ways: resolving the issues or reaching an impasse. Although at first blush these two opposite results hardly seem to warrant a chapter, the manner in which a negotiation concludes affects not only the current negotiation but also may impact the future relationship between the parties. The L in TABLE discusses when and how to determine if it is time to let go of either the particular negotiation session or, more drastically, the entire negotiation process, or to continue to try to resolve the matter. Chapter 5 also discusses

when parties reach a resolution and the steps that they should take to ensure the agreement accurately reflects the parties' understanding. The transition from a handshake at the end of a negotiation to a signed agreement is fraught with missteps. This chapter guides the reader through that process.

Ethics and Equity: Throughout a negotiation session, negotiators should expect honesty and fairness from their fellow negotiators. The E in table is a reminder that effective negotiators must embrace ethical behavior, and that bias and discrimination have no place at the table. Despite these aspirational goals, realistically, unethical behavior will occur in some negotiations. Chapter 6 focuses on recognizing this type of behavior and discusses some responses.

Once empowered with the TABLE method described in Chapters 2–6, Chapters 7–9 provide opportunities for practicing the method in a variety of scenarios by introducing fundamental legal principles to use with numerous negotiating problems. Combining the TABLE method with legal principles is a unique feature of this book and provides a realistic approach to developing effective negotiating skills, as researching and recognizing the law is integral to the negotiation process.

A word of caution is in order regarding the laws referenced in this book. This book is designed to teach negotiations skills. It is not intended as a primer in any specific area of the law nor intended to provide legal advice. Rather, general legal principles in certain areas of the law are introduced to emphasize the importance of examining and understanding the law when negotiating. Although this book describes general legal requirements for some states, the statutes and cases cited are subject to revision and local rules may somewhat vary the analysis.

Authors' Notes on the Exercises and Problems

Mastering a skill, such as negotiating, requires many hours of practice. Throughout the book, we have provided numerous exercises and problems for you to practice your negotiating skills before you arrive at an actual negotiation table. We distinguish between exercises and problems for specific reasons. In Chapters 2–6, we introduce and explain the TABLE method, and provide exercises to reinforce the various components of the method. These exercises should be completed after you have read the portion of the book to which the exercise is directed. Minimal preparation is needed for these exercises, and most of them can be completed in five to ten minutes.

Chapters 7–9 provide full-length negotiation problems centered on the specific events addressed in each of the respective chapters. After you read the legal principles in each chapter, you are given the general information of the problem, which consists of the basic facts of the negotiation. All negotiating parties will know the general information. You should consider that the facts in the general information presented are accurate and true.

Following the general information, you are given the structure for developing confidential information. Confidential information means what it says. It is information that is known to one side only and is not meant to be shared initially with other parties to the negotiation. Typically, in order to preserve the confidentiality of that information, negotiation books will separate confidential information from the general information by placing the confidential information in the back of the chapter or leaving a blank page and separating the confidential information in that way. However, we know that some readers just cannot help themselves and will read confidential information that is intended only for the other side. Once they know that confidential information, the negotiation problem is tainted and loses its realism. While we would hope our readers would not succumb to temptation, especially after reading the Ethics section of this book, we did not want to offer that temptation. Therefore, the confidential information in our problems is given in a different format. We refer to the confidential information as bargaining positions. In essence, we permit you to create your own confidential information within the parameters of the problem. We pose questions to you in which your answers become your confidential information. For example, when you are asked to state your bargaining position as to the maximum amount you are willing to offer to settle the matter, if you decide your bottom line is $10,000, that amount is your confidential information and included on your Tactical Planning Worksheet. How do we know that you will not "change your mind" in the middle of the negotiation and come up with different bottom line than was reflected as confidential information in your worksheet? At the end of each negotiation session, you will be asked to exchange planning worksheets with the other side. This exchange not only allows you to see the planning process undertaken by the other side, but also is a check on the accuracy of your confidential information. Obviously, what was written as confidential before the negotiation must remain part of your confidential information (and worksheet). Furthermore, while you are permitted to reveal confidential information during the negotiation as needed, you may not change confidential information. By presenting the problems in this manner, we hope for a more realistic negotiation experience.

Many of the problems in Chapters 7–9 are self-contained. You will be able to practice several complete negotiations, using the TABLE method, by referencing the legal principles given in each chapter. These chapters also contain several problems where you will be asked to conduct legal research to discover the applicable law. For both formats, however, there are many ways to expand on the problems. For example, in a classroom, you may be asked to conduct more extensive research geared to other jurisdictions. Also, the facts of each problem can be modified. Further, in a classroom, confidential information could be dispersed in a more traditional format, such as by the instructor distributing copies of confidential information to each side. We are confident that either way, the problems in Chapters 7–9 provide many opportunities to practice negotiating skills.

This second edition aims to empower negotiators by equipping them with updated tools and insights to negotiate and resolve realistic life problems effectively, whether for themselves or on behalf of others. Practicing the TABLE method helps develop confidence in your negotiating skills. After reading this book, you will be ready to sit confidently at the head of the table in all your negotiations.

PART I

The TABLE Method

CHAPTER 2

Tactical Planning

Just Winging It

Planning for a negotiation may be extensive or may be limited but having a negotiating plan is critical. Negotiators should proceed with a six-step planning process to achieve their goals. The six-step tactical planning process requires: (1) identifying the relationship; (2) conducting research; (3) setting an optimal realistic goal and determining a minimum acceptable level; (4) formulating alternative options; (5) devising questions and responses to anticipated questions; and (6) preparing opening offers, concessions, and counteroffers. The time dedicated to each of the six steps will vary depending on the particular negotiation. Moreover, the actual number of steps is semantics, with lists with fewer steps generally combining several tactical steps into more general categories and lists with more steps elevating subgroups into full-blown steps. Moreover, as discussed in Chapter 4 on Bargaining, once the negotiations are underway, additional adjustments may be necessary. There is a constant, however. Preparation is key and completing a planning worksheet (see Tactical Planning Worksheet in Appendix A) prior to negotiating can lead to more successful negotiations. This planning process is the beginning of an adventure and an opportunity to develop your bargaining position.

Step 1: Identifying the Relationship

Your initial step in preparing for an upcoming negotiation is to identify the relationships involved. This brief moment, which includes honest self-reflection, can help to provide necessary perspective. It is an invitation to consider the bigger picture in light of the relationships and personalities involved. This self-reflection moment is an important initial step in the planning process. It can often be completed quickly but should not be overlooked. Identifying the relationship includes determining whether the upcoming negotiation is arms-length or arms-open, understanding the balance of power, and assessing personality styles.

Arms-Length, Arms-Open

Negotiations generally involve two distinctive relationship types. An arms-length negotiation presumes the parties are independent and unrelated and involve parties with no prior or continuing relationship. For example, a buyer negotiating a contract for the purchase of a house from a stranger may be willing to walk away from the table if the offer is not desirable. If the parties come to an agreement, the title to the house will transfer, and they are likely never to meet again.

By contrast, an arms-open negotiation involves dependent or related parties such as family members or business partners who know each other. An arms-open negotiation requires protecting that relationship as a goal. Since the parties have a prior relationship, each side must determine if they want to risk that relationship through negotiations. For example, assume a father rents a room in his house to his son for $500 a month. If the son stops paying the rent, the father must decide if he is going to demand the payment or have the son move out, negotiate alternative terms, or simply forgo asking for the rent. By demanding payment or negotiating alternative plans, the father runs the risk of ruining the relationship. However, if the father needs the income from the room and has given up the opportunity of leasing it to a third party, the father may negotiate, even if the process puts the relationship at risk.

Finally, there are situations where one type of relationship could transition from arms-open to arms-length or vice versa. For example, family members who had an arms-open relationship may transition to an arms-length relationship when involved in an intra-family will contest. This type of negotiation is particularly difficult. The parties were initially connected, and therefore the parties may have emotional reservations about negotiating. Further, the family members may be unclear as to whether they want their relationships ultimately to end up with the parties together or separate. Conversely, a relationship may start as an arms-length relationship and transition into an arms-open relationship. For example, assume two neighbors who had not previously met, have a confrontation about one neighbor's loud music at night, which is disturbing the other's sleep. After several repeated incidents, the loud playing music neighbor takes the initiative and invites his sleep-deprived neighbor to his next party. The sleep-deprived neighbor attends the party, and the neighbors begin to discuss compromises so they can live in harmony. Subsequently, they become social friends, not just neighbors, and now have an arms-open relationship if, and when, they need to negotiate any future disputes that arise.

In order to determine if a particular negotiation is arms-open or arms-length, you should answer the following questions:

1. Do you have personal knowledge of the other side that is helpful in planning the negotiation?

   Yes ___ (arms-open) No ___ (arms-length)

2. Do you want a continuing relationship with the other side once the negotiation has concluded?

   Yes ___ (arms-open) No ___ (arms-length)

It is important to consider these questions carefully. For example, assume you are planning to negotiate a prenuptial agreement with your fiancé. In this case, both questions would hopefully result in a "yes" answer and the relationship would be clearly characterized as arms-open. In other words, presumably before contemplating marriage, you have acquired significant personal knowledge of your spouse-to-be and you also want the relationship to last "till death do you part." In identifying the relationship as arms-open, you are including your insights into your fiancé's negotiating style and interests in your planning, while, at the same time, being mindful that one of the goals of the negotiation is to preserve the relationship. Moreover, because this is an arms-open relationship, you may be willing to make more concessions, make fewer demands, and negotiate more openly than in a different type of negotiation.

By contrast, assume you were involved in a car accident with a stranger. Since you have no prior knowledge of the stranger and do not want the relationship to continue, your answer to both questions would be "no," and the relationship is properly characterized as arms-length. In identifying this relationship as arms-length, since you do not have insights into the other side's negotiating style or interests, you will need to focus carefully on your own negotiating style so that you are ready to respond to their unknown style. Moreover, because this is arms-length and you are not interested in continuing the relationship, you may plan to make fewer concessions and may even make higher demands than you would in an arms-open relationship.

Sometimes the answers to the two fundamental questions are not self-evident. Also, as mentioned above, a relationship may transition from one type to the other. For example, assume you are casually acquainted with a competitor in your area of business and are now contemplating buying his business. Since he is only an acquaintance, you may not have sufficient knowledge about his negotiating style or interests to be helpful in planning the negotiation. Thus, your answer to the first question of personal knowledge would be "no." However, your answer to the second question of whether you want a continuing relationship might not be a simple "yes" or "no" and may actually be a "maybe." In this example, even though you have no personal knowledge about the business owner prior to the negotiations, you recognize that you might want the relationship to continue in some form, such as keeping the original owner working for the business for a couple of years as a consultant after you acquire the business. In this case, this relationship is more properly identified as arms-length, which may transition to arms-open. In planning this type of negotiation, you have to be particularly flexible in your bargaining positions. You may plan on making more or fewer concessions depending on how the relationship develops during the negotiations.

Balance of Power

Parties rarely have equal power in negotiations. Usually, one party has more to lose or more to gain than the other party. Sometimes one party holds all the power and has no incentive to negotiate. For example, assume a Hollywood producer is auditioning actors for a walk-on role in a new television series. The producer may have auditioned hundreds of actors, all eager to get the nod. When he finally selects the actor for the role, there may not be a need for a salary negotiation at all. The actor is so thrilled to have received the part that the producer may, in fact, be able to say, "this role pays $50, take it or leave it!" If the actor tries to negotiate a higher fee, there are a few hundred other actors waiting in line, ready to take the role. In this example, the producer has all the power. The actor in effect has no power. This power struggle is not just limited to Hollywood but may occur in everyday negotiations. For example, assume Ava is the hiring partner at a law firm. The job market is full of promising young attorneys with outstanding resumes for associate positions. Ava has narrowed her search to three candidates. Ava and her partners have set a very lucrative starting salary, aligned with starting salaries at similar firms. If the final candidates want to negotiate a higher salary, will Ava engage in that discussion? Probably not. The risk of losing one of these candidates may not justify paying a higher salary. If Ava can hire a great associate for the standard salary, she would likely forgo the negotiation. She holds all the cards.

In the above examples, one party may be like the character Oz from the classic movie, the Wizard of Oz. In that film, Oz's voice emanated from behind a curtain, and his demanding and stern voice made him appear as all-powerful. However, once the curtain was removed and Oz appeared in person, he appeared quite vulnerable. At this point, Dorothy and her crew could "negotiate their demands." As in the Wizard of Oz, if a party cannot get behind the curtain in dealing with an all-powerful person, the all-powerful person will dictate, not negotiate, the terms of the agreement. However, if a party can get behind the curtain, they may acquire negotiating power. For example, remember the actor with no negotiating power. Now assume that actor's research had uncovered that the Hollywood producer wants a certain A-list actor to star in his feature film and that A-list actor will be unavailable. If the non-A list actor, or his agent armed with this knowledge, can convince the producer of his unique acting "similarities" to the A-list actor, he may gain some negotiating power. The producer still retains more power since, after all, there is no film without his decision. Now, however, there is an opportunity for a negotiation. Both parties have something to gain, as well as something to lose. The producer may lose his best substitute for the A-list actor, and the non-A-list actor may lose the opportunity to get his big break!

If the parties are willing to negotiate initially, the power may be more balanced. Keep in mind that if you are negotiating with someone who has more power than you, he is likely to negotiate less and demand more. Therefore, in planning the negotiation, you should make an initial determination as to your relative power, as this determination will allow you to plan the limitations and expectations of your negotiation strategy. Remember that determining this initial relative power encompasses many of the other tactical planning steps, including conducting research and formulating options, as discussed below. Furthermore, even if you start the negotiations with less bargaining power, you may be able to increase your power during the course of the negotiations as information is exchanged and concessions are made. Recall the example above involving the hiring of a new associate for a law firm. Assume Ava offered the job to Brett for the standard salary. Brett attempts to negotiate a higher starting salary. Ava initially suggests she will not negotiate the salary and that the salary is fair because it is the going rate. In response to Ava's position, Brett informs her that he is more qualified for the job and deserves a higher salary than the standard set salary because he will be able to bring to the firm several corporate clients based on his connections. By providing this information to Ava, Brett has not only distinguished himself from other job applicants but has also moved towards equalizing the power in this negotiation.

Personality Styles

Once you have examined the initial balance of power, it is important to determine the personality styles of those involved in the negotiations. People tend to overestimate or underestimate their negotiating abilities, based on their successes and failures over the years in negotiating life events. Negotiation experience develops early in life. It includes negotiating allowance money from parents; negotiating which restaurant to go to with friends; and negotiating with a spouse over who is going to walk the dog after work. Even if none of these negotiations involved formal negotiating sessions, people have developed a personality style as to how they negotiate. Nevertheless, they may not have thought much about their negotiating personality and more importantly, whether it can or should be improved. While they may have been told that they are a tough negotiator or a pushover, these terms are better described as competitive or cooperative. Professor Charles B. Craver, a renowned expert in negotiations, in discussing different negotiating styles, notes that "[m]ost negotiators tend to exhibit a relatively "cooperative" or relatively "competitive" style."[1] The chart on the next page describes some of the typical characteristics of these negotiating personality types.[2]

Competitive Negotiator	Cooperative Negotiator
Appears confident, often to the point of being boastful	Appears open and trusting
Appears experienced, often highlighting the actual or perceived inexperience of the other side	Does not boast about their experience or highlight the other side's inexperience
Makes high, often unreasonable offers and demands	Makes reasonable, sometimes too conciliatory demands
Takes an aggressive posture, often with threats	Takes a collegial posture, rarely uses threats
Tries to maximize their position by working against the other side	Tries to maximize their position by working with the other side

While some individuals are consistently competitive, and others are consistently cooperative, most negotiators develop characteristics of both styles. In fact, Professor Charles B. Craver maintains that "[m]ost successful negotiators are able to combine the most salient traits associated with the cooperative/problem solving and the competitive/adversarial styles."[3]

In planning a negotiation, you should first determine your own personality style as to whether you are more cooperative or competitive. Figuring out your own negotiating personality style may not be particularly difficult as long as you are willing to assess your style honestly based on your prior negotiating history and you are willing to listen to outside assessments of your style.

The next step in personality analysis is slightly more difficult. In fact, it may be quite difficult to determine the personality style of the other side. In an arms-open negotiation, that task may be easier in that you are familiar with and have some insights into the other side's personality. In an arms-length negotiation, however, you may have no insight into the other side's personality at all. Research may help. For example, you may seek out other persons who have negotiated with the other side in other deals. Your research may uncover that your negotiating opponent has a reputation as a competitive negotiator. This research must be evaluated carefully to ensure it is reliable and that others' assessments as to what is competitive conform to your definition of competitive.

Recognizing personality styles of the negotiating parties is particularly important during bargaining, especially if the styles differ greatly. For example, if the negotiating opponent tends to be the competitive type, a cooperative negotiator may want to try to adjust his cooperative tendencies in order to stay in the game and not get bowled over by his opponent's extreme demands and competitive behaviors. Cooperative negotiators tend to adopt an integrative bargaining style. Generally, integrative bargaining is a collaborative approach, where the parties to a negotiation seek solutions that will benefit all parties. The object of the negotiators in integrative bargaining is to increase the total payoff through cooperation—a win-win situation. In an integrative negotiation, parties need to identify and understand their mutual problems, communicate their interests, offer several possible solutions, and then choose a solution that will benefit both parties. To accomplish this result, the parties must avoid interpersonal conflict; thus, communications are usually more inviting and cooperative. In contrast, distributive bargaining is a more competitive and adversarial approach, where each party attempts to maximize their own interests regardless of the other side's loss. This distributive negotiation strategy is often used when distributing or dividing a finite amount of resources such as money, assets, etc. between the parties. The goal under a distributive approach is not a win-win situation, but that one side win as much as possible. In a distributive negotiation, each party is guided mainly by his or her expectations of what the other will accept. In turn, parties usually try to obtain as much information as possible from the other side while at the same time trying to disclose as little information as possible about their own real interests.[4] Adjusting to differing negotiation styles is more fully discussed in Chapter 4 on Bargaining.

Step 2: Conducting Research

After this self-reflection moment, it is time to proceed to step two of the tactical planning process. Tactical negotiation planning requires research. In their well-known negotiation book, the authors Roger Fisher and William Ury, suggest that effective negotiators should find objective criteria to support their negotiation goals and positions.[5] The term objective criteria is sometimes referred to as standards or simply sources of legitimacy. Another way to think about this is to recognize that research is necessary to determine if goals are realistic. The research involved in finding objective criteria often includes discerning the significant facts and determining the applicable law. There are often other sources of objective criteria. For example, when a homeowner is planning on selling her house, comparable sales in the neighborhood within a relevant period of time may serve as objective criteria. In a litigation example, assume Dylan is seeking $10,000 for injuries caused by a fall on a supermarket's floor that he claims was wet. Dylan will need to support his claim with relevant proof of his related expenses such as medical bills. In addition, Dylan or his attorney would need to research and determine the applicable law related to a supermarket's liability for wet floors. Once this objective criterion is determined, Dylan is prepared to make demands with confidence because he has the law and facts to back up his offers. Moreover, research also requires becoming familiar with the norms and standards of the industry involved. For example, the standard percentage for licensed talent agents for union actors is 10%.[6] Research is not complete without factoring in these norms.

It is also important to make sure your objective criteria are truly objective, especially when researching online. With so many sources available online, it may be difficult to determine if the information you obtain from researching online is accurate or fake. In conducting research, follow some simple guidelines. First, investigate your sources. Look behind the information from the site and determine if it is a legitimate site; in essence research the site. Is it a recognized source such as a newspaper or periodical? Is it a post to a social media cite that does not have supporting information? Is the website created or sponsored by a group, individual or organization that is supporting a particular agenda? Second, do not be fooled or captured by the headlines. The headline may be a slanted or exaggerated description of the actual text of the piece. Moreover, the information may have popped up on the screen because your search terms were exactly what you wanted to find. While you might say of course "I searched for exactly what I wanted," there may be a drawback to only searching in this way. For example, if you are researching for the lowest price on a microwave, in addition to doing an internet search "What are the lowest prices on microwaves" you might also try "Compare prices on microwaves." The "lowest prices" search may give you advertisers who may be advertising a low price on a microwave as a marketing promotion for their other products. By contrast, a "compare prices" search may give you a price comparison site from independent sources that has recently researched and reviewed various models. Both search terms are useful but be aware of the sources of information. Third, check the date of the source. You may be surprised to find that what you think is current information may actually be dated. Always try and get the most current information to use as objective criteria.

Furthermore, artificial intelligence (AI) tools are often used to enhance research for negotiations. These tools are capable of analyzing vast amounts of data, including market trends, competitor pricing, and industry benchmarks, which can supplement the foundational research required for effective negotiations. Moreover, these AI tools can generate historical pattern recognition to analyze past transcripts, contracts, and emails. This analysis could help to reveal previously employed tactics and concessions, providing valuable insights into negotiation strategies. AI tools can be particularly advantageous in the context of business negotiations. For example, AI can compile SEC filings, news articles, and earnings calls to help identify the other party's financial pressures and strategic priorities.

Clearly, the more complex the transaction involved in the negotiations, the more research is needed. If, for example, the negotiations involve a possible merger of a company with a competitor, the research involved even in the planning stage would be extensive and multifaceted. In such complex negotiations, typically, the research planning requires the engagement of advisors to investigate legal, regulatory, and financial hurdles. These advisors would often be further deployed once negotiations were underway, for due diligence, valuation, and financial evaluation. Note that research, even in less complicated negotiations, may be adjusted during bargaining.

EXERCISE 2-1: CONDUCTING RESEARCH

Your local professional basketball team is playing this weekend, and your college roommate is flying into town. You want to surprise her with tickets. Research and find the best price for courtside seats and describe the results of your research. If no courtside seats are available, research the next best level of seats available. If basketball season is over, research another professional sports team. If you are in an area without a professional sports team or if your team's overwhelming losing record makes tickets too easy to obtain, try this exercise with other ticketed events such as a music concert or theater performance.

Step 3: Setting An Optimal Realistic Goal and Determining a Minimum Acceptable Level

The third step in tactical planning requires significant thought. Not only do you have to plan your optimal realistic goal, but you also need to formulate your minimum acceptable level. Your optimal realistic goal is the best outcome you hope to achieve in the negotiation.[7]

Your minimum acceptable level is the minimal outcome you would accept. This minimum acceptable level for the negotiation is often referred to as your reservation point. For example, in the case of a home sale, if the seller would not sell for less than $600,000 that is the seller's minimum acceptable level (*i.e.,* the lowest price the seller would be willing to accept). If you are negotiating on behalf of a third party, the minimum acceptable level is the lowest outcome the third party would be willing to accept.

Setting your optimal and your minimum levels allows for a range of acceptable outcomes between those two markers. This range is often referred to as ZOPA, which is an acronym for the zone of possible agreement. Depending on the particular negotiation, the range may be wide or quite narrow. In order to determine both your optimal realistic goal and your minimum acceptable level, you need to conduct research to support them with objective criteria as discussed in Step 2 above.

Having an optimum realistic goal leads to significantly better outcomes in negotiations. Research has shown that negotiators who set their optimum goals achieve objectively better outcomes than those who focus on a more moderate levels.[8] Moreover, social psychology studies have shown that individuals perform significantly better when they set harder goals rather than moderate or easy goals.[9]

There are, however, psychological hurdles to overcome when setting high goals. Certain personality types fear failure and thus are hesitant to set high goals unless they are confident in the outcome. In cases where this fear of failure concern is admitted or obvious, it may help to discuss the high goal setting objectives with someone the negotiator implicitly trusts, such as a friend or relative. Moreover, if the negotiator is adamant about setting a significantly lower than optimal realistic goal, it might be productive to switch negotiators. For example, assume a will contest involving the children of the deceased against the director of a nursing home. Suppose further that the will in question was executed by the parent in the last stages of dementia, was signed under suspicious circumstances, and left the parent's entire estate to the director of the nursing home who had only known the parent for two months. After researching the issue, the children determine that they have an excellent chance of successfully challenging the questionable will and inheriting their parent's entire estate under the laws of intestacy. Assume, however, that one of the children decides that the goal of the negotiation is to obtain 20% of the estate, because that child fears failure. The other children may, and perhaps should, talk to that one sibling and convince him to allow the other siblings to take the lead in the negotiations. If the sibling agrees to step aside, the remaining siblings could attempt to negotiate the settlement of the will contest themselves.

The optimal goals also need to be realistic. Poorly designed high goals that are unrealistic can backfire in spectacular ways, even in non-negotiating settings as illustrated by the experience of Wells Fargo, one of the United States' largest banks. Previously, Wells Fargo had implemented an aggressive sales goals incentive program for its retail bank employees. Under that sales goals incentive program, retail bank employees were urged to sell at least eight financial products per bank customer.[10] Those cross-selling sales goals were unsustainable and were so unrealistic that they were deemed to have encouraged cheating and the opening of fictitious accounts. In addition to reputational issues and losses of thousands of jobs, Wells Fargo's fake account practices, which was attributed in significant part to its unrealistic sales goals, cost the bank $185 million in fines, including a $100 million penalty from the Consumer Financial Protection Bureau, the largest such penalty the agency had issued. Wells Fargo's revised compensation and incentive program for its retail bank employees now focuses primarily on customer service.

Setting realistic goals is critical not just for major banks, but also for everyday negotiations. Assume a couple, Lucas and Victoria, are contemplating a prenuptial agreement. Suppose Lucas sets the goal of keeping everything he brings into the marriage and, in the event of divorce, obtaining everything earned during the marriage by either of them and keeping any income earned from their marital property for himself. That goal is not realistic. Rather, such a one-sided goal perhaps suggests that Lucas is not truly ready for the current romantic relationship to progress into a legally binding relationship, because he is not setting a goal that indicates a willingness to negotiate.

Similarly, setting an unrealistically high sales price of a house that far exceeds comparable house sales, and does not factor in the poor condition of the house, can backfire on the prospective seller. An unrealistic sales price could lead to the house remaining on the market for a significant time period, which can make it appear less desirable to prospective buyers. Furthermore, having to keep lowering the price because it was set too high initially leaves the seller in a particularly weak bargaining position.

In addition to realistic goals, the goals need to be specific and take into account monetary and non-monetary concerns. Focusing on specific, rather than general goals, helps to motivate the negotiation strategy. Keeping with the sale of the house example, assume a realistic goal is to sell the house at a price that is slightly above comparable sales in the neighborhood, because the house includes additional amenities. That goal may be realistic but may not be sufficiently specific to be as helpful as possible. In truly setting the negotiation goal, it is important to think through additional questions. For example, how quickly must or should the house sell? Does the seller need to move within a few weeks because of a pending job transfer? Alternatively, does the seller have time flexibility? Might the seller with an external deadline consider renting the house, if the house might not sell at her realistic price within her expected or needed time period? In addition, how much higher over comparable sales is the seller anticipating receiving?

Another transactional example where setting specific goals is helpful is putting together a partnership agreement. Many clients might have the general goal of creating an equitable partnership agreement. That is a fine general goal, but again it is more helpful to have in mind a specific goal for the negotiations. For example, if one partner is expected to contribute more initially, or to be more actively involved in the ongoing partnership, the goal for an equitable partnership agreement needs to be examined carefully before entering into the negotiations and needs to include those issues as part of the goal. The more complex the transaction is, the more likely that there will be numerous components to your goals.

Specific optimal goal setting is also important in negotiating litigation issues. For example, a client's general goal may be to settle a dispute for a reasonable amount and to avoid a trial. That could be worthy and valuable information, but without specificity, it is not particularly helpful in settling the dispute. It is important to translate the client's idea of a reasonable amount for avoiding a trial to specific monetary and non-monetary goals.

In addition to setting your realistic, optimal goal and minimum acceptable level, it is important to attempt to predict the other side's likely optimal goals and minimum acceptable levels. Consider particularly how important non-monetary factors or related issues might be for the other side. Moreover, as discussed further in Chapter 4 on Bargaining, in many negotiations, the negotiated outcome could actually result in both sides ending up in a better position than their individual optimal specific goals might have initially suggested. By anticipating the other side's goals in the planning phase, the negotiator is in a position to achieve a better combined synergistic result in the negotiation. This high synergistic result requires both parties to be willing to think collaboratively and creatively to discover areas where their combined interests work to achieve a goal that singularly they could not achieve. This synergistic result is often referred to as increasing the pie.

Conversely, information may be obtained during the bargaining that requires you to reevaluate your minimum acceptable level. Both sides might wind up accepting an agreement below their anticipated minimum level once new information comes to light during the bargaining phase of the negotiation. Even in this unlikely event, the planning is crucial because it provides a framework for the negotiations.

EXERCISES 2-2 AND 2-3: SETTING GOALS

2-2. Assume your high school reunion will take place in 3 months. Since you will be seeing many of your old high school classmates whom you have not seen in many years, you want to "get in shape" for the event. How would you formulate your general goal of "getting in shape" to a specific, realistic goal? How would you achieve your "optimal realistic goal?" In formulating your specific optimal goal, take into account the following:

(1) Monetary and non-monetary factors

(2) Your personality type

(3) Necessity of consulting with others (*e.g.*, trainers, doctors) to facilitate setting your goals

(4) Additional information you may need to obtain before setting your goals

2-3. Assume you have accepted a job in a different city and need to sell your current house. You have conducted research and determined comparable prices for houses in your current neighborhood range between $400,000 to $600,000. You have to move within two months to start your new job, and you need to net a minimum of $300,000 from the sale of this house in order to be able to afford a comparable home in your new city. Your outstanding mortgage on your current house is $100,000. You expect closing costs to be about $20,000. The housing market has been somewhat sluggish with the last comparable home in your neighborhood taking four months to sell. If your house does not sell within two months, you will need to rent in the new city and rents for the size you need for you and your family and convenient to schools and your job average between $4,000 and $5,000 a month. Currently, you have $40,000 in savings and your monthly expenses, not including your mortgage on your current home, are $5,000 a month. Based on these facts determine:

(1) What is your optimal realistic goal and why?

(2) What is the minimum acceptable level you would accept for your house and why?

(3) What alternatives do you have if you fail to negotiate the sale of your house within the two-month period?

(4) What other information would be helpful in preparing your worksheet?

Step 4: Formulating Alternative Options If Negotiations Fail

The fourth tactical planning step is to consider options if the negotiations fail. If you do not come to an agreement, what happens next? What is your best alternative? Is maintaining the status quo acceptable? This concept of exploring alternatives to the negotiation is often referred to as determining BATNA (the Best Alternative to a Negotiated Agreement).[11] Regardless of the nomenclature, the one with the power to leave the table often has the upper hand. Accordingly, it is important to formulate specific and viable alternatives to negotiations.

For example, when a buyer is negotiating to acquire a company, the buyer should consider whether his current company would be able to continue to thrive in his existing business if the acquisition negotiations fail. If the buyer's business could not continue without an acquisition, the buyer's alternatives are limited. The buyer's research should include an analysis of other potential available acquisition targets. All of this information is critical in planning the buyer's range of acceptable outcomes in the negotiation with the designated acquisition target company.

In a litigation context, if the parties do not settle, the alternative to a successful negotiation may be going to trial. The risk of going to trial with an uncertain outcome and its additional costs, and time, are all important factors to consider in planning the range of outcomes for the failed negotiations. As with the acquisition example above, the research in this litigation context should include a determination of the additional costs, both monetary and non-monetary, of going to trial.

In addition, this step of the planning requires attempting to forecast the other side's alternatives to a negotiated agreement. For example, looking at the acquisition example from the lens of the target company, it is important to try to forecast whether that company needs to be acquired for its continued existence. Is the target company attractive to other buyers such that the target could easily walk away from this negotiation? In the litigation context, if the other side's reputation would be harmed by the publicity of a trial, would the other side be less likely to walk away from the negotiation?

EXERCISE 2-4: FORMULATING ALTERNATIVE OPTIONS

You flew across the country for an important client meeting. Unfortunately, when you arrived at your destination, your luggage did not arrive with you. Your meeting is in a few hours. The airline believes that they will be able to locate your luggage and get it to your hotel shortly. Since your meeting is within a few hours, and the gym outfit you wore on the plane is not appropriate for the meeting, you reluctantly decide to purchase a suit. You do not want to spend much, however, because you have perfectly good suits at home and you are on a budget. The hotel directs you to two stores. In the first location, you find a suit that is appropriate for the meeting, is priced at $400, but unfortunately does not fit you properly and needs slight alterations. The store can do "emergency" alterations for an additional fee of $50. They promise that it can be done at least an hour before your scheduled meeting. You decide to run to the other location to see if you can just buy a suit there. The second location is a vintage shop that has a perfectly fitting designer suit, priced at $600. You look great in this suit, and you clearly prefer this one in terms of style. When you tried it on, however, you noticed that it has a slight, barely noticeable, tear on the left sleeve, which might be difficult even for a professional tailor to repair. The store clerk agrees immediately to give you a ten percent discount due to the damage. To get a larger discount you would need to speak with the manager. The manager is at lunch and will return in half an hour. Your meeting with the client is now due to start in three hours.

In deciding whether to purchase the vintage suit now with ten percent discount, what factors are relevant in weighing your alternatives of (a) waiting a half hour for the manager in the hopes of getting a lower price or (b) returning to the first store and purchasing the suit that needs alterations? After considering these factors, which choice would you make?

Step 5: Preparing Opening Offers, Concessions, and Counteroffers

After conducting research to uncover objective criteria and having determined your optimal, realistic goal, your minimal acceptable level, and your BATNA, you should generally be ready to formulate your opening offer for your worksheet. In fact, in an arms-open negotiation your optimal realistic goal may be your opening offer. In an arms-length negotiation, however, your opening offer may be slightly more optimistic than your optimal realistic goal. Professor G. Richard Shell defines an optimistic first offer as "the highest (or lowest) number for which there is a supporting standard or argument enabling you to make a presentable case."[12] He explains that this optimistic opening offer "need not be supported by your best argument, just a presentable one."[13] Notice, however, that an optimistic first offer is still one supported by objective criteria. It is not a random or an extreme number. Once the negotiations get started, however, as discussed further in Chapter 4 on Bargaining, you may not use your planned opening offer. If, for example, at the start of the negotiation session the other side appears extremely motivated to enter into an agreement, you may obtain an even better outcome than your optimal realistic goal or even your proposed optimistic first offer by opening with a more aggressive opening offer. Moreover, sometimes the opening offer has already been made before any negotiation planning has taken place. For example, if a tenant breaks a lease that contains an early termination clause requiring the tenant to pay four months' rent, then the landlord may demand the four months' rent from the tenant and that constitutes the landlord's opening offer.

Even if you have prepared your opening offer, during the actual negotiation, the other side may make the first offer, so your prepared opening offer now becomes a counteroffer and may need to be adjusted in response to the other side's opening salvo. It is important to prepare an opening offer but to be aware of the necessity of maintaining flexibility during the actual negotiations. Of course, having an opening offer at-the-ready does not mean introducing that offer first. See the Chapter on Bargaining for strategies on making and responding to offers.

Step five of tactical planning also requires formulating concessions. Concessions are used by parties throughout negotiations to help reach a settlement range. Although making a concession implies you are "conceding" or giving up something, think of concessions more like an exchange or trade off with the other side. You make concessions not just to give up something but to trigger the reciprocity of getting something in return, which moves the parties toward settlement. Therefore, in planning, you should make a list of concessions you are willing to make, and prioritize them based on your goals and interests, and the projected goals and interests of the other side. What concessions are you willing to make? How likely is the other side to value each of your concessions? Concessions can be monetary or non-monetary. For example, you may be willing to agree to an earlier closing date than you initially wanted on the sale of your house in order to get your price. Skilled negotiators make a list of proposed concessions. The list should rank the concessions in order of importance. Concessions serve many purposes including keeping the negotiation going if they stall. Also, non-monetary concessions may serve to preserve a higher monetary result.

You will also need a strategy as to the timing of making concessions. Do you want to begin with a small concession to show goodwill, or do you plan to save concessions for a time in the negotiation session when the process is stalled, and you need to move things along? In determining your concessions, you need to consider your relationship with the other side. If you are attempting to establish a long-term relationship, as in going into a business partnership, you may be more willing to use concessions to establish a good working relationship that shows your flexibility. Conversely, if you are trying to settle a matter subject to litigation, you may use concessions sparingly to maximize the best result for your client without giving too much away.

Your plan also needs to anticipate concessions the other side may make. What is the strategy for handling the other side's concessions? For example, in negotiating an employment agreement the employer might be willing to concede two days a week of remote work if the employee is willing to work one Saturday a month. This employer's concession on remote work might be the first one made, especially if the employer already offers some other employees that option or if the employer was planning to make that offer to all of her employees anyway. Keep in mind that even if this is the least important concession to the employer, the employer may have insight that this is a perk that the prospective employee values highly, so it is a valuable concession to make. Many companies are adept at offering concessions that appeal to prospective employees that are relatively easy to concede.

Concessions and counteroffers go hand in hand. As you plan your counteroffer, you should anticipate their concessions. For example, if you are attempting to buy a house and the seller offers the house for $400,000, you may plan to counter with an offer of $350,000, because the roof needs replacing which will cost $50,000. You should anticipate that the seller may disagree that the roof needs replacing but concede that the roof needs repairing. In this example, by anticipating that the seller may concede the need for repairing but not replacing the roof you are prepared to adjust your counteroffer.

One of the most difficult parts of the six-step tactical plan is anticipating the other side's concessions and counteroffers. If you do not have enough information to determine what concessions are valued by the other side, you should conduct research as part of your planning process. If you are new to an industry or profession, researching the business norms and practices will be most beneficial in anticipating the other side's concessions. Research can involve anything from talking to those in the industry or reading articles or manuals about an industry. For example, a negotiation with federal regulators may not follow the standard concession dance. Assume Bob, an officer of a public company, is being investigated by the federal Securities and Exchange Commission (SEC) for a securities law violation. In trying to negotiate with the SEC, Bob might think that if he agrees to a larger civil money penalty, the SEC might agree not to impose a long-term ban on Bob serving in the future as an officer or director of a public company. Such an assumption might not be appropriate, however. In this industry, sometimes regulators expect large money penalties to be tied to longer time sanctions. In other words, if Bob offers to increase the amount of his penalty in the hopes of reducing any time sanction, his higher monetary penalty offer could backfire as the SEC will now want to increase the time sanction to match the higher monetary penalty. This example simply shows that before preparing offers or concessions it behooves the negotiator to truly research, not just the law and the facts, but also the norms of the industry or practices of the opposing side.

In planning your offers and concessions, in addition to preparing the planning worksheet, it is sometimes helpful to role-play the negotiation with a colleague or friend prior to entering the actual negotiations. By actually "acting out" the negotiation, you have the opportunity to see how your planning plays to the other side, and gives you practice in responding to offers and concessions on the spot. Role-playing can be invaluable in bringing the planning worksheet to life. You receive immediate feedback as to the strengths and weaknesses of your plan. It is the difference between simply reading a script and a live rehearsal. While your plan may play well on paper, your performance may be lacking. By rehearsing offers and concessions, you have the opportunity to observe the process before the actual negotiation.

AI platforms may assist you in role playing your negotiation. Certain AI platforms are able to perform real-time simulations using multiple AI generated scenarios. For example, Stanford University's M&A negotiation simulator allows users to engage in role play on various negotiation scenarios and provides feedback on the user's negotiation strategies and concession pacing.[14]

EXERCISE 2-5: PREPARING OPENING OFFERS, CONCESSIONS, AND COUNTEROFFERS EXERCISE

You have rented an apartment in a twenty unit building in downtown Atlanta for the past year. You pay $2,000 per month for a one-bedroom apartment. Your lease is up for renewal in two months, and you indicated to the landlord that you would like to renew the lease for an additional year. Thus, your landlord sent you a renewal lease contract for your review. According to the lease, your rent will be increased by $200 per month. You happen to know that there are currently five apartments that are not leased, and two other apartments with leases expiring at the same time as your lease. You have talked to the two tenants whose leases expire when your lease does. One tenant has told you he does not plan to renew his lease. The other tenant, who lives a few doors down from you and is very friendly with the landlord, told you he is unsure of his plans to renew and you should "work your own deal," and he does not want to discuss it further. You do not know the status of the remaining apartments.

You have also looked at two comparable apartment buildings in your neighborhood. One of those apartment buildings has a one bedroom available for $2,000 a month. However, that apartment is 100 square feet smaller than your apartment and located right next to the elevator and trash disposal. The other apartment building is fully occupied with the next one-bedroom apartment available in four months for $2,100 per month.

You really prefer to remain in your apartment as you do not want to go through the hassle and expense of moving. You also love the location of your apartment on the top floor of the building and enjoy the gym and swimming pool amenities. However, you do think your apartment should be painted and the refrigerator replaced. You also would like the landlord to improve the security in the building by installing security cameras at the entrances and hallways. While you can afford to pay the extra $200 per month, based on the information you know, you decide you are going to try to negotiate a lower renewal rent. If your landlord ultimately does not budge on the rent, however, you will stay in the apartment and pay the rent increase.

(1) What would be your opening offer? (Note: this is really a counteroffer since the lease renewal has set the opening offer at $2,200). You may include both monetary and non-monetary offers.

(2) What concessions are you willing to make? Make a list from the least important to the most important concession.

(3) What concessions do you anticipate the landlord is willing to make?

(4) What do you think the landlord is willing to accept?

Step 6: Devising Questions and Preparing Responses to Anticipated Questions

Skilled negotiators know the benefit of having prepared questions. Preparing questions to ask the other side is often omitted from negotiation planning but should be included. The process of preparing questions crystalizes for the planner information that he might be missing about the other side's case. For example, in a sale of a house, the seller might want to prepare a question asking the buyer how soon the buyer needs to move in. If the buyer needs immediate access to the house, because, for example, he has recently sold his prior house and is temporarily living with in-laws, that information could be useful either as a bargaining chip for the seller or as an agreed upon term facilitating the rest of the negotiations. Also, questions, if asked properly, can be a way to show the other side that the negotiator is interested in seeking common ground by getting their input. Finally, questions break up the negotiation intensity of making and responding to demands, which often leads to an escalation of stress and anxiety. Questions do not need to go just to the substance of the negotiations but can also be used to establish rapport. For example, asking the other side how they coped with the ten inches of rain in the last three days can be an easy way to establish a rapport. However, asking a follow-up question of whether he believes the rain is due to climate change may be a way of destroying the rapport. Again, planning is key.

In preparing questions, focus not only on the subject matter of the question, but also on the type of question. The two main types of questions asked during negotiations are close-ended questions and open-ended questions.[15] Close-ended questions are questions that require a brief answer, usually just a yes or no. For example, a close-ended question would be, "Did you run the red light?" This question simply requires a yes or no answer. An open-ended question usually requires a detailed answer because the question as framed does not lend itself to a yes or no answer. The question often begins with who, what, when, where, why, or how. For example, instead of the leading question, "Did you run the red light?" you could ask an open-ended question such as, "How did the accident occur?" This open-ended question will likely elicit a detailed response and will allow the responder to tell his version of the story of the accident. Of course, it is probable that the story of the accident will be very favorable to the responder, but at least the question leads to a discussion and to an opportunity to gather information.

In planning for the negotiation, you should prepare both closed and open-ended questions. Open-ended questions tend to be non-threatening and are likely to further the discussion. Close-ended questions can be helpful to turn to if during the negotiations the other side is not forthcoming in sharing information. In such cases, the planner can resort to a relatively easy closed-ended question to try to pinpoint the answer and continue the negotiating process. Asking close-ended questions can become somewhat tedious, in that the repetition of a yes or no answer to a question can lull both the questioner and responder into a pattern that hinders establishing a rapport between the parties. The best method may be to intersperse closed and open-ended questions during the negotiation.

In addition to closed and open-ended questions, other types of questions serve objectives beyond gathering information. A leading question suggests the answer with an objective of getting the responder to adopt the questioner's position. For example, "you were texting on your phone right before the accident occurred, weren't you?" This question attempts to get a response desired by the questioner (most likely a plaintiff's attorney) that the responder (most likely the defendant) was texting before the accident.

Confrontational and complimentary questions are two additional types of questions with different objectives. A confrontational question is an assertive question whose objective is to confront the other side when they have taken a seemingly disingenuous or aggressive position. For example, assume the other side starts with an extremely low offer that is completely unrealistic. A confrontational question might be something to the effect of "are you really expecting me to believe that you cannot offer more than this paltry sum of money?" Another version might be "are you really telling me that your client has not authorized you to offer more than that sum to settle the case?" Parties should use confrontational questions sparingly, if at all, because these questions may completely derail the negotiation. However, if you know or suspect that the other party is an overly competitive type of negotiator who tends to take an aggressive stance during negotiations, it is prudent to plan some confrontational questions in case the need arises. Conversely, a complimentary question is one whose objective is to build up the other side. An example of this type of question would be, "since you have so much knowledge and experience in these matters, would you mind explaining to us your position in detail?" It is probably best not to use too many of these questions either, as the party may give the impression to the other side that he values the other person's opinion more than his own, which will weaken his bargaining position. Therefore, a party should have a few confrontational and complimentary questions "in the bag," but delay putting them on display in the negotiation unless necessary.

The planning worksheet should prepare for questions to be interspersed throughout the negotiation. Questions should be centered on subject areas or particular goals. As in the example above, a party may want to ask questions to find out more about how the accident occurred and may also want to gather information about the damages. Instead of just listing all the questions together, separate liability questions about the accident from damages questions. This approach to organizing questions will allow you to quickly refer to questions during the negotiation on the same topic.

Preparing your responses to anticipated questions from the other side is as important as preparing your questions. Negotiators should expect that if they are going to ask questions, they will be answering questions as well. In planning for the negotiation, you should recognize weaknesses in your positions and decide your approach if asked questions by the other side concerning these areas. A particularly important area of concern for planning is how to respond to questions that seek to elicit confidential information that you wish to protect or have a duty to protect from disclosure. This dilemma often arises when a party is negotiating in a representative capacity on behalf of another person, such as an attorney negotiating on behalf of a client. In that situation, the representative must make sure to reveal only the information that the client has authorized them to reveal.[16] If the client has not authorized the client to reveal confidential information, the attorney should decide in advance how he will handle these types of questions. For example, if you are a lawyer representing a client in a car accident and you are asked if your client ran the red light, there are three possible answers: (1) yes; (2) I am not revealing that information; and (3) no. If you choose option one and answer "yes," but your client has not authorized you to reveal this information, you are likely revealing confidential information that is protected. You may subsequently be sued by your client for malpractice, or disciplined by a court, or your state's bar association, for this breach of fiduciary duty.[17] If you choose option two and answer, "I'm not revealing that information due to attorney-client privilege," the other side may interpret the reluctance to reveal the information as the same as a "yes" response and infer that your client ran the red light. If you choose the third option and answer no and your client had actually told you that he had not run the red light, then the "no" response is one you are most eager to give as it benefits your client. What if, however, your client had told you that he ran the red light? In that instance, a "no" answer would be a lie. Not only would the lie be unethical and should compromise your moral code, but it could also have significant legal consequences for both you and your client. For example, if the case eventually settles, and that other side's attorney relied on that "no" response in entering into a settlement, the settlement is subject to being set aside for material misrepresentation.[18] Additionally, as the attorney, you may be subject to a claim for fraud based on the lie.[19] See Chapter 6 on Ethics and Equity.

Not every question needs a direct answer. If a party does not want to respond to a question directly for whatever reason, he should plan some diversionary responses. Diversionary methods include answering the question with a question, changing the subject matter, being offended by the question and refusing to answer, or simply ignoring the question. In planning such diversionary non-responses, you should be aware that any of these methods you use will likely be mirrored by the other side in responding to your questions. This diversionary interplay can result in little or no exchange of information during questioning. Therefore, it is best to plan to reveal some useful information to the other side and encourage them to do the same and use diversionary methods sparingly.

EXERCISES 2-6, 2-7, 2-8, AND 2-9: DEVISING QUESTIONS AND PREPARING RESPONSES TO ANTICIPATED QUESTIONS

2-6. Closed-Ended Questions (*two-person exercise*). Assume you and a friend are having coffee. Your friend is interested in pursuing a profession other than the one than the one in which she is currently employed.

Pair up with a person who will play the role of your friend. Instead of asking your friend what other professions would interest her, ask only close-ended questions (*i.e.*, ask only questions in which the answer is yes or no). For example, you may ask, "Does your new profession require a college degree?" or "Does it require an advanced degree?" Your friend must limit her answers to a "yes" or "no" response only. By asking a series of closed-ended questions, see if you can discover your friend's desired profession. After completing your questioning, switch roles and repeat the exercise.

2-7. Open-Ended Questions (*two-person exercise*). Assume your 15-year-old son took the family dog, "Mellow Mary" to the dog park. While at the park, your son tells you that Mellow bit another dog. Your son then begins texting on his phone because he believes he has given you all the necessary information and that the conversation is over. You, of course, are quite upset at the situation and are imagining all kinds of fallout from the event, from Mellow having psychological issues to receiving a call from the owner of the other dog or his lawyer.

Pair up with a person who will play the role of the 15-year-old son while you play the role of the parent. Using only open-ended questions, try to uncover details about the incident from your less than talkative son. Remember these questions are describing and explaining questions, not questions that elicit only a yes or no answer.

2-8. Mixing Closed-Ended, Open-Ended, Complimentary and Confrontational Questions (*two-person exercise*). Assume you stopped by a garage sale on your way home from work. You immediately see a television for sale that attracts your attention. You have been contemplating buying a television to use in the spare room in your apartment. You notice a tag on the television with a price of $50.00.

Pair up with a person who will play the role of the seller while you play the role of the buyer. In order to gain as much information about the television as possible, ask the seller questions as to both the price and quality of the television.

2-9. Mixing Close-Ended, Open-Ended, Complimentary and Confrontational Questions. A seller has posted a television for sale on the OfferUp app. The television is a Toshiba 20 inch "smart" television and is two years old. The asking price is $499.00. Make a list of questions you would like to ask the seller.

CHAPTER 3

Arranging the Negotiation

Sensing that an in-person negotiation may not work, Petra was ready to switch to negotiating by text.

After completing your tactical planning, it is time to determine the logistics of the negotiation. In other words, deciding the when, where, and how of the negotiation. This is an important component often overlooked by participants. One consideration for determining logistics is whether the negotiation is arms-length or arms-open. An arms-length negotiation often requires a more formalized setting than an arms-open negotiation. For example, if Zoe is interested in purchasing a house owned by her sister, Zelda, they may have a series of in-person casual, informal negotiations in a variety of settings before they come to the actual agreement and specified terms. By contrast, if Zoe is negotiating with a seller with whom she has no relationship, the negotiations will likely be more formalized and be prearranged, often through an agent or attorney. As part of the planning process, the parties should determine the timing and location for their initial negotiation. Furthermore, present day technologies allow the parties to negotiate in numerous formats other than in-person, including videoconferencing, phone, email, and texting.

The COVID-19 pandemic dramatically altered the landscape of negotiation. While in-person meetings were once the standard, the need for social distancing and remote work forced a rapid shift towards virtual methods. This led to increased reliance on phone, email, and, most notably, videoconferencing platforms like Zoom. Even post-pandemic, the changes in negotiation styles and preferences are likely to be long-lasting.

A negotiation may entail one or a mixture of several formats. In deciding which format to use initially, it is important to recognize the pros and cons of each.

Various Platforms for Negotiations

In-Person

An in-person negotiation is the traditional method of negotiation. When parties contemplate conducting a negotiation, they most likely imagine scheduling a time and place to meet to attempt to resolve their conflict. In-person negotiations have some advantages. Parties who meet in-person have already gone to the trouble of arranging their schedules and exerting the effort of arriving at a meeting place. These steps indicate a certain commitment to the negotiation process. Presumably, parties would not waste their time to meet in person, if they were not seriously attempting to work out their conflicts, unless, of course, these parties are ordered to do so by a court or by an aggressive human resources department.

Beyond the believed seriousness of the negotiation process, in-person negotiations also offer other advantages. When parties get together in a conference like setting, they are afforded a sense of privacy that may be lacking when conducting videoconferencing, email, or text negotiations. Given that sense of privacy, parties may be able to more freely exchange information that they may feel reluctant to do by videoconferencing, email, or text.

In-person negotiations also allow parties who do not have a prior relationship to get to know one another through informal conversation, initially through ice-breaking and subsequent small talk that may take place throughout the negotiation. Perceptions as to a person's warmth are important in a negotiation. In fact, one study has shown that our perceptions of others' warmth and competence make up for 80% of our judgment of them.[1] Contrary to what many would believe, negotiators observe warmth before competence and in some negotiation contexts, actually value warmth over competence.[2] Warmth encompasses traits such as trustworthiness, sincerity, friendliness, and kindness. These traits are undoubtedly discovered more easily in-person than through email or text. Through ice-breaking and small talk, the parties may be able to establish a rapport and assess each other's warmth quotient. See "Ice-Breaking" in Chapter 4 on Bargaining. While a certain amount of competitiveness is an important negotiating trait, overly competitive negotiators are generally perceived by other negotiators as suspicious. The ability to assess these traits is a positive aspect of having an in-person negotiation.

In-person negotiations also allow the parties the opportunity to complete the negotiation more efficiently. Since the parties have made the effort to get together in person, there may be a tendency to stay in the room until a deal is reached, especially if there is a positive rapport and the parties have found common ground. While there are many stories of the person who storms out of the room while shouting, "you're wasting my time," those stories are usually what makes good television drama. As noted, except for a few cases in which the parties are required to meet to negotiate, parties who voluntarily agree to meet may have a greater incentive to come to an agreement.

Phone Negotiations

Another traditional method of negotiating is by phone. Phone negotiations can be used to conduct the entire negotiation in certain cases, especially when you want to make a quick deal. Or phone negotiations can be valuable when used in conjunction with in-person or other formats of negotiations. Phone negotiations can be used early in the process of the negotiation for introductions and to gather some initial information from the other side. Phone calls later in the process are often valuable to follow up on a prior session or to settle issues that remained open from a prior session. For example, if a prior negotiating session was halted because there was a need for further research or investigation into certain issues, follow-up by phone would be appropriate once that research or investigation has been conducted.

Phone negotiations have both advantages and disadvantages. Negotiating by phone allows the parties to have real time negotiations much like in-person negotiations, but without the delay and expense of travel. While phone negotiations do not permit the parties to observe non-verbal clues of expression and body language, they do provide for interpretation of tone and inflection. Due to its somewhat informal nature, phone negotiations allow parties flexibility. For example, you could end a negotiation session that is heading in the wrong direction more easily than when negotiating in-person by saying "unfortunately, I need to jump off this call now." Conversely, it is just as easy for you to start a negotiation session by phone because a call can be made at any time or any place. In addition, phone negotiations allow for others to participate in the negotiations through the use of speaker phones or multi-party calling. Of course, all persons participating in the phone negotiations should be identified to maintain confidentiality and avoid deception.

There are some risks associated with telephone negotiations. Unlike an in-person or video session, since you are not in "view" during a phone negotiating session, you might be tempted to multi-task during the conversation. This multi-tasking distraction may result in a less than optimal performance. In addition, negotiating by cell phone while you are commuting or are otherwise on the go may make it difficult to memorialize the terms of an agreement until a later time. At that time, you may not accurately remember the agreed upon terms. Another concern is that with the ease and informality of phone negotiations, you may be tempted to answer a call and start engaging in negotiations before you are properly prepared. This impulse to answer the call is generally a mistake. You should be sure to check the caller ID before answering. If not prepared to negotiate, you should perhaps not answer the call or send the call to text.

Email Negotiations

Negotiation by email has many advantages not found in face-to-face or phone negotiations.[3] Due to its asynchronous nature, parties may send and respond to emails at any time and any place. Thus, email erases time and distance impediments that may act as stumbling blocks to in-person negotiations. Whether it is first thing in the morning or very late in the evening, a party can make an offer, accept an offer, or just keep the conversation going. No worries about cancelled flights, late arrivals, or any other actual or created obstacles to not show up. Although it is not unheard of for an email negotiator to complain that their server was "not working," or that they did not receive a prior email, such excuses should not lead to the significant delay that a cancelled in-person negotiation may entail.

Consistent with the ability to negotiate at the parties' convenience, email negotiation often proves cost effective. Costs associated with travel for face-to-face negotiations are avoided. If the negotiation involves multiple parties, email avoids perhaps several in-person meetings if all parties cannot attend at the same time. Furthermore, if the negotiation involves represented parties, clients can be included in email communications as they occur, thus avoiding time spent by attorneys updating clients as to what occurred in the negotiations. All of these benefits should result in reduced costs for clients.

Email negotiation also allows the parties to take a break from the discussions if emotions are running high, or if they have reached an impasse. Furthermore, the theatrics associated with in-person negotiations are mostly eliminated by email. For example, a negotiator who erupts in anger in an in-person negotiation is stymied from this behavior in an email negotiation. Even the negotiator who resorts to all capital letters wording in an email, trying to express anger, is unlikely to produce more than indifference or even a laugh from the other party. In addition, a party's failure to respond at all to an email can be interpreted in different ways. Are they done negotiating? Are they angry? Are they conferring with others to formulate a counteroffer? Did they decide to take an impromptu vacation or take ill? While ambiguity may afford the party taking a break time to collect their thoughts, the party not receiving a response may become frustrated or angry such that it derails the negotiating process. Thus, you want to ensure that your email responses are not misinterpreted. See Chapter 4 on Bargaining for more ideas on responding to others.

Email also provides a verifiable way to prove what occurred since it is memorialized in writing. This written communication, as opposed to the verbal communication in face-to-face negotiations, may have both a positive and negative effect on the process. A party may be more reluctant to put in it in writing, since there will be a record of what occurred that cannot be easily erased. By contrast, in a face-to-face negotiation, there can be considerable disagreement as to what was said, or simply a denial that something was said.

Email negotiations, however, do not provide the opportunity to observe non-verbal clues from the other side. Some studies laud the ability to read non-verbal clues during an in-person negotiation.[4] For example, facial expressions such as lip biting may indicate anxiety. Body language such as crossed arms might indicate that the person feels defensive. Constant fidgeting may suggest impatience. However, other studies show that these non-verbal clues are greatly overvalued and may in fact be misleading, particularly where the negotiators are from different cultures.[5] Therefore, while in-person negotiations allows the opportunity to observe non-verbal conduct, the resulting benefit is mixed as a negotiating strategy. Without visual or vocal clues, email negotiators are left to convey their proposal solely with words. For some who enjoy the game of negotiation, this option may prove too mundane. However, other negotiators are bolstered by the clear meaning of words and prefer avoiding the distraction of deciphering non-verbal clues and emotional outbursts.

Because of the asynchronous nature, the effect of negotiating by email may result in more thoughtful exchanges. While there is no suggestion in this book to ever "wing it" for any type of negotiation, those involved in face-to-face negotiations may be derailed from their plan by an aggressive party whose tactics throws them off. In an email negotiation, one is afforded the opportunity to take time to plan when responding, which may provide for more reflective and thoughtful responses than in-person negotiations. Further, the more strategic planning you apply in drafting your email responses, the more likely the negotiation will be successful.

Videoconferencing

In our first edition, we discussed the option of videoconferencing. Little did we know the pandemic was right around the corner and videoconferencing was about to become the preferred and exclusive method of negotiating for an extended period of time. Its popularity continues to the present. Videoconferencing is, in effect, a combination of in-person, phone, and email negotiations. Videoconferencing affords many of the advantages of email, phone, and in-person negotiations with some disadvantages. Many of the benefits of an in-person negotiation translate to a videoconferencing negotiation. Due to its synchronous nature, videoconferencing provides face-to-face contact like an in-person negotiation. Thus, the parties may have the ability to read verbal and visual clues. Videoconferencing also occurs in real time, unlike email or text-based negotiation. This real-time effect allows the parties to take the time to ice break and establish a more comfortable rapport. It further allows the parties the ability to wrap up the negotiation and make decisions more efficiently since, similar to meeting face-to-face in a conference room, they are meeting in the virtual conference room.

In addition to having some of the benefits of face-to-face negotiations, videoconferencing also has many of the benefits of email negotiations. Like email negotiations, videoconferencing saves time and money in that the parties do not have to physically meet, thus eliminating travel time and related expenses. As during the pandemic, videoconferencing not only saves time and money but is the only option when travel is difficult or suspended. Furthermore, videoconferencing can be recorded with ease and thus the conversations can be memorialized. Even if the parties do not wish to record the video conference, just the fact that a party is "on camera" may prompt a more thoughtful exchange of information and a decreased likelihood of spontaneous outbursts.

Despite the many advantages of videoconferencing, there are some downsides to using this method for negotiating. First, although videoconferencing allows the parties to "see" each other, it is less personal than in-person meetings. Unlike an in-person meeting, negotiating by videoconferencing requires the parties to stay on screen and in the picture, thus offering a somewhat stilted image of that person. With this fixed picture, the parties are not able to move around the room or display anything more than their image from the neck up. Therefore, it is possible to misread visual or verbal clues on the screen given the fixed image. Moreover, as with phone negotiations, with a fixed screen, the parties may be unaware of others in the room who are not visible on the screen. Second, there may be technical difficulties with videoconferencing that may greatly interfere with the negotiating process. Remote connections are often shaky, networks are subject to intermittent failures, and the hardware or software may have compatibility issues that interfere with the connection. Third, since the parties are meeting in real time, they must be aware of time zone changes. While one party may want to have a video conference at 10:00 AM, that time may translate to 2:00 AM for the other party. Differing time zones may eliminate some of the advantages of not meeting in-person.

Zoom and similar platforms offered a significant upgrade from pre-pandemic videoconferencing. First, user-friendly interfaces and wider availability across devices made videoconferencing accessible to a broader range of individuals, regardless of their technical expertise. Second, technological advancements led to more stable connections and fewer disruptions compared to earlier videoconferencing systems. Third, features like screen sharing, breakout rooms, and virtual backgrounds enhanced collaboration and allowed for more dynamic and engaging negotiation sessions.

Pandemic Zoom negotiations have revealed more drawbacks to this virtual method but with simple solutions. One drawback to videoconferencing is when only a facial view is on the fixed screen as opposed to in person where the parties see the whole person. One solution is for the parties to back up their cameras so that they show more than just a facial view. While those negotiators who prefer to wear a coat and tie with their gym shorts may find this burdensome, allowing parties to view hand and body gestures, along with facial expressions, may lead to a more positive and relaxed atmosphere and more in line within in person negotiations. Further, in videoconferencing it is important to note that using the tiny screen of a smartphone diminishes communication, as opposed to larger screens.[6] In fact, larger screens, such as a 32-inch monitor, are associated with greater trust, presumably under the theory that the more you see, the more you know.

Second, while Zoom has allowed negotiators to see themselves when negotiating with the other side, this "selfie" aspect can lead to self-consciousness and self-criticism, as well as distracting from the conversation at hand. Turning off the selfie feature may improve concentration and mirror a more in person experience.

Third, Zoom and other such video platforms also allow the parties to multi-task during the negotiation sessions. For example, parties on such video platforms may be tempted to check their text messages and emails on their phones during the session. Research has shown that multi-taskers perform worse during negotiations and, if discovered, the multi-tasker is deemed less trustworthy by the other side.[7]

Finally, because Zoom negotiations are so prevalent, many of us suffer from videoconferencing fatigue. It is very tempting to resolve all the issues by hopping on a video conference. However, constantly resorting to videoconferencing can result in lackluster performance and, eventually, in poorer outcomes. To combat videoconferencing fatigue, incorporate other platforms such as email and telephone conferences to start, continue, or finalize negotiations. This combination of platforms will likely keep the parties interested and engaged. Further, during a video negotiation, build in breaks away from the screen as you would in leaving the room during an in-person negotiation. Suggest taking a break to review documents, or simply to refresh your coffee. These breaks will allow some down time so that the parties feel refreshed once they continue. Of course, use judgment wisely. Too many breaks may be interpreted as a stalling or as a non-cooperative tactic (see Chapter 4 on Bargaining Tactics).

Studies have shown that videoconferencing and other virtual negotiations favor the less powerful party.[8] Research found that the party with less power did better in virtual forms of negotiation than in face-to-face negotiations. The research suggests that when people negotiate remotely, power hierarchies have less impact on the outcome. Virtual negotiation particularly tends to level the playing field. Therefore, in situations such as an employee negotiating a raise from his boss, negotiating virtually may help to balance the power. That is, of course, if the employee can get the boss to respond on screen.

With many advantages but also disadvantages, it may be difficult to decide if negotiating by videoconferencing is the best method for successful negotiations. The type of dispute, the parties' locations, time restraints, and costs, are factors that may determine if this method is appropriate. As with other methods, videoconferencing should be considered as a viable negotiation platform.

Text Messaging

Text messaging can also serve as a significant platform for negotiations. It has both advantages and disadvantages compared to other platforms. One benefit of text messaging is that it is a quick and easy way for the parties to communicate, especially when used as part of the overall negotiation process. Text is often used to initiate or continue the negotiation in another forum, such as by email, phone, videoconferencing, or in-person. Another benefit of texting in the negotiation setting is that it is generally viewed as more informal than email, which can be beneficial particularly in certain arms-open negotiations where the parties are amicable when starting the negotiations. Also, unlike an email where the other party might have blind copied another person into the conversation and thus made it difficult to know who is "in the room," the members of a group text are generally visible, with a click or two, to all parties. There is no hiding in the text room. Texting can also be used as an advantageous alternative to a phone call. Although texting is not truly real time as a phone call, the ability to provide multiple rapid-fire responses with text can mimic the real time effect of a phone call. Unlike a phone call, however, since a text is not actually in real time, a party may be able to avoid direct responses more readily than by phone.

There are certain disadvantages to negotiating by text. Text messages are generally short, often use abbreviated words, and may lack content or details. The lack of explanation can lead to text being misinterpreted. Also, text messages are typically sent immediately after they are composed without the drafter first reviewing or editing. By contrast, email systems provide easier methods for saving drafts and editing and thus encourage the drafter to review before hitting send. Also, those who send text messages may try to clarify or amplify their texts by including emoticons (emojis). However, the use of such emojis can have the opposite effect and actually lead to more confusion. Emojis are not uniformly interpreted. For example, in a text, emoji tears may be intended by one party as signifying laughter and happiness but interpreted by the recipient as frustration. While this may not be a problem with texts among friends, in the negotiation context it could derail negotiations or even lead to a lawsuit. For example, in one case a prospective tenant, in discussions by text with a landlord, sent the landlord a series of emojis that included a smiley face, a comet, a champagne bottle, dancing bunnies, and a chipmunk.[9] Partially because of the emojis, the landlord believed an agreement had been made and took down the listing. When the potential tenant backed out of renting the apartment, the landlord sued. The judge agreed with the landlord that the prospective tenant had negotiated in bad faith and awarded rent to the landlord. Accordingly, use of emojis during negotiations should be used sparingly and with caution.

While some traditional negotiators would not generally use texting for negotiations, text messaging is often the preferred method of communication for millennials, and members of Gen Z, and must be considered as an available negotiation format. In fact, text messaging has long been used as part of the negotiating process in high stakes negotiations involving law enforcement agencies. For example, in 2011, police negotiator Andres Wells was pursuing a suspect in a gas station robbery who was threatening suicide.[10] The suspect began ignoring Officer Wells' telephone calls. Instead, the suspect sent the officer a text message. This was the first time Mr. Wells had ever encountered a suspect using a text message as a form of communication. The suspect in a text demanded the officer contact his girlfriend. Then, in a subsequent text, the suspect demanded water. Recognizing that he would be unable to successfully resolve the crisis solely through text messaging, Mr. Wells' strategy was to get the suspect to stop texting and pick up the phone. Eventually the officer was successful, as the suspect agreed to accept phone calls from the officer and the matter was resolved. Officer Wells was forced to use text messaging as a way to communicate in this high stakes situation. Because of negotiations such as these, law enforcement agencies are training their officers to address the challenges of crisis negotiations through text. In a situation such as crisis negotiating with a suspect, determining the suspect's mental state is crucial, and thus verbal cues are very important. In order to decipher these verbal clues, officers are now trained to encourage suspects to switch from text messaging to in-person or telephone methods of communication. Most negotiations do not rise to the level of a crisis. Nevertheless, negotiating by text messaging may be an integral part of the process.

EXERCISE 3-1: TEXT MESSAGE

You are trying to sell your car and negotiating by text message with a potential buyer. You have never met the buyer, and the negotiation has been conducted solely by text messaging. You are moving and need to sell your car within the next five days. You have had several text exchanges with the buyer with multiple offers and counteroffers. You intend to text your final offer to the buyer and believe the price will be acceptable to him. However, you also want the buyer's payment to you to be in full and an all-cash deal. Finally, you want to arrange the delivery of the car to the buyer within five days.

A. Translate what you believe buyer was texting. Do you believe you have a deal with the buyer?

B. Prepare the following responses to the buyer:
   (1) Respond to buyer using only emojis to convey your message.
   (2) Respond to buyer using only words to convey your message.
   (3) Respond to buyer using both emojis and words to convey your message.

C. Compare the responses. What are the advantages and disadvantages of responding using emojis in this negotiation? What are the advantages and disadvantages of responding using words without emojis?

Choosing the Initial Platform for Negotiating

Which initial form of communication the parties decide to use in their negotiations is based on many variables including the relationship of the parties. For example, in an arms-open negotiation, such as negotiating a prenuptial agreement, it would be unusual to think that the engaged couple would start the negotiation on any other platform than in-person. In an arms-length negotiation, however, such as the purchase of a house from a stranger, the initial format for the negotiation may not be significant and would likely be determined by personal preference or practical issues such as time and costs.

Furthermore, similar to the crisis negotiator scenario above, the parties may begin a negotiation using one platform for the negotiation and move to another platform during the process. For example, a person negotiating a car purchase may meet with the car dealer in person, but if the deal is not completed on the lot, they may continue the discussion by email or phone and finalize it by text message, confirming the agreed upon purchase price.

EXERCISES 3-2, 3-3, AND 3-4: CHOOSING THE INITIAL PLATFORM FOR NEGOTIATING

3-2. You and your fiancé have decided to have a destination wedding in the Bahamas. You saw an advertisement in Wedding Weekly for a hotel in Nassau that specializes in destination weddings. The ad quotes a price of $30,000 for a four hour "all in" wedding, which includes a decorated room for the ceremony and reception, a DJ, a cocktail reception, a five-course meal, and a wedding cake. The hotel will even include a person to perform the ceremony. This offer is for a wedding party of up to 50 guests. The advertisement lists an email address to contact the hotel manager for further information.

Draft an email to the hotel manager. Introduce yourself and ask a few questions in order to gather more information about the package. Also, lay the groundwork to negotiate for either a price reduction or more services. You plan to have only 30 invited guests. This is an introductory email only. Do not attempt to conduct the entire negotiation by email.

3-3. *(Two-Person Exercise)* Assume the same facts as in Exercise 3-2. However, for this exercise, assume that the hotel has an affiliate hotel near you and there is a representative, Mr. Representative, available to discuss your destination wedding. You made an appointment with Mr. Representative to meet in person to discuss the wedding.

Pair up with a person who will play the role of Mr. Representative. Introduce yourself and begin the groundwork to negotiate a lower price. Do not attempt to conduct the entire negotiation. You will have 5 minutes to complete this exercise.

After conducting both **EXERCISE 3-2** and **3-3**, answer the following questions.

(1) How did the email introduction differ from the in-person introduction?

(2) Which method did you find was preferable in this situation? Why?

(3) Would you successfully be able to conduct the entire negotiation using either email or in person?

(4) Would a combination of email and in-person negotiation achieve the optimum result? Why or why not?

3-4. Assume you interviewed for a marketing position at a start-up company located in California. You live in Tennessee. Your interview was in person in their California offices. You left after the interview and two days after you arrived home to Tennessee you received a text message offering you a position for a salary of $70,000 per year with significant benefits. While the salary is more than you are making currently in your present job, your research suggests that the salary offered is slightly lower for comparable jobs in California given the high cost of living. They have given you a one-week deadline to accept the offer. You have decided that you want to ask for a higher salary. Since you cannot do an in-person negotiation for practical reasons, you will need to use one of the other platforms discussed above to negotiate a higher salary. Answer the following questions for each possible platform.

(1) Assume you choose to negotiate by email. How would you draft an email regarding the salary?

(2) Assume you choose to negotiate by text. How would you draft your text message? Would your text be different than your email and why?

(3) Assume you choose to negotiate by either phone or videoconferencing. Draft an outline of the initial conversation you would use to introduce a negotiation concerning the salary under either phone or videoconferencing. How would videoconferencing be different than phone?

(4) Which platform do you think would work best for this exercise? Do you anticipate switching platforms at any point during the negotiations and why?

CHAPTER 4

Bargaining

I know you're really enjoying this ice-breaking, but it's time to negotiate.

Ice-Breaking

Once the parties have chosen their initial negotiation platform, it is time to meet and begin the process of negotiating. No matter which platform the parties choose to initiate the negotiations, the start of the negotiation is often the most awkward part. The parties should think of the start of the negotiation as the beginning of a first date. Most people on that first date want to make a good first impression. Similarly, the beginning of the first negotiating session should strive for that good first impression objective.

Many inexperienced negotiators will just start the negotiations with their opening offer. Such an abrupt opening may not be optimal. Or there are some negotiation pretenders who show up with no real intent to negotiate, but rather show up and make an unrealistic demand, appear miffed when it is rejected, and storm out of the room in a dramatic fashion. Why do they show up? Perhaps they were ordered to do so by a court or were under some type of outside pressure to make an appearance. Perhaps they did not read this negotiating book and believe this dramatic posturing is most effective. Such posturing is unlikely to succeed. This posturing signals to the other side that there is no genuine interest in negotiating an agreement. Parties who intend to negotiate in good faith would not start a negotiation in such a volatile manner. Rather, like a first date, the parties should spend some time getting to know each other and finding common ground before launching into demands. Parties that approach a negotiation in an overly aggressive manner, believing that establishing a rapport and seeking cooperation shows weakness, are often surprised by how quickly the negotiation dissolves. It is important from the outset for parties to show they are willing to collaborate to reach a successful outcome.

No matter which platform you are using for the initial negotiating session, if you have never met the other side, you should take a moment to introduce yourself. If you are meeting in person for the first time, you should formally introduce yourself even if you have previously called, texted, or emailed the other person. A formal introduction may also save you the potential embarrassment of starting a negotiation with the wrong person or mispronouncing their name.

After the introductions, it is advisable to take a few minutes for ice-breaking. Ice-breaking is best accomplished by finding common ground with the other side. That common ground may be as insignificant as the weather. However, to avoid the mundane, if you are negotiating with a person you have never met you should do some homework to obtain basic information about them. Your biographical research may uncover common ground. Perhaps you attended the same college as the other party or grew up in neighboring cities. You may have a common interest in certain sports. A brief discussion on any of these topics helps to put the parties at ease.

After the introductions and ice-breaking, it is helpful for you to make a statement showing your willingness to make a deal. For example, "I'm happy we could meet today, and I hope we can work this out." You may think this shows weakness, but it does not, and is usually quite effective. A willingness to settle should be the reason you are meeting. Of course, this does not mean that if ten minutes into the negotiation the other side is making unreasonable demands and refusing to make counteroffers, that you should continue your amicable posture. At that point, you should make firm demands that are clear and supported by objective criteria. If there is no reciprocal willingness to negotiate in good faith, it may be time to end the session.

At this beginning stage of the bargaining phase of the negotiation, it is a good idea to present your proposed agenda to the other side. If your negotiation session has a time limit that you did not communicate when the negotiation was scheduled, inform the other side at this time. For example, "I have a hearing in an hour, so we will only have about 45 minutes to discuss this now." If you are limiting this negotiation to one issue in a case, for example medical expenses and not liability, state that at the outset.

In other words, try to outline for the other side the scope of what you believe can be accomplished in this session. Also, be open to meeting again, if things are not resolved in this session. If the negotiation goes badly, you may not be eager to schedule the next session. In the beginning, however, it is a good idea to let the other side know that you expect an open line of communication that will continue beyond this session, if necessary.

After ice-breaking, it is time to start negotiating. Since you have a negotiation plan, you should feel confident to proceed. Recall, however, that this plan is just a guideline, as you may be off your game plan very quickly. if for example, the introductions did not go as amicably as hoped, or if the other side institutes their game plan before you. However, no matter how the negotiation begins, negotiations typically include offers, counteroffers, and concessions.

Offers, Counteroffers, and Concessions

There is considerable debate on who should make the first offer in a negotiation.[1] As noted in Chapter 2 on Tactical Planning, sometimes a first offer has already been made prior to the negotiation. For example, if you are negotiating for the purchase of a home, the first offer may be the seller's listed sale price for the home. In that case, your first offer is really a counteroffer. In addition, the other side may make the first offer before you have a chance to take the lead. You will likely have to adjust your planned opening offer, if the other side makes the first offer. However, in many negotiations, the first offer has not been made. In these cases, you have to determine whether you should make that first offer or wait for the other side to make it.

Some experts believe making the first offer gives you the upper hand in the negotiation in that you have set a starting point. By making the first offer, you have "dropped the anchor," which often results in what is referred to as anchoring bias. Anchoring bias, which applies in numerous contexts not just negotiations, is a cognitive bias and describes a "common tendency to give too much weight to the first number put forth in a discussion and then inadequately adjust from that starting point, or anchor."[2] If the parties eventually settle closer to the initial offer than to the other side's counter offer, it may be the result of an anchoring bias. Negotiation research on anchoring bias "has shown that negotiators may be able to gain an edge by making the first offer and anchoring the discussion in their favor."[3]

A study on anchoring bias involving a sale of a house demonstrates the powerful effect of making the first offer. Professors Greg Northcraft and Margaret Neale conducted an experiment in which they provided real estate agents with different randomly chosen list prices for a house that was for sale.[4] The random prices for the house in the experiment ranged from $119,900 to $149,900. The real estate agents were also given information about the house such as comparable prices and other data. In addition, the agents all took a tour of the house. After the agents were each given their individual randomly designated "list price," they were then asked to set their own list price for the house. The result of the experiment was that agents who were given a higher random list price set their own list price higher than those who were given lower list prices. Even though all the real estate agents were given the same additional information about the house and all took a tour, they were likely influenced by the initial randomly designated "list price" they were given, suggesting an anchoring bias. Interestingly, all the agents rejected the idea of an anchoring bias and justified their estimates on unique features of the properties they were assigned.

Anchoring bias may be especially effective in situations where there is an unequal balance of power or when one party has more knowledge about the subject matter than the other and attempts to drop the anchor by making the first offer. For example, in a salary negotiation, typically the employer has more power and knows more about the salary range of their company than the potential employee. In this situation, the employer almost always drops the first anchor and makes a salary offer. How should the potential employee respond to the employer's attempt to anchor? The potential employee needs to be armed with objective criteria to uproot that anchor and perhaps pull the salary into a range more desirable to the potential employee.

A first offer does not always, however, result in anchoring bias. Generally, in a situation where there is a long-standing relationship between the parties, anchoring bias may lose its effect.[5] If, for example, a car manufacturer has been shipping cars to a car dealer for many years, the parties' negotiating pricing may be somewhat routine. Each side has nearly equal power and the same access to knowledge, such as profit margins and because of this awareness, each side will resist being anchored.

Furthermore, making the first offer may, in fact, be a disadvantage in certain negotiations. You may decide to let the other side make the first offer in the following situations. First, despite the risk of the other side attempting to drop an anchor as discussed above, it may make sense to hear the other side's offer when he possesses more knowledge about the matter at hand than you do, and you are unable to obtain that information through any further research. Second, it may make sense to allow the other side to make the first offer when your highest, specific, realistic offer is so novel and innovative that it is difficult to estimate its value. For example, Thomas Edison went to Western Union with a new invention to improve the telegraph machine. He had initially planned to ask for $2,000, but when Western Union asked his price, he decided to let them make the first offer. Western Union offered $40,000, which he accepted and used the funds to build a laboratory where he would later develop a better known invention—the light bulb.[6] A third instance in which it may make sense to have the other side make the first offer is where it is customary practice in a business or industry.

Notwithstanding certain situations where you should not or cannot make the first offer, in instances where you have significant information, you should plan to make the first offer. Making the first offer signals to the other side the value you have placed on the negotiation. An overly aggressive first offer may suggest a long battle ahead. Conversely, too low an opening offer may indicate to the other side a too eager willingness to settle, which may suggest weakness in your case. Since your planned offer is supported with objective criteria, you should feel comfortable in taking the lead and making the offer.

Communicating Objective Criteria behind Offers and Counteroffers

Experienced negotiators recognize the value of communicating objective criteria in support of their offers and counteroffers.[7] For example, you should not say, "I am willing to offer you $10,000 to settle this case." Instead, say, "I am willing to offer $10,000 because that amount represents half of your property damage and based on well-established law, you are 50% at fault." If the other side doubts your criteria, it helps to offer proof. Be prepared to offer to show the other side the case law, comparables, or other objective criteria and be ready to do a quick internet search, if there arises a question about such criteria. Similarly, if the other side makes an offer and does not support it with objective criteria you should ask her to support that offer with her objective criteria. If she has no basis, or if she tries to bluff a justification, you should refer to your planning worksheet to prove that her offer is not realistic and to justify your rejection of that offer. For example, assume you want to purchase a boat, which is listed for sale for $80,000. You meet to negotiate with the seller. After initial ice-breaking, you offer to buy the boat for $40,000 and you provide the seller with objective criteria supporting your offer. Assume the seller rejects your offer and reiterates that the list price is $80,000 but provides no objective criteria supporting that price. Instead of raising your offer, you should ask the seller for her justification for the list price. The seller should provide some objective criteria as to why $80,000 is a realistic price. If she is unwilling or unable to provide objective criteria as to why the $80,000 is justifiable, you should reiterate your criteria for the $40,000 offer. For example, if your criteria included a range of comparable sales you could explain that the seller's offer is clearly outside the range. This discussion should cause the buyer to reconsider her initial list price.

Sound negotiations have a healthy exchange of offers and counteroffers supported by objective criteria. Obtaining a counteroffer from the other side typically propels the parties towards a resolution. Even if the counteroffer is not particularly attractive, it serves several purposes. First, it demonstrates a willingness of both parties to participate actively in the negotiation. Second, the counteroffer when coupled with the offer, serves to bracket the negotiation.[8] In other words, the offer and counteroffer reveals the upper and lower settlement limits of the negotiation. Bracketing indicates the actual range that the negotiating parties are in and should protect against future extreme offers outside the range.

Once the negotiation is bracketed, it is important to check your planning worksheet and compare that bracketed range to your minimal acceptable level. If the negotiation bracket includes your minimal level, you know that you are now in a range to settle, although you should continue to work towards moving the needle closer to your optimal, specific, reasonable goal. If the bracket does not meet your minimal acceptable level, then you know that there is a lot of work ahead in this negotiation. For example, assume when preparing your planning worksheet, you determined that your optimal realistic goal was $50,000 and your minimal acceptable settlement was $20,000. In negotiations, you offered $50,000 to the other side, and she responded with a counter offer of $10,000. The negotiation is now bracketed, with the potential range of settlement between $50,000 and $10,000. However, since your minimal acceptable settlement is $20,000, even though the negotiation is bracketed, you are not in the range in which you planned to settle. Regardless, bracketing is beneficial, as you and the other side have now set the parameters of this negotiation with a settlement range between $10,000 and $50,000.

Bracketing can also be understood in the context of the sale of a house. Assume a seller determines that his optimal realistic goal for the sale of the house is $500,000 and that the minimum he would accept for the house is $440,000. The seller lists the house for sale for $500,000. Assume further that a potential buyer makes an offer of $460,000 for the house. When the buyer's offer comes in, the negotiation is now bracketed. That is, the parameters for the negotiation are set within the range of $500,000 to $460,000. Since $460,000 is higher than the seller's minimal acceptable level, the parties are well in a range to agree in the negotiations and the negotiations should go well. What if, however, the buyer's offer was only $420,000? In that case, the negotiation is bracketed, with the range between $500,000 and $420,000, but the range is below the seller's minimal acceptable level of $440,000. In that case, the negotiations may be more challenging. Once the negotiation is bracketed, there should continue to be a healthy exchange of offers and counteroffers supported by objective criteria.

There may be instances, however, where the other side rejects your offer, does not make a counteroffer and thus no bracket is established. If no counteroffer is forthcoming, ask for one. If the other side is attempting to get you to revise your first offer before making a counteroffer, hold firm. If you adjust your initial offer, you have just made a counteroffer to your own offer. In essence, the other side has managed to get you to negotiate against yourself to obtain a better deal without putting an offer on the table. Stick with your negotiating plan and communicate that you will not make any further offers until you receive a counteroffer. Also, make sure that you check your plan, so you do not accept below your bottom line and be aware of what your alternatives are to settlement. While it would be highly unusual to accept the first offer or counteroffer, bracketing will give you the ability to see how much work is ahead before you make a deal.

Along with offers and counteroffers, concessions are an integral part of the negotiations. Generally, once an initial offer and counteroffer have been made, the parties typically begin making concessions.[9] In other words, concessions should be interwoven throughout the negotiation. The timing of making concessions is a critical factor in a negotiation. Further, making smaller concessions at appropriate times is usually more productive than making one large concession. Also, making rapid concessions is often associated with a weak position, while holding off on making concessions is associated with a reluctance to engage in any meaningful bargaining. Getting the other side to make the first concession is advantageous in accessing flexibility. If you have taken the lead and made the first offer in the negotiation, the other side's counteroffer may in fact include a concession. However, if no concessions appear forthcoming, it may be necessary for you to start the concession exchange.

Since you have prepared the Tactical Planning Worksheet, you have prepared concessions you are willing to make and the order in which you plan to make those concessions. You would usually begin with the concession that you have determined on your worksheet is of least importance to you, but is something valued by the other side. Furthermore, with thorough research, you are likely aware of the value the other side has placed on this concession. For example, assume Sally's dog allegedly bit her neighbor Cory in front of his house, causing a minor bite wound to his leg. Cory has sued Sally for monetary damages, including medical bills and emotional distress. However, the dog bite required minimal medical intervention, with no stitches or scarring. Since Sally's dog had all of his shots, there are no known diseases transmitted from the dog to Cory. Yet Sally may know from speaking with others in the neighborhood prior to the negotiation that Cory has strongly suggested that Sally's dog be removed from the neighborhood, even hinting to other neighbors of a drastic remedy that her dog should be euthanized. During the negotiation, after first offers and counteroffers were rejected, Sally may now decide to make a concession that she will not walk her dog on Cory's street in the future. This small concession is of minimal importance to Sally but based on information Sally has learned from the neighbors, is of great importance to Cory. Sally's concession may prove to move the needle on the big issues in this case, the amount of damages, and hopefully delay or avoid discussion of a more drastic remedy such as removing the dog from the neighborhood or euthanizing the dog.

Concessions are rarely made in isolation and are usually tied to offers. Therefore, the ultimate success of a concession may likely depend on the seriousness of the first offer. If the other side perceives the first offer to be frivolous, the concession will also appear lacking in sincerity and depth. For example, in the dog bite case discussed above, assume Cory presented medical bills of $800 to Sally in support of his damages claim. If Sally's first offer is $25 and she states to Cory, "that's all you deserve," Cory will likely not value Sally's subsequent concession of not walking the dog on Cory's street. Further, just as offers must be supported by objective criteria, so should concessions. When offering a concession, explain how the concession benefits the other side and that you are truly given up something of value.

While offering a concession should lead to a reciprocal concession and counteroffer, negotiations rarely run so smoothly. Generally, negotiation protocols suggest that when one party concedes certain issues the other party is expected to make similar compromises. Experienced negotiators know, however, that some parties do not follow negotiating protocols, at least not on every occasion. It is possible that a concession will be rejected with no reciprocity in the hope that an outright refusal to cooperate may spur additional concessions and offers. It is important that you never get to the point where you are the only one in the room making concessions. In that situation you are increasing the attractiveness of your offer while the other side simply sits back and waits until the terms become acceptable. Similar to bargaining against yourself by making repeated unreciprocated offers, if you see that you are in the situation where the other side is simply rejecting whatever concessions you put on the table, it is time to put the brakes on making subsequent concessions. Instead, you should ask the other side for their next offer or concession. If none is forthcoming, it may be time to end the negotiation session.

Some negotiators like to avoid the possibility of unreciprocated concessions by making a contingent concession.[10] In other words, I will make this concession if you make that concession. In this way, your concession is contingent on a reciprocal concession. By using a reciprocal concession strategy, you have clearly communicated to the other side that you not only expect him to make a reciprocal concession, but that there is a specific concession you want him to make. A contingent concession does have some drawbacks, however. By tying your concession to the potential concession from the other party, you have narrowed the possible concessions the other side may have made in response to your concession. In fact, the other side may have made a more beneficial concession in response to your concession than the one you proposed that he offer. Recall Sally's biting dog. If Sally simply makes a concession that she will not walk her dog on Cory's street and waits for Cory's response, she has left open all possible concessions Cory may make. However, if Sally says, "I will not walk my dog on your street if you agree to not pursue quarantining or euthanizing my dog," she has effectively made a reciprocal bargain of those issues only. If Cory says, "I was never going to pursue that course of action and give me my $800," her contingent concession has weakened her bargaining power. If she had simply said, "I will not walk my dog on your street," Cory may have lowered his damage request in response. However, if the continued welfare of the dog was in fact priceless to Sally, then she was wise to use the contingent concession even though she may wind up paying more in damages. Given the uncertainty of contingent concessions, it is of the utmost importance that you conduct research prior to the negotiation, so that you are in the best position to place a value on the concessions you are making and accepting from the other side.

Remember during the bargaining phase of the negotiation to refer to the concession order you outlined in your Tactical Planning Worksheet. Also, remember to check off the concessions as you offer them and write down the concessions you have been offered during the negotiation. Some of the offered concessions will hopefully match the anticipated concessions you tried to predict in your planning worksheet. Keeping track of the concessions will ensure you make those concessions in order and will give you a quick picture of the number of concessions you have made in relation to the concessions made by the other side.

EXERCISES 4-1 AND 4-2: OFFERS, COUNTEROFFERS, AND CONCESSIONS

4-1. Assume that six months ago, you started an online meal prep delivery service. You place an ad on a popular food delivery platform advertising customizable weekly meal plans for busy professionals. You advertise that in addition to standard meals, you also offer low calorie, low carb, vegan, and gluten free options. Your ad includes your contact information and states that pricing depends on the number of meals and dietary preferences. Kate, a potential client, messages you through the platform and explains her needs for five meals per week, tailored to a vegan and gluten free diet. Kate also states she needs the meals delivered within two days of placing the order. She then asks for a price. You respond that based on the information provided, your price for five meals delivered within two days would be $200 ($40 per meal). Kate responds that she does not want to pay more than $150 for the five meals. You counter with $170, explaining that at this price, you will need three days to prepare and deliver the meals due to ingredient sourcing for vegan and gluten free options. Assume that Kate states your terms are unacceptable and asks for a better price but does not counter further. Assume that your business is doing reasonably well after six months and while you are eager to add new customers, maintaining consistent pricing is paramount for the success of your business. You have only had two prior customers who requested vegan and gluten free meals and you charged them $40 per meal for standard three-day delivery. However, both customers only wanted three meals per week. How should you respond to Kate?

4-2. You are a salesperson for a large electronics store. The store is currently trying to sell a well-known manufacturer's latest mobile phone. The manufacturer mandates that the phone must be sold for its retail price of $1200. However, the manufacturer will allow the store through its salespersons to offer perks, or concessions, to buyers that are not tied to the price. These perks include free service contracts, free service activation, a generous trade-in policy of no less than 75% of its value in the next two years, and a 50% discount on a case for the phone. What would be your strategy for selling this phone? How would you order these concessions to a potential buyer? Why?

Questions

Questions used during the bargaining process can be very effective for many purposes. They are valuable for general information gathering and for clarifying or justifying positions taken in the negotiation. They are also helpful for establishing a positive rapport or for altering the tone of the negotiation when needed, such as tempering an angry exchange.

As discussed in Chapter 2 on Tactical Planning, a thorough planning worksheet will include your proposed questions. However, it is not possible to plan all questions you may ask. Moreover, it is not effective simply to run through all of your prepared questions in the order you planned in your worksheet. Questions are best interspersed throughout the bargaining process. Good negotiators will constantly adjust questions during the negotiation depending on the answers they receive. Once an answer is given, a follow-up question may be necessary.

Listening is a critical part of the questioning process.[11] When and how to ask questions requires you to listen to what is being said by the other side and to pay close attention to the tone and manner in which it is being said. For example, assume you represent a client involved in a car accident. The other side claims that your client failed to yield the right of way at an intersection and hit his client's car, causing injuries. In your worksheet, you planned to ask a question early in the negotiation in order to gather information as to how his client perceived the accident occurred. However, before you can ask that question, the other side begins the negotiation by saying, "Let me tell you how this accident happened. Your client sped through the intersection and was totally negligent in hitting my client's car. End of story." In this scenario, if you were not really listening but reviewing your planning worksheet as he was making this testy statement, and you now ask, "Can you tell me how your client said the accident occurred?" it will be obvious that you were not listening at all to what was just said. Unless the other party thinks you were making a not too funny joke, your question will probably infuriate him and may put a damper on the negotiation. However, hopefully, you were paying attention to the question, and you abandoned your scripted question and asked follow up questions to get more details about their version of the accident. By asking follow up questions, you will be able to gather additional information, since it is highly unlikely that the other side presented a complete detailed version of the accident. It is more likely the other side presented a version very favorable to his client's position and thus left out key information that you would like to know.

Skilled negotiators use both open-ended and closed-end questions as appropriate. Since you should have a prepared list of closed and open-ended questions in your Tactical Planning Worksheet, during bargaining you should strategically decide the best approach to interspersing these types of questions in order to receive optimal answers from the other side. Failing to use a strategic mix of questions could result in receiving unsatisfactory answers or no answers at all. For example, while you may have started with open-ended, non-threatening questions, if the other side's answers are not forthcoming, you may need to reframe your questions as more direct, close ended, or narrow questions. These types of questions may be successful in that they may only require a yes or no answer. Of course, there is a likelihood that the other side may refuse to answer some or all of your questions. If you receive an answer such as "I am not going to answer that," or the more forceful, "Are you kidding me?" you should try to encourage the party to answer. You should explain that an answer would be helpful in moving toward a resolution of the case. For example, if you ask the other side "Was your client on the phone at the time of the accident," you may get the response, "I'm not going to answer," or "I don't know," or "You can ask my client in a deposition." If you receive any of those unhelpful answers, you may explain to the other side that providing an accurate answer will help determine how to apportion liability and that delaying this answer will only serve to delay a resolution. This type of encouragement may prompt a helpful response. However, it is human nature that people (and those who represent them) are reluctant to answer questions that may hurt their case, even though the answer will eventually be revealed. In the situation where the other side will not answer because his client has instructed him not to answer, especially if the information is protected by the attorney-client privilege, you may in fact have reached a dead end. In that instance, it is better to change course and move to a different issue or topic, which will lead to more effective bargaining.

As discussed in Chapter 2 on Tactical Planning, questions serve purposes beyond simply information gathering. Questions may also be used for purposes such as establishing a positive rapport with the other side. For example, during ice-breaking, you may want to ask a non-threatening question such as, "How was the drive to our office today?" Unless the other side was stuck in a two-hour traffic jam, this type of non-threatening question allows the parties to establish a rapport before getting down to the nuts and bolts of the negotiation. However, even the best non-threatening question may go astray. If you sense that the other party is simply not a person who enjoys any small talk, you may abandon the small talk questions and move forward with your agenda.

Questions may also help to clarify matters arising or justify positions taken by a party during the negotiation. For example, if the other party has offered a settlement proposal that is 1% of sales revenue calculated from the first date on the shelf to the expiration date, you should ask questions for clarification. For example, is the percentage based on gross or net revenues? Also, when is "on the shelf" determined? Do not assume that the terms will be explained more thoroughly when the terms are included in the contract. If you cannot explain the deal to others as it was explained to you, you do not have a clear understanding of it. Do not be concerned that you may appear less knowledgeable by asking questions. In fact, asking questions may highlight that there are missing links in the other side's proposal that can now be corrected.

Furthermore, questions are effective in situations where a party makes an offer without providing objective criteria. In those situations, you should ask, "What is your basis for the offer?" This question will help to uncover the other side's objective criteria, if there are any.

Questions can also be usefully employed when negotiations become contentious. They allow the parties to step back. For example, if you make an offer perceived as unrealistic or perhaps insulting, the other side may respond angrily, "That offer is absurd." In order to diffuse this anger and hopefully put the negotiation back on track, you should calmly ask, "What about the offer raises concerns for you?" Hopefully, a question like this would prompt the other side to offer a reasoned response and move the parties towards a productive negotiation session.

Just as you prepared questions to ask in your Tactical Planning Worksheet, your worksheet should reflect questions you expect to be asked and how you plan to respond. Since you have likely anticipated many of the questions posed by the other side, you should be ready with answers. The way in which you answer questions may be mirrored by the other side in the way she answers your questions. Similarly, if you plan to use some diversionary techniques to avoid answering questions, you can expect those diversionary tactics to be used by the other side. For example, in the car accident case discussed above, if you asked the question, "Was your client on her phone at the time of the accident?" you may receive this mirrored question as a response: "Was your client on his phone at the time of the accident?" This question to a question response is fine as long as you have a satisfactory answer. But if you do not want to answer that question, you should not ask it.

Finally, do not be discouraged if many of the questions you prepared go unanswered or unasked. There will be other opportunities to obtain information. You do not want questioning to consume the negotiation process. Use questions strategically and purposefully, but do not lose your focus on bargaining by asking an excessive number of questions.

Bargaining Tactics

Ideally, negotiators will deal fairly and honestly with each other and not resort to game playing or devious tactics. Unfortunately, negotiations do not take place in La La Land and many negotiators do employ these tricks. Thus, you should be aware of some of the most common tricks and tactics and how to respond effectively to them. Tactics involving lying and bias are covered in Chapter 6 on Ethics and Equity.

While there are a myriad of negotiation tricks and tactics, some of the most widely used tactics are described below.[12] Coupled with descriptions of the tactics are some suggested responses.

> ***Extreme opening offer/demand:*** A negotiator may make an extreme offer or demand. This tactic may be used by a competitive, aggressive, negotiator who believes that the shock value of an excessive offer or demand will serve to send a message that he is no pushover and, in fact, may be the bullying kind. An extreme offer may also be used by a negotiator who is not adequately prepared and decides to just shoot from the hip with an extreme offer. Not surprisingly, extreme offers or demands are usually not accompanied by objective criteria.
>
> *Response:* If you receive an extreme offer or demand, your first response should be to ask for the basis of the demand, *i.e.*, the objective criteria, in a non-threatening manner. It is likely that the other side does not have an objective basis for the demand but more likely he will provide an emotional basis, such as "your client needs to pay for what he has done." If this is the case, you may explain why his criteria are lacking. You may further wish to make your own reasonable offer, highlighting the objective criteria you have employed. If the other side will not budge from his extreme position, this negotiation may be over before it has a chance to get started.
>
> ***Take it or leave it:*** A negotiator may set forth an offer followed by the statement, "take it or leave it." This ultimatum may have been preceded by an extreme offer or preceded by an offer worth further consideration but not necessarily acceptable on the spot. In either case, the negotiator employing the ultimatum of "take it or leave it" is attempting to circumvent any further discussion about the offer.
>
> *Response:* While you might be tempted to respond with a hearty "I'll leave it," such a response would likely lead to an escalation of an already tense situa-

tion. Instead of responding by directly addressing their ultimatum, it is better to ignore the "take it or leave it" ultimatum and keep the focus on the offer or demand. You should ask the other party to explain the objective criteria for the offer and continue with further questioning if necessary regarding the basis of the offer. Also, be sure not to fall into the trap of bargaining against yourself and continuing to make offers that are not reciprocated.

Threats: There are many different types of threats a party may resort to in a negotiation. Assuming a threat is not illegal or criminal, such as extortion, a threat used in a negotiation is generally a desperate attempt to force a settlement when a party believes that things are not going well. One type of threat is a scare tactic that interjects a peripheral issue into the discussion in order to intimidate the other side. In these cases, the party using the scare tactic generally does not have the ability to follow through with the threat. For example, assume the other side says, "If you don't accept our offer to purchase your company, we will smear your reputation in the industry." Another type of threat is when the party may or may not have the intention of following through with the threat. For example, the party says, "If you don't settle, we are going to file suit tomorrow." The threat may be simply grandstanding, if the party has no intention of ever filing suit. The party may, however, believe he has a better chance of success in court than you do, and will actually file suit if you do not agree to his negotiating terms. Other types of threats may be grounded in fact and have to be given consideration. Sometimes, a party uses a hardline threat to set forth a viable alternative not previously discussed. For example, if the other side says, "If you do not accept our offer to purchase your company, we will continue our talks with one of your competitors, and if we purchase their business, you will likely not find a buyer in the near future, since we know we are one of few buyers available to purchase this type of business." This type of threat may prove to be an accurate assessment and must be considered more seriously than empty threats.

Response: When a party issues a threat during a negotiation, before you respond, you must first diagnose and try to understand the motivation behind the threat. Was the threat made out of frustration or was it made to introduce a viable alternative? If negotiations have become heated and the other side is simply venting frustration, you should try to express your concern and move the discussion back to the realistic proposals on the table. However, if the threat is actually an alternative that the other side is in a position to employ, you should ask questions to uncover additional information and determine the strength of that alternative. If you are unsure of the viability of the threat and a party persists in using the threat, it may become necessary to call them on the threat and if necessary, respond with a threat. For example, back to the example, "If you do not settle, we will file suit tomorrow," you may feel confident to call them on it if you feel they are bluffing. You might point out that a lawsuit would be costly and the time it would take to get the case resolved would cause a disruption to their business. If the party is unmoved by this reasoning, it might be best to offer a counter threat such as, "If we do go to trial, legal precedent is in our favor and I believe a jury will be much more sympathetic to our position than to your position." Of course, you need to be prepared to back up these statements or else you are simply issuing an empty threat as well. In situations where you are unsure of the legitimacy and strength of threat, the best approach in confronting the threat may be for you to use a mix of aggressive questioning and accommodating questioning.

Limited/lack of authority: You may get to a point in the negotiation where you believe you are close to coming to an agreement, when suddenly the other side says, "This all sounds good, but I have to go back to my client, boss, husband, preacher, or mother before I can make this deal." If disingenuous, this is a classic stall tactic and an attempt to delay a resolution of the matter. If negotiations are going well, it may be baffling as to why a party would want to delay, but the "blame someone else" tactic is likely an attempt to get you to sweeten your offer by interjecting uncertainty of authority.

Conversely, there are cases in which a settlement requires approval by another person, such as where an attorney needs client approval, but the negotiating party refuses to try to obtain that approval. The party may respond to your offer by saying, "This offer is so insulting that I am not going to take this offer back to my client." In this instance, the party is using the ultimate insult tactic, *i.e.*, your offer is so unworthy it is not even worth repeating to the client. The refusal to obtain the authority may be a stalling tactic.

Response: You should never be in a position where the other side can surprise you with a claim of a lack of authority. Before you begin negotiations, you should confirm that the party you are negotiating with has the full and complete authority to enter into a settlement. If the party does not have such authority, you should establish a procedure before negotiations begin for obtaining such authority. However, if you have not had a pre-negotiation discussion concerning authority, and you are surprised by this lack of authority during the negotiation, you should now establish the procedure for getting this authority by asking, "When will you get a response from your client?" If you receive a vague or unconvincing answer on authority, you can infer that the other side probably has no procedure set up to convey settlement proposals to his client and this authority issue is probably a bluff. In that case, you may want to set the parameters by setting forth a time frame for a response such as "how about calling me later today with your client's response." However, if you are in the position where the attorney will not even take the offer to his client, you should remind him that attorneys have an ethical duty to convey all offers to clients, and his client may later be surprised upon learning the attorney rejected your offer without notifying him. Then you can tell the attorney you expect a response once that offer is conveyed to the client.

Time pressure: Many times, there are real time constraints in a negotiation. For example, if you are negotiating a matter in litigation with the other side and the trial is set to begin the next day, time is an important factor both parties must confront as the negotiation proceeds. Or, if the parties are negotiating a prenuptial agreement and the wedding is in a month, the pressure is on to come to an agreement, ditch the prenup, or the heart wrenching decision to cancel the wedding. However, you should be aware of a party who imposes a time constraint when no such constraint exists. For example, if a party says, "This is our offer and you have 24 hours to accept it," and does not give any reason for the 24 hour limitation, it is likely this is a fake deadline imposed by the other side to try to prompt you to quickly accept the offer for fear it may expire. Sometimes time constraints may be subtler. A party who states during a negotiation that he suddenly must leave in 20 minutes, or a party negotiating by email who writes that he will be unavailable by email for a week is attempting to assert time pressure on you to quickly come to a resolution.

Response: You should be able to prevent a party from asserting an artificial time constraint during the negotiation by setting up a time schedule when planning the negotiation. If you are planning to meet in person, discuss the length of time you are available for the negotiation and inquire about time constraints for the other side. If you are negotiating in other formats, this may be more difficult. Since email and text are not in real time, setting a time frame is difficult. You should, however, try to set an endpoint during such exchanges. For example, if you sent the last email or text and have not heard a response for 24 hours, you might send another text or email trying to prompt a response. If you still receive no response, it is time for you to back off from the exchange as the other side may purposely be trying to ignore you in the hope that his silence will cause you to make a better offer.

Anger, sadness, and related personality traits: Negotiations tend to be emotional, and not all negotiators are adept at keeping a poker face during bargaining.[13] Further, there are instances when showing emotion is not a tactic but is genuine. Showing emotion may humanize a party and bring the parties closer to a resolution. For example, assume that Grandma passes away, and two sisters are negotiating over who will get possession of her silverware. Sister 1 becomes teary eyed after telling Sister 2 that she would like Grandma's silverware to eventually pass down to her daughter, who is a chef. Sister 2 is moved by her emotion, and Sister 1's emotional statement may in fact help to resolve the dispute. However, in the same scenario, if Sister 1 produces tears that appeared feigned, and says Grandma said to her before she passed away, "Sister 1, I want you to have the silverware after I go," Sister 2 may believe the tears and the story are fake, and this emotional statement may actually escalate the matter.

Anger is also a common emotion expressed during negotiations. In most instances, anger complicates bargaining, and it is not helpful in resolving the conflict. A party may become angry simply because he has lost control during the negotiation or the anger is a tactic to intimidate the other side and force a solution. Furthermore, whether the anger is real or fake, when a party expresses anger, the other side often responds with anger. Anger is often expressed in personal attacks, which have no legitimate purpose in effective bargaining.

Response: In most negotiations, it is best to try to maintain composure when confronted with an emotional outburst from the other side. By keeping your emotions steady, you have the opportunity to consider the other side's emotional display in context. It may be that the party's expression of emotion is genuine and will bring you closer to a resolution. In arms open negotiations, where the parties have a personal relationship, emotions may be easily triggered as negotiations become tense. However, if the emotion is a recognizable tactic, and does not serve to facilitate the negotiation but in fact makes the negotiation more tense, you should try to stay calm and get the negotiations back on track. This calmness is especially effective when responding to anger. Do not allow yourself to be bullied or intimidated. Unfortunately, in some circumstances, your composed demeanor in the face of anger may serve to make the other side angrier. If that is the case, you should take a break until the other side can approach the negotiation without anger. Furthermore, avoid the temptation to respond to anger with anger. If you start a yelling exchange, you will lose your focus, and it will be difficult to get the negotiation back on track.

The above tactics are only a select few of the myriad of possible gamesmanship employed by negotiators. If you are involved in an arms-length negotiation, you should be on guard to potential tactics and be prepared with responses. If you are involved in an arms-open negotiation, however, because of your familiarity with your counterpart you are probably well aware of what, if any, tactics they may attempt and are already prepared with responses and you can move right on to Chapter 5 on Letting Go or Resolving.

CHAPTER 5

Letting Go or Resolving

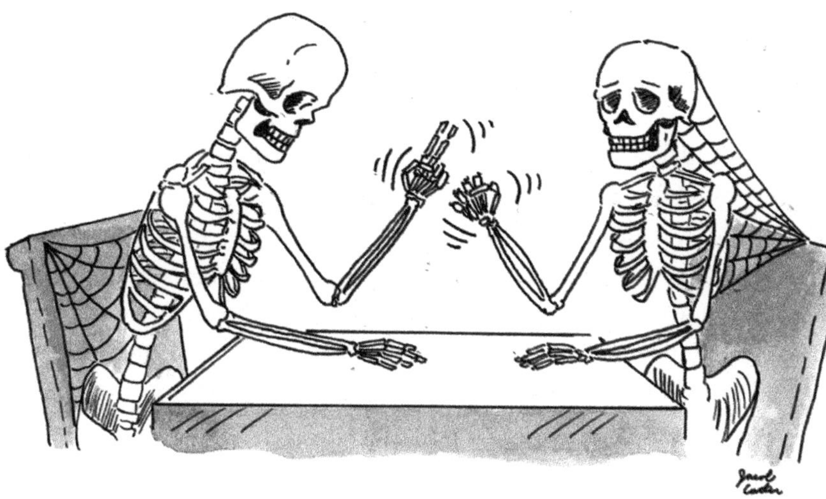

"We're so close, we can't give up now!"

Letting Go or Resolving

If you bargain effectively and efficiently, you will hopefully reach an agreement during bargaining and will not need to confront the letting go or resolving dilemma. However, there is a point in many negotiations where you begin to doubt whether there will be a resolution. This doubt may arise whether you have been involved in a series of negotiations on the matter or it is only the first negotiation. If the offers and concessions have slowed to a crawl and frustration is becoming apparent, it is time to either kick the negotiation up a notch or call it, either for the day, or for good. However, there are many factors to address before deciding if you should stay or go. These factors are considered below.

Time Constraints

Prior to or at the beginning of the negotiation, as discussed in Chapter 4 on Bargaining, you likely set the agenda, which hopefully included any time constraints on the upcoming negotiation session. There may be rigid time constraints that are out of the parties' control, such as pending trial dates, shipping deadlines, or expiration of contracts. If any of these are in play, then both sides know the clock is running and there may be a greater desire to keep the negotiation going, especially if alternatives are not attractive. There may also be more flexible time constraints set by a party, such as needing to adjourn for another appointment or catching a flight. These are flexible time constraints because they are self-imposed by the parties, and although the party may believe these future obligations are not movable, there is no third party deadline imposed as in a trial date. There may also be time constraints that are not preplanned but arise abruptly during the negotiation. These abrupt time constraints may be real emergencies that arise or may be manufactured predicaments by a party who just wants to leave the negotiation. For example, a party's phone may suddenly ring followed by an announcement that she must leave. Was this a real or manufactured excuse? If the negotiation was stalled or emotions were running high, it may well be a subtle way of ending it.

If the negotiation is headed towards a time constraint that you are aware of, it is appropriate to take a moment to assess your progress and determine whether it is desirable to continue with the pending deadline looming ahead. In order to make that assessment, you should examine your current bargaining position and determine how close you are to resolving this negotiation and your alternatives if you do not settle.

Assess Your Progress

Determining if you are close to resolving the matter will help you decide your approach to the remainder of the negotiation. At this stage of the negotiation, you may be making real progress, some progress, or no progress at all.

Assume the negotiation session has been going well, with mutual offers and concessions, when it slows to a crawl and suddenly you are at an impasse. In order to get back on track, you should try to return to questioning, especially non-threatening questions.[1] Try to determine, through questioning, why the offers and concessions have stopped. It may be that the other side has reached his bottom line, or that he has reacted negatively to information you have given to him and does not want to continue. By asking questions, you may be able to uncover the reasons for the disruption.

It also may be that your negotiating counterpart is reluctant to make a deal for emotional reasons, not business reasons. For example, assume that Nate has owned and worked at his family deli for 40 years. He took over the business from his father, who had started the business. Nate is in poor health, and he needs more liquid assets. His family members have not been significantly involved in the business and do not want to take over and run the deli. You want to purchase his deli and after several rounds of negotiations, you and Nate are very close to making a deal when suddenly Nate says, "That's it. I don't think we are going to make a deal." He then begins to gather his belongings and starts to leave.

It is apparent that Nate is having an emotional reaction to selling his business and trouble letting go. At this point, you should try to show compassion and discuss with him the difficulty of leaving his business. You should also try to brainstorm some creative solutions to keep Nate peripherally involved in the business. Perhaps Nate can be a consultant, or you might agree to consider hiring some of his family as future employees. However, these solutions must also be compatible with your goals. You should also ask Nate to examine his alternatives if he does not sell the deli to you. It is likely his best alternative is not as good as your offer. After exploring these options, you may now have convinced Nate to go through with the sale.

Sometimes, you may notice the mood in the room shifts for no reason that is apparent to you. In this case, you should examine the reasons for the shift in mood. If you had been having a professional and courteous exchange, you are much more likely to get the negotiation back on track.[2] However, if the mood and tone has been strained or negative, you, or the other side, may have reached the breaking point and the negotiation is collapsing under the strain. It is important to examine if there was a mood changing event that occurred during the negotiation, and attempt to get back on track. In this case, a short recess may be able to get the sides to break the ominous mood and return to productivity.

If your negotiation never progressed past the ice-breaking and initial offers stages, and now you are faced with a time constraint, it may be that this was never going to be a successful negotiation and it is time to quit. You are not really deadlocked because this negotiation was DOA. Any attempt to resuscitate it at this point may lead to a hurried bargaining phase with the potential for you to make too many concessions in the hopes of making a quick deal. If you believe there is still a possibility of working a deal, and are not confined by a rigid time constraint, you may want to suggest ending the negotiation session for the day, and reconvening at another time. However, do not make this suggestion unless you think the next negotiation will be different from this one. Moreover, if you have gained any information from this session, you may legitimately need to do additional research and investigation before the next session. Even if that is not the case, you should not meet again if there are no plans to take the negotiation in a more successful direction. Therefore, you will need to review your Tactical Planning Worksheet and determine if there is a different strategy you may need to implement the next time. Of course, it takes the other side to act reasonably also. If you were negotiating in good faith, but the other side was simply unreasonable, refusing to make offers, counteroffers, or concessions, there is no amount of strategy or revising of your worksheet that will help. In that instance, it is better to either agree to meet again only if the other side truly wants to attempt to reach a resolution and will put more effort into bargaining.

In many negotiations, the bargaining is not all smooth or all rocky. You may be at a point where there have been some offers and concessions on both sides, but the brackets are wide and not close to your settlement range, and progress has halted. If you have proposed the last offer on the table, and no counteroffer is forthcoming from the other side, as previously discussed, make sure you do not make another offer and bargain against yourself in an attempt to move the negotiation forward. You should also maintain your composure and not be frustrated by the lack of progress, even if the other side vents his frustration. Asking open-ended questions, such as "What can we do to move the negotiation forward?" may get the other side to talk and lead to further progress. But be prepared for a response such as, "offer us more money." If you are unable to move past this point, and other attempts to move the negotiation forward fail, it is appropriate to evaluate whether there is anything else to accomplish in this session. If there was real progress that has temporarily slowed, you may be more readily able to suggest a recess or schedule another session. If there is a time constraint, a break may be possible but scheduling another session may not. At this point, it is time to examine your alternatives.

Examining Your Alternative Options

Before pulling the plug on any negotiation, it is important to compare the offer on the negotiation table to your alternative options if you do not reach an agreement. The offer on the table may be within your range of an acceptable agreement, but not at the top of the range, or the offer may not be within your range of an acceptable settlement. In either situation, you must decide whether to push for more or accept their offer and consider your alternative. If you are within your range, you may breathe a little easier, because you are likely assured of a positive outcome. However, if you are not in range, you may be sweating a bit. Either way, you should determine if the status quo or alternative is better than the last offer. Since you have prepared a planning worksheet, you have pre-determined your BATNA. Further, you have also estimated what the other side's best alternative is as well. During the course of the negotiation, you may have gained information that you must now factor in and adjust the other side's alternative. Taking in all these factors, assess the most desirable outcome for the negotiation. It may well be that continuing the negotiation and seeking a better resolution is better than accepting your alternative. If this is the case, you should assess time constraints and decide the best approach to keep the negotiation process going.

Splitting the Difference to Reach Agreement

Sometimes parties are stuck in the process and no matter how much they debate and use objective criteria, neither party is willing to budge from their last offers. Splitting the difference is a well-known technique implemented by parties to try to reach an agreement by using simple math.[3] For example, let us assume Buyer and Seller are in the midst of negotiations over the sale of a house. Buyer's last offer was $275,000 and Seller's last offer was $285,000. Despite offering objective criteria and asking questions to obtain more information, Buyer and Seller refuse to budge from their last offers, but neither party wants to walk away (even if they pretend they do). Buyer may now suggest that they "split the difference" and agree to a selling price of $280,000, which is the midpoint between $275,000 and $285,000. This technique may prove successful in that it seems a fair way to raise/lower offers without an emotional component.

Splitting the difference should be used sparingly and with caution. First, you should rarely split the difference in the early stages of the negotiation or never when your respective offers are far apart. Splitting the difference between $275,000 and $285,000 is significantly different than splitting the difference between $300,000 and $800,000. It is likely with this vast range that you have not acquired information from the other side or fully stated your position. Negotiations should not be reduced to simple mathematical equations when there are real differences in offers and desired outcomes. Your Tactical Planning Worksheet set forth your research and objective criteria for you to use in order to make offers, counteroffers, and concessions. Do not abandon your planning to do mathematical computations when your bargaining position is so far apart from the other side's bargaining position as reflected in the offers.

Second, splitting the difference may simply be a tactic used by the other side and does not promote fairness at all, despite the use of non-judgmental math. For example, refer back to the sale of the house. Assume Seller had first offered the house at $300,000 and Buyer's first offer was $220,000. After small concessions and counteroffers by Seller, Seller's last offer was, as stated in the example above, $285,000 while buyer's last offer was $275,000. They now decide to split the difference and agree on $280,000. However, under this scenario, Buyer has increased his original offer by $60,000, while Seller decreased his offer by only $20,000. Unless Buyer's opening offer was not justified by objective criteria, Buyer did not succeed in obtaining an equitable result by splitting the difference. Therefore, it is important to keep track of offers, counteroffers, and concessions during the negotiation so as not to fall into the trap of splitting a lopsided difference.

Third, splitting the difference may result in re-bracketing of your offer. Therefore, it may be wise for you to avoid being the one to suggest the split the difference option. Even with this warning, you may still be tempted to use this technique in the throes of a negotiation when a deal may be imminent. If you decide to suggest splitting the difference, be aware that a savvy negotiator may use this split the difference offer as a chance to re-bracket the negotiation and ultimately make a better deal. For example, assume you are an attorney representing a doctor, who is the defendant in a medical malpractice action. During the negotiation with the plaintiff's attorney, your last offer on the table was $100,000 and the plaintiff's attorney's last offer was $120,000. It is late in the day and you are ready for this negotiation to end, so you throw out a "let's just split the difference at $110,000." Instead of jumping at your offer, the Plaintiff's attorney replies, "So you're willing to go to $110,000?" As you mumble "yes," he says, "Ok, let me take that back to my client and get back to you." A few hours later, he contacts you and says, "my client will not go to $110,000 but will agree to $115,000." You are likely to either agree to $115,000 or you may try to get his client to split the difference again and agree to $112,500. At this point, because you are still close to settling, you are most likely eager not to derail the deal. However, your splitting the difference technique became an offer which permitted the other side to counter one more time for a higher amount.[4]

Scheduling Another Negotiating Session

If in fact, you cannot reach an agreement during the negotiation session but have decided it will be beneficial to continue the negotiation at another time, and have convinced the other side to continue, it is important to make sure you schedule the next meeting before you adjourn for the day. It is not enough to leave simply with a casual, "I'll be in touch." It is much more effective to attempt to set the next meeting at the end of this session. In this way, not only do you have a commitment from the other side to continue, but you have shown your willingness to try and further work toward an agreement.

When scheduling the next meeting, you should first determine the forum in which to continue.[5] While you may have met in person for this negotiation, you are certainly not bound by that forum for the next meeting. In fact, logistics may prove it to be difficult for the parties to meet again in person, so alternatives should be suggested. As discussed in Chapter 3 on Arranging, videoconferencing, email, phone, and text are all viable formats for negotiation and may be an easy and cost effective way to keep the discussion going.

After determining the forum, you should also try to schedule the next negotiation session sooner rather than later. Obviously if you are bound by a rigid time constraint, that time limitation will influence the next meeting time. However, if there is no immediate time constraint, it is still preferable to not allow too much time to pass before continuing the negotiation. If you delay the next meeting, the incentive to continue the negotiation may decrease. Also, unanticipated issues may arise in the interim recess, which may complicate or derail the progress you have made. Further, although absence makes the heart grow fonder in personal relationships, in negotiation, out of sight, out of mind may prove applicable. This saying may be especially true if you are negotiating the purchase of a business or a job offer. In these situations, there are other fish in the sea and delaying discussions may prove the kiss of death for the deal.

Draft 57: "If you agree to put a semi-colon instead of a period at the end of the second sentence in paragraph 32, I will agree to put a subheading before paragraph 64 as you requested."

Executing the Agreement

If you reached an agreement during the negotiation, congratulations! Even if less desirable than you expected, hopefully your agreement was within your acceptable settlement range and was better than your alternative. While you may think the hard work is over, there is still much to do in order to finalize your agreement, which is the conclusion of a successful negotiation.

If you were negotiating in person, it is likely that you and the other party came to a verbal agreement, shook hands, and said, "I'll be in touch." At this time, it is unlikely that you will have the time or resources to reduce that verbal agreement to writing and draft an immediate settlement agreement and make it legally binding. However, as is often noted, a verbal agreement is not worth the paper it is written on. While oral contracts may be enforceable, it will be a difficult road to prove the terms in the absence of a writing.[6] Therefore, before you adjourn, convince the other side to take a few minutes and reduce the key terms to writing. Memorializing key terms in writing at this time will ensure that you are both in agreement, and if not, allows time to resolve matters in which there remains confusion. If there is no time to reduce the terms to writing before adjourning, you should send an email confirming the terms to the other side as soon as possible after you leave. Hopefully, the other side will acknowledge the representations made in your email, and you will now have written confirmation.

If you have been negotiating by email or text, you have the luxury of already having some terms of your agreement in writing. However, negotiating through email or text rarely translates to a completed agreement. Nevertheless, emails or texts may serve as a written basis from which you can springboard to a completed agreement.

If your negotiation was recorded, the recording will be useful in several ways. First, it will confirm the terms to which you have agreed. Next, it will clear up any confusion as to what was said during the negotiation. Finally, it will help to prevent a party adding terms not agreed upon. Any discrepancies between the parties can be cleared up by playing the recording.

The next and final step in the process is to prepare a formal agreement. Most often the parties will draft a contract, which when finalized, becomes the operating document that controls the parties from this point forward. If a party does not live up to the terms of the agreement, he may be considered "in breach" of the agreement.[7] If the parties are unable to work out their differences, the aggrieved party may need to file a lawsuit or attempt to resolve the dispute through arbitration or mediation.[8]

Whether or not you were able to write down key provisions at the end of the negotiation, you should discuss whether you or the other side will be preparing the final agreement. In some situations, it is standard for one party to prepare the final agreement. For example, in the purchase of a house, the seller, most often through their agent, prepares the sales agreement. This agreement is usually a series of forms containing boilerplate language in which the key provisions, such as sales price, are filled in on the form. Similarly, the seller of a business usually prepares the agreement. However, if you are settling a matter subject to litigation, either party may prepare the settlement agreement, depending on the circumstances. Notwithstanding an industry standard, if there is no objection by the other side, it is wise for you to prepare the agreement so you have the control and the ability to get the document finished in a timely manner.

Once it is decided who will prepare the agreement, the parties should agree to a schedule for completing the agreement. It is customary for the person who prepares the agreement to send it to the other side, who may make non-substantive corrections, additions, or deletions to the agreement before returning it to the preparer. This back and forth may continue until the agreement is acceptable to both sides. Therefore, it is important to try and set a time frame for completion. For example, you might say, "I will prepare the agreement and send it to you by Friday. If you have any changes, I hope we can work on them at the beginning of next week and have this signed by next Thursday." In this way, both parties will have a completion date to strive for. In general, the sooner you can finalize the agreement, the better. Further, there may be valid time constraints in place which will dictate completion of the agreement, such as a pending trial date. If so, you will obviously be bound by those limitations.

In drafting the agreement, do not add any terms not agreed upon in the hopes of playing a game of "gotcha." Conversely, if you receive a prepared settlement agreement, make sure no additional terms were added as well. Changes made by either side should be merely formal or stylistic, not substantively altering the terms of the settlement. The preparation of the settlement agreement is not an opportunity to continue the negotiation, but rather should memorialize the agreed upon terms.

While you hope the process of finalizing the agreement goes smoothly as described above, unfortunately there may be times when a party does add terms to the agreement, either intentionally or mistakenly or he may suggest that the changes are not substantive. If you do not have any written or recorded proof as to what was agreed upon, you may need to jump back to negotiation mode to work out the differences. If you do have to re-negotiate terms, you should first try to narrow the discussion to the new disputed terms and resist the temptation to bring up other terms not in dispute. For example, if a home buyer now disputes that he agreed to a ten-day closing, instead insisting he agreed to a thirty-day closing, the seller should attempt to resolve the closing date instead of moving to other issues. For example, in response to the closing date dispute, the seller should not say, "Well I've decided not to repair that broken window that I had agreed to do." However, if the parties are unable to come to an agreement on the disputed terms, it may be necessary to open up other related issues in order to resolve and salvage the deal. In the home purchase example above, if the parties cannot resolve the closing time frame, and the buyer is insistent on thirty day closing, seller may now say, "well if it is going to be a thirty day closing, you will need to pay me $500 over the agreed selling price as I will incur an extra twenty days of expenses with the house." Note how the disputed closing time frame has prompted the seller to renegotiate the selling price by linking the extra closing time to more added costs. Even though the seller takes the risk by renegotiating terms, he has tied the closing date to the objective criteria of increased expenses.

Drafting the Agreement

The actual drafting of the agreement can be a lengthy and time-consuming process. As noted above, if you are in an industry in which forms are standard, or even required by law, you have a great head start in putting together the agreement. Even if you do not have standard forms, good research, including using AI tools, should provide you with sample forms for whatever contract you are preparing. For example, if you are preparing a settlement agreement for a slip and fall case, you will be able to find many samples of settlement agreements, even tailored to personal injury cases. However, a form is just a starting point and can only provide a framework for your document.

In drafting your agreement, keep the language simple. If you are drafting the agreement, make sure you understand every word you are placing in the contract and avoid the temptation to use complex language and opt for plain language. For example, instead of writing, "the undersigned," simply use their name. This is especially important if you are an attorney drafting a contract on behalf of a client. Attorneys often believe they must use complex legal language to impress clients with their "legal talk." Certain legal terminology, however, may be crucial in some contracts, and if so, that language should be explained to the client. Further, since this is the client's agreement, they need to thoroughly understand the language of the agreement. A client should not have to hire another lawyer to explain the agreement to him. Also, drafting a contract with simple language provides protection for the attorney as well. If the client thoroughly understands all the language used, that client cannot come back at a later date to the attorney and now say they were confused by the terminology.

If you did not draft the agreement, thoroughly check the contents of the agreement once you receive it. While it is paramount to make sure the substance of the agreement is what you have agreed upon, it is also important to check even seemingly minor details. For example, check dates, times, and spelling of names of parties. A checklist that is specific to the type of agreement you are preparing may help. An agreement settling a lawsuit will have a much different checklist than a lease agreement. If you are unsure if the agreement thoroughly represents the terms you have agreed upon, you should enlist the help of a third party to review the document. This person may be a trusted associate, or even a friend with knowledge of the matter. However, if you are not a lawyer or being represented by a lawyer, when in doubt it is best to use the services of a lawyer since you want to make sure the agreement conforms to the requirements of the law.

Once the agreement is acceptable to all parties, it should be properly executed. Many times, the applicable law will require that the agreement be notarized. After those formalities, the agreement should be binding on the parties.

EXERCISE 5-1: EXECUTING THE AGREEMENT

(30 min) Assume Chad sued The B Restaurant for injuries allegedly resulting from a slip and fall in the restaurant's dining area. Chad alleged that he slipped on water that had accumulated on the floor after a waiter accidentally spilled a glass of water. Chad claims The B Restaurant was negligent in failing to clean up the spill in a timely manner. The parties' attorneys met to attempt to negotiate a settlement. After several hours of negotiations, the attorneys reached an agreement. Before leaving the negotiation session, they wrote down the following terms:

1. The B Restaurant will pay Chad total damages of $20,000 in one lump sum payment within ten days of the execution of this agreement.
2. The B Restaurant will give Chad a voucher for five free meals at the restaurant for selected dates, excluding major holidays.
3. The B Restaurant and Chad agree to a mutual release of all present and future claims.
4. The B Restaurant and Chad agree to keep the settlement confidential.
5. The B Restaurant and Chad agree that there is no admission of liability by either party.

Use an AI tool to draft a settlement agreement based on the terms outlined above. Ensure that the AI-generated draft includes standard clauses for personal injury settlements, such as confidentiality, mutual release, and non-admission of liability. Edit and tailor the draft to ensure it aligns with the specific terms of this case (*e.g.*, payment amount, meal voucher details, etc.). Remove any language you do not understand or that does not apply to this scenario. Do not simply fill in blanks. If you do not understand the language, do not put it in the agreement.

CHAPTER 6

Ethics & Equity

A thorough analysis of the negotiation process requires examining ethics and equity, the E of the TABLE method. One would hope that negotiators would act ethically and treat all parties equitably, and therefore there would be no need to discuss effective responses to lapses in such conduct in a negotiation. However, the often private setting of a negotiation seems to be conducive to these troubling types of behavior, in that many negotiators believe the absence of formal proceedings or witnesses in a negotiation embolden them to behave in such a manner. Therefore, every negotiator should anticipate and prepare to respond to both unethical behavior and inequitable treatment.

Ethics

Negotiators often fail to consider ethics when approaching or conducting negotiations. In fact, many negotiators are unsure as to what is considered unethical behavior. They would not be entirely wrong in their uncertainty. Generally, unethical behavior means engaging in conduct that violates accepted moral principles, social norms, or professional standards. It involves actions considered wrong, unfair, or harmful to others. Nevertheless, it is difficult even for experts to agree as to what is unethical in a negotiation, and certain types of conduct may be considered ethical by some and unethical by others. As discussed in Chapter 3 on Bargaining, employing questionable ethical conduct in a negotiation may be considered acceptable tactics by many negotiators. For example, bluffing may be considered lying and unacceptable by some, or a legitimate part of negotiation strategy and acceptable by others. Professionals, such as attorneys, are guided by codes of conduct, which may help to delineate ethical conduct, but other negotiators are simply left to make decisions based on their individual moral and ethical standards.

Some negotiators do not concern themselves with ethical challenges because they take the approach that since the negotiating process is unrestricted in terms of both forum and format, whatever they say or propose is not easily discovered or proved outside of the negotiation room. Therefore, their conduct will not be subject to scrutiny for its ethical component. However, the "I can do it because I will not get caught" approach is shortsighted and potentially weakens a negotiator's effectiveness, especially when his conduct undoubtedly crosses acceptable ethical boundaries.

Furthermore, notwithstanding the frequent ineffectiveness of lying, negotiators who engage in unethical behavior can be penalized in many ways. For example, as noted in Chapter 2, on Tactical Planning, material misrepresentations relied upon by one party in entering into an agreement may result in that agreement being set aside when those misrepresentations are discovered. In addition, many professions have their own ethical rules and codes that impose penalties on negotiators who engage in unethical behavior in a negotiation. Furthermore, negotiators who act unethically run the great risk of gaining a reputation as one who is not to be trusted, a label that diminishes their bargaining power in future negotiations.

Most unethical conduct in a negotiation is linked to the exchange or withholding of information, usually in the form of dishonest communication.[1] Lying, misrepresenting, and deception are terms used interchangeably under the general heading of untruthful information and is the most prevalent type of unethical conduct that occurs in negotiations. It can often be very difficult to discover and address during a negotiation.

Why Do Negotiators Lie?

Negotiators lie to improve their bargaining position. They may feel backed into a corner, having run out of truthful approaches to making offers, counteroffers, and concessions, and are unhappy with the offer on the table. In order to move the negotiation forward, they tell a lie. Alternatively, negotiators may feel that the other side has deceived them during the course of the negotiation, and their reciprocal lies are simply a tit-for-tat strategy.

Frequently, parties lie in a negotiation for the simple reason that they believe that everyone lies, and in fact, the other side expects such behavior. Even more confusing is that certain types of lies have long been supported by various professional codes and negotiation experts, under the theory that certain types of lies are part of the negotiation game. For example, in the legal profession, a lawyer will not be disciplined for unethical conduct if he claims during a negotiation that he has no authority to offer a higher settlement amount when he does have that authority.[2] However, a negotiator who claims his client told him he did not run the red light when in fact the client told his attorney he did run that light would be subject to attorney discipline. Under the Model Rules of Professional Conduct, making false statements of material fact is unethical but the rules carve out an exception for certain statements made in negotiations. Under the Model Rules, "estimates of price or value placed on the subject of a transaction and a party's intentions as to an acceptable settlement of a claim" are not statements of material fact and hence not unethical, because these types of statements are made under "generally accepted conventions in negotiation."[3] However, the attorney's lie about his client not running the red light is a false statement of material fact and thus a violation of the attorney's ethics code. The Model Rules make it clear that not all statements made during negotiations will fall under the "generally accepted conventions" exception that escape penalties under the ethics rules.[4]

In line with the exception in the Model Rules for attorneys involved in negotiations, many negotiators believe lies concerning settlement amount authority and similar negotiation statements are so integral to the negotiation process that lying in these areas is not problematic or unethical. False demands and misstatements about authority seem to be expected in negotiations and often set bargaining ranges for the negotiation.[5]

Types of Lies

There are generally three types of lies used during negotiations: 1) statements that are affirmatively false; 2) statements considered half-true, such that the statement in and of itself is true, but the negotiator has omitted a material fact making the statement misleading (this type of lie is referred to as paltering);[6] and 3) lies of omission, which involves a negotiator who knows the truth, but intentionally conceals the truth, misleading the other party.[7]

While outright lies are your typical everyday untruth, paltering, and lying by omission are more intricate and likely take some practice. The following example demonstrates the differences in the three types of lies.

Assume you have decided to rent a house for the weekend for a 4th of July party. You find the perfect house and are in the process of negotiating with the homeowner about the rental. You especially like the backyard area because it has an outdoor kitchen complete with a large grill. You ask the landlord if the grill is in working condition. If the grill is not in working condition and the landlord answers, "Yes" he has made an affirmative false statement. If, instead, the landlord answers, "Last July 4th, we had a huge party here and cooked up dozens of hamburgers and hotdogs on that grill." This statement is an example of paltering. Assuming he had that huge party last 4th of July and cooked on the grill, his statement is true. However, he omitted the material fact that the grill is not presently working, which makes his statement misleading. Finally, instead of an affirmative false statement or paltering, the homeowner answers, "What would the 4th of July be without a cookout!" and he then points to the grill. This statement is a lie by omission. He has not answered the question about the grill's condition affirmatively "yes" or "no," or made a truthful but misleading statement about the grill. Instead, he has made a comment about the 4th of July, and cookouts in general, while omitting the answer to the question as to whether the grill is in working condition.

Consequences of Lying

Negotiators may feel that if challenged about lying, they will simply lie again and deny they ever made a false statement and therefore there are no consequences to lying. This repeated denial may only compound the initial problem and now the negotiator is caught in a vicious cycle of lies. Furthermore, once a party lies and is "caught" in that lie, it may be difficult to believe any further representations made by that party during the negotiation. This distrust may even occur when negotiators tell those "acceptable" lies. For example, assume an attorney falsely states that "My client has not given me authority to pay more than $10,000 to settle this case." However, after trading counteroffers and concessions with the other party, the attorney now states, "I am prepared to offer you $15,000." The other party is immediately thinking (maybe even out loud) what happened to his $10,000 authority? Once the other party heard the $15,000 offer, he will now realize the lie, and the consequences may be that any further bottom line given by that attorney will quickly be discounted as not factually true. Therefore, even though the attorney may be within his ethical bounds to state a false authority under generally accepted conventions of negotiation, the consequences may result in a less effective negotiating posture.

Even negotiators who believe they have gotten away with the lie during the negotiation find their lies often discovered in later proceedings in the same matter, through depositions, or through other investigative methods. Then, once cornered, they engage in further unethical conduct to try to remedy the situation. There is a reason why prosecutors often say the cover up is worse than the offense.

Furthermore, deceitful negotiators develop reputations as untrustworthy, which greatly diminishes their effectiveness in subsequent negotiations. Negotiators who develop reputations as known liars have great difficulty in future negotiations in proving they are making honest representations. The "once a liar always a liar" label may stick to that person and greatly diminish his effectiveness in negotiations. For example, Professor Leigh Thompson describes one study where negotiators were observed over a 10-week period.[8] After that time, they were classified as either liars, tough-but-fair, or cream puffs. Those negotiators who were classified as liars had much greater difficulty resolving disputes in subsequent negotiations. Due to their reputations, their negotiations involved aggressive exchanges as they were consistently challenged on statements and representations they made during the negotiation, resulting in fewer settlements than the tough-but-fair or the cream puff negotiators.

The consequences of lying go beyond ruining your reputation and potential ethics violations. Lying can rise to the level of fraud. A negotiator commits fraud when he makes a statement that he knows is a misrepresentation of a material fact upon which the other side reasonably relies to his detriment, causing damages.[9] For example, an obvious case of fraud would be a car salesperson who knows that an odometer on a car was reset from 20,000 miles to 5 miles but represents to a buyer in a negotiation that the used car is in fact new, since the odometer shows 5 miles. If the buyer purchases the car, he will have an action for fraud because the salesperson knowingly made a material misrepresentation about the mileage on the odometer. Further, the buyer has damages in that he has purchased a car of less value since it is a used car when he believed he was purchasing a new car.

Other cases of fraud in negotiation may not be as obvious. For example, courts have struggled in fraud cases that involve negotiators making representations that they have other offers when they do not. Professor G. Richard Shell in his article describing risks associated with lying in negotiations, references an Oklahoma case where a real estate agent was held liable for fraud when she told a prospective homebuyer that if the buyer did not purchase the home now, another buyer was going to purchase the house and pay the asking price later that day.[10] In that case, however, the other buyer did not exist, and the court held given all the facts and circumstances that this misrepresentation was material and fraudulent. Further, courts have also found that self-serving statements about the value of a person's business may rise to the level of fraud in a negotiation, if the statement is verifiably false.[11]

The lesson to be learned from these cases is that best practices for negotiators is to avoid the temptation to lie during a negotiation. Although there is some leeway in professional codes as to what constitutes unethical behavior, you may find yourself before a court who will decide if your factual statements rise to the level of fraud. If it does, you may be subject to damages and the potential unraveling of the deal you have made. Furthermore, if you develop the reputation as someone who plays fast and loose with the truth, you may find it difficult to effectively bargain with the other side in a negotiation, as each and every representation you make would likely be subject to scrutiny.

Uncovering Lies during Negotiations

Even though you have read this book and have been convinced not to lie in a negotiation, the other side may have missed the opportunity to read this book and will in fact decide to lie during negotiations. Many theories have developed on the ways in which to spot a liar, and just as many theories have dismissed these lie spotting theories. Most people believe they can spot a lie, when in fact even those who are adept at lie detection are only at best 60% accurate,[12] a statistic that is only slightly better than flipping a coin. Still there are some indicators that may seem more telling than others, and it is helpful to be aware of some of these and how to respond when you believe the other side is using lying as a bargaining trick.[13]

Inconsistent Statements

A negotiator who makes inconsistent or contradictory statements may be lying. For example, at the beginning of a negotiation, if one party says, "I must leave this negotiation at 3:00 PM because I have another appointment." Accordingly, at 3:15 you remind him of his declaration that he had to leave by 3:00, and he answers, "No. I said 4:00." or "No. I never said I had to leave at a specific time." At this point, you may begin to question your own memory of his first statement, but if you are certain your memory is accurate, his inconsistency may point to dishonesty. However, be aware that while your memory may be accurate, perhaps the other side is not lying, but in fact does not remember his prior statement. Therefore, his inconsistency may not be intentional, just forgetful.

When the stakes are higher than simply what time a party is leaving a negotiation, an inconsistent story may point more clearly to lying. For example, if you are negotiating the purchase of a house and you ask the seller if the neighborhood is safe and he answers, "There were a couple of stolen car incidents." Later on in the negotiation, as you are getting closer to making a deal, you repeat the question about crime, and he now says, "There has never been a crime in this neighborhood." His now inconsistent statement may point to dishonesty. Since he is now trying to close the deal, he may want to make his house seem especially desirable to entice the buyer by now claiming there is no crime in the neighborhood.

Saying No

No is a key word used by negotiators when making misleading or dishonest statements. A negotiator who says no after hesitating, or says no and changes the subject, may be struggling with the truth. Further, a person who answers a question no and refuses to add details may be hesitant to advance a lie with further untruthful details.

Changes in Behavior

A change in a negotiator's behavior may signal lying. For example, a person who begins speaking more formally may be lying. Pay attention to a person who was using contractions such as, "I'd like to hear your proposal" and now says, "I cannot accept your terms." Also, pay attention to how he emphasizes words, changes the tone of his voice, or uses superlatives, such as, "My client DID NOT run the red light. He is an AWESOME driver." A person who is lying may also tend to stumble on his words, clear his throat often, or talk too fast. While these are generalized behavior signs, any behavior that is out of the ordinary or a change for that person may indicate lying. Therefore, it is important to establish a baseline for a person if possible. For example, when a person has never raised her voice in previous discussions, and that person is yelling when recounting a detail, she may be lying. However, a person who regularly clears their throat when speaking and who is now clearing her throat when recounting a fact may not be lying, just in need of a throat lozenge.

Truth Emphasizers

People who are lying often strangely emphasize that they are not. Statements such as "in all honesty," or "to tell you the truth" are sometimes just the opposite. The lying person is so emphatic because he knows his statement is a lie. We should assume that people are telling the truth. Thus, the need to make statements that you are telling the truth may be a cover for the lie that is on the way or in the mix.

Physical Signs

Lying may have some physical manifestations, according to researchers.[14] Liars are more likely to press their lips together, and their smiles often look forced. Also, their mouth and eye combination may be a giveaway. Truthful people tend to smile with their whole face, exhibiting expressive eyes and crow's feet, if they have them! People tend to fidget when they are not telling the truth. Then again, they just may be nervous. However, if they had been sitting still during the negotiation and then suddenly started fidgeting, this may be a sign that what they are now saying is not truthful. However, one physical sign many once believed to indicate lying has been mostly disproved, namely that liars cannot look the other side in the eye while telling a lie. Apparently, most liars have perfected the technique of looking directly at the person, perhaps in response to hearing that this was a telltale sign of lying.

Responses to Lying

It is difficult to confront someone on a lie during a negotiation, especially where the proof may be lacking. Furthermore, the moment you make the accusation, the tone of the negotiation will change, especially if there has been cooperative behavior by both sides up until the point of the lie. Therefore, you should first analyze if the other side has actually lied, simply misremembered, or is innocently mistaken.

In order for you to determine if a negotiator is really lying, you should ask specific questions concerning the troubling statement and try to zero in on the lie. It is helpful to maintain a positive tone and begin with non-threatening questions. For example, in a negotiation about a price dispute over the purchase of a used computer, you might ask "Just to clarify: You said the buyer first offered the seller $3,000 to purchase the item, and now you said the buyer first offered the seller $2,000." Asking questions will highlight inconsistencies in a liar's story. Furthermore, liars who use paltering or lying by omission are often uncovered when asked specific questions. For example, in the house rental problem discussed above, when the homeowner answers that he used the grill for his own party last July 4th, an easy follow up question such as, "Is the grill in working condition now?" may have uncovered the truth. However, instead of telling the truth, the homeowner may now choose to make an affirmative lie by answering "yes." If he does confirm his paltering statement with an affirmative lie, and you have your 4th of July party and the grill does not work, it will be much easier to prove your case when you sue the homeowner for misrepresentation as you can recount how the homeowner affirmatively lied as opposed to paltering.

Another response to lying is to give the other side information that will point out that their story cannot be accurate. For example, if a party states that a traffic light was malfunctioning at the time of the accident, you may be able to show a picture taken by a store's street camera that shows the light functioning normally at the time of the accident. However, having a smoking gun picture is often not available, and such a "got you" moment takes place mainly in movies. Therefore, if your attempt to correct lying conduct is not successful, and the lying rises to the level of a material misrepresentation, you may decide to simply say, "I don't think we are making any progress" and end the negotiating session. At this point, if the other side seems confused as to the abrupt end, you may decide to confront the party's lying conduct. Since the negotiation is derailed at this point anyway, confronting him about lying may serve to put him on notice that such conduct will not be tolerated in the negotiation, and perhaps he will correct this behavior.

EXERCISES 6-1 AND 6-2: ETHICS

6-1. *(2-person exercise) (6 minutes, 3 minutes each side)* The purpose of this exercise is to test your ability to recognize when a party is lying in everyday conversation. You and your partner will take turns and exchange eight points of information about a vacation you have taken to a city or country. You can share details such as where and when you went, who was with you, what did you enjoy or dislike about the trip, and any other information that is pertinent. However, when you reveal the information, two of the items you disclose must be false. As you disclose the information about your vacation, the other side may ask questions, but they are limited to five questions. After you have both taken turns exchanging information, you should each separately write down the two items you disclosed that were false and the two items you believe the other side disclosed that were false. Then exchange papers and see how accurate your assessments were.

Feedback and Discussion: How accurate were your assessments of the other person's lies? If you were accurate, how did you reach the conclusion that the statements were false? If you were not accurate, what would you have done differently to discover the false statements?

When you revealed the false statements, do you think there was any difference between the way you delivered the false and accurate statements? Did you use paltering, omissions, affirmative false statements, or a combination of the three methods? If you used different forms of lying, which form, if any, worked best for you? Why?

6-2. *(2-person exercise) (5 minutes)* The purpose of this exercise is to test your ability to recognize if a party is lying during a negotiation. You and your partner will role-play as a buyer and seller of a used car. This exercise will consist of a prospective buyer asking a series of questions to the seller to determine if the buyer can detect false statements made by the seller. The buyer will ask the seller the following questions:

1. What is the condition of the tires, and have they been replaced or repaired?
2. Has the car been in any accidents and if so, was there damage to the car?
3. Does the car currently have any mechanical issues?
4. Was the car ever vandalized or stolen and recovered?
5. Has the car been regularly serviced?

Instructions for the seller: If you are playing the role of the seller, before beginning the negotiation, you should write down answers to the above questions as representative of truthful answers. However, when you begin negotiating, you should change your answer to two of these questions and answer falsely (*i.e.*, the answer is different from what you wrote down). You may either make an affirmative false statement, engage in paltering, or lie by omission.

Instructions for the buyer: If you are playing the role of the buyer, you may ask these questions in any order you deem appropriate. During the initial questioning, you are not permitted to ask follow up questions.

After receiving initial answers to your questions from the seller, try to determine which two of the seller's answers are false. After making that determination, during the negotiation, you may address your concerns to the seller about the suspected falsehoods using one of the response methods discussed above. You may decide to confront the seller or ask more follow up questions. You may also choose to ignore his false statements. At the end of the 5-minute session, write down which two of the seller's answers you believe are false.

Feedback and Discussion: At the conclusion of the negotiation, the buyer and seller should then exchange papers and see if the buyer correctly determined the seller's untruthful statements. If you were the buyer, and you correctly determined the false statements, how did you come to that determination? If you were the seller, do you detect any differences in the way you delivered the false answers as opposed to the truthful answers?

Equity

In addition to ethics, the "E" in TABLE requires reflecting on equity. Recognizing and understanding the role of equity in the context of negotiations is important for several reasons. First, as a practical matter, participants are more likely to feel invested in negotiations conducted equitably. This buy-in may result in the participants viewing any subsequently negotiated agreements as legitimate as opposed to unfair or unconscionable. Moreover, certain inequitable or biased behaviors, even if not illegal, can cause significant harm to the participants, their organizations, and to society. Second, alertness to bias can provide tools for thwarting or confronting negative bias actions in ways that may allow negotiations to proceed successfully. Bias during a negotiation can appear in both subtle and overt forms. For example, the other side may interrupt a female speaker more often than a male speaker or address a male in the group more often than the female. More disparagingly, slurs, obscene gestures, or nicknames may be inserted into the negotiation in order to disorient or alter behavior. Being aware of such actions may serve to negate some of their effects, provide necessary information during the negotiation, or signal the likelihood of a viable future relationship. Finally, on a broader level, awareness of bias is the starting point towards challenging conscious or unconscious biases' pernicious effects.

Unconscious biases influence evaluations and decision making in numerous contexts, including in negotiations. Generally, people use unconscious biases to balance competing ideas and make quick decisions. The terms implicit bias and unconscious bias when applied to others are often used as a short hand for ways in which people group others including by race, gender, ethnicity, age, sexual orientation, or other aspects of identity. Cognitive research studies reveal that implicit biases based on cultural and historical beliefs about groups are pervasive and operate "under the scope of human consciousness, and that they influence the ways in which we see and treat others, even when we are determined to be fair and objective."[15] Moreover, scholars on racial bias have observed, "implicit racial biases can influence the behaviors and judgments of even the most consciously egalitarian individuals."[16]

There are powerful studies demonstrating the negative effects of implicit bias in negotiations involving housing and in the criminal justice system.[17] In the context of negotiations for consumer goods, a series of influential studies on the effects of racial and gender bias conducted by Professor Ian Ayers are particularly instructive.[18] One of those studies sent testers of different races and genders posing as potential buyers to hundreds of car dealerships in Chicago. The testers entered new car dealerships separately and bargained to buy similar new cars, using a scripted uniform negotiation strategy. The focus of the study was whether automobile retailers would react differently to this uniform negotiation strategy when the potential car buyers differed only by gender or race. The study revealed systematic negative bias towards African Americans and women. For example, even though the testers used the same negotiating bargaining script, the dealers' salespersons initial sales price offers to the African American buyers and the salespersons' "final offers," which ostensibly represented the lowest prices the salespersons could offer to sell the cars, were much higher for African American potential buyers after several rounds of offers and counter offers. Professor Ayers' studies on racial and gender bias found overwhelming evidence that in a variety of markets – retail car sales, bail bonding, and kidney transplantation – racial minorities are consistently at a disadvantage. More recent studies continue to find implicit racial bias negatively affecting African Americans in negotiations.[19]

Many of the identity-based employment negotiation studies focus primarily on gender. Studies on gender bias in the negotiation context are instructive and can be used as a guide to studying racial, ethnic, and other types of bias in negotiations. More than thirty years of research have yielded a complex picture. In one of the first studies on gender in negotiations, the researchers observed how the gender of the negotiator affected the negotiations.[20] In their report, they described instances of women being more competitive than men in some contexts, while in other instances, women appeared less competitive. The researchers theorized that the observed differences might occur because women have a greater emphasis on interpersonal relationships, which results in them being more competitive or cooperative depending on their counterparts.

Some studies focus more on the social and institutional processes that might activate gendered behavior rather than gender differences.[21] Studies discussing contextual factors that trigger gender dynamics often rely on characterizing negotiations as either integrative or distributive with different styles of communication associated with each approach.[22] As discussed in Chapter 2 on Tactical Planning, integrative bargaining is an approach where the parties seek to collaborate for mutual benefit. By contrast, distributive bargaining is where the parties use a more competitive and adversarial approach, and each party attempts to maximize their own interests regardless of the other side's loss. Stereotypes would seem to suggest that women would excel at the integrative negotiations, which rely on stereotypical feminine attributes such as cooperation and compassion. In turn, males should stereotypically excel at distributive bargaining, which emphasizes an adversarial approach. However, despite the stereotypes, the results are not that different when the game structure changes between integrative and distributive systems. Interestingly, some studies found that results do change depending on whether the women were negotiating on behalf of themselves or others. One study in particular describes how "women are significantly more effective and aggressive negotiators when negotiating on the behalf of others, rather than for their own benefit."[23]

There are important caveats to gender negotiation analysis. First, gender differences may be overstated.[24] With regard to communications, for example, "many people believe that men and women communicate differently, and that belief is buoyed by researchers who argue that women's verbal style is best described as supportive, egalitarian, and personal, while characterizing men's as instrumental, competitive, and assertive."[25] Studies, however, rebut these characterizations. Several studies have shown that there are no differences in outcomes that can be attributed solely to the negotiator's gender and men and women are equally capable of learning and applying effective negotiation strategies.[26] A meta-analysis of numerous studies on gender differences in negotiations found "a bargaining advantage for men under conditions of highest predictive incongruity for women."[27] Examples of such conditions of predictive incongruity for women include "when negotiators are not experienced" and when the laboratory negotiation experiments are designed with "high structural ambiguity." Generally, a negotiation experiment has high structural ambiguity when the negotiators are not provided information to lessen ambiguity, such as the bargaining range, standards for agreement, and values. This meta-analysis also found "a bargaining advantage for women under conditions of lowest predicted role incongruity."[28] Studies with "lowest predicted role incongruity for women" included those where the negotiators had some negotiating practice and experience; where the experiments involved women negotiating on behalf of others; and where information to lessen structural ambiguity, such as bargaining ranges or values, was available.[29]

Additional caveats to gender negotiation studies are in order. First, gender identities can fall outside the male/female dichotomy. Second, individuals have multiple intersecting social identities. For example, a person can identify as female, lesbian, grandmother, and professor and all of these can inform and affect her negotiations. Focusing solely on gender as the difference between men and women fails to account for simultaneous dimensions of identity that may become salient during a negotiation. Moreover, focusing on individuals and their negotiating proclivities misses the cultural and institutional mechanisms and implicit biases that can create identity inequities in negotiations.

As each of us attempt to disrupt our implicit bias by engaging in self-reflection, becoming more culturally competent, and practicing inclusive behaviors, we can help shape our personal and professional lives, our organizations, and our communities. More specifically, in the negotiation context, averting implicit bias and practicing inclusive behaviors may encourage the negotiating parties to hear multiple points of view and allow for innovative solutions.

Recognizing that race and gender, age, sexual orientation, ethnicity, religion, and other aspects of identity can affect the outcome of a negotiation, it is important to discuss some of the tools that negotiators can use to lessen these prejudicial effects and negotiate more effectively.

Awareness

The single most important tool against bias in negotiations is awareness. Being aware enables you to have an intention, choose behaviors to implement your intention, monitor your counterpart's reaction, evaluate whether you are achieving the outcome you intended, and if not, change your negotiation behavior.

Mindfulness Meditation

Mindfulness meditation has been shown to help regulate attention and emotions and may help negotiators in stressful negotiations. It may also be helpful to reduce bias and increase empathy towards underrepresented or stigmatized persons.[30]

Preparation

As mentioned in Chapter 2 on Tactical Planning, being prepared is crucial for any negotiation opportunity. Preparing for the negotiation process involves examining priorities, ranking their importance, and knowing your leverage. Being prepared to reference relevant and objective standards during bargaining situations is especially important. The use of objective measures may provide negotiators with the confidence to initiate a negotiation and to ask for an outcome that is in line with that of their co-workers, counterparts, or the market.

In addition, in preparing for negotiations AI tools can be helpful in recognizing and reducing potential bias. By analyzing vast datasets, identifying patterns, and offering impartial recommendations, AI tools help parties focus on factual evidence rather than subjective assumptions. AI tools can use natural language processing and machine learning to evaluate historical negotiation outcomes, market trends, and counterparty behavior, providing strategies grounded in empirical data rather than intuition. This approach minimizes the influence of unconscious biases, such as gender or racial stereotypes, which often skew human judgment. However, AI's effectiveness hinges on collaboration between technology and human judgment. While AI can surface equitable options and mitigate overt prejudice, negotiators must critically evaluate its inputs, cross-reference recommendations with ethical guidelines, and remain accountable for final decisions. As the American Bar Association's Formal Opinion 512 (2024) explains, AI is a tool that can assist an attorney but is not a substitute for professional responsibility.[31] By combining AI's analytical rigor with principled human oversight, parties can navigate negotiations with greater fairness and integrity.

Mentors and Social Networks

Having strong ties, as protégés, mentors, or just individuals in social networks can be a strong asset. Having mentors, or being a part of a social network, can open the doors to new opportunities within an organization and provide important information that can be used during negotiations. For example, information gleaned from social networks may serve to provide salary ranges for positions in an organization where such information is otherwise not easily available.

Activate Egalitarian Goals

There is some support for the theory that alerting the other party in the negotiations to fairness and egalitarian goals may help alleviate some negative implicit bias. Suggestions for activating such goals include remarking on the other side's unbiased views or fairness.[32]

PART II

Applying the TABLE Method

CHAPTER 7

Negotiating Business Relationships

In this chapter, you will practice negotiating in business settings using the TABLE method. The chapter includes various business-related negotiations including salary offers with and without non-disclosure agreements, the acquisition of a small business, and a dispute involving a homeowners' association (HOA).

Each of the various problems in this chapter will require you to think about multiple issues involved in the relationship. For example, in the problem on salary offers you will want to think about the components of the offer such as the base salary, bonuses, frequency of reviews, promotion opportunities, job title, benefits, and flexible work schedules. A separate problem on salary offers includes a discussion of, and a problem for, negotiating salary offers that are coupled with a non-disclosure agreement. For that problem, in addition to the issues involved with the salary offer you will also need to think about the terms of, and the importance to the parties of, the non-disclosure agreement. Similarly, the problem on acquiring a business requires analysis of various issues involved such as licensing requirements and the need for due diligence before the acquisition. The final problem in this chapter, involving a HOA, is designed as a multi-party negotiation involving a dispute among a homeowner, the HOA, and an outside contractor. For this problem, you will need to analyze the role of an HOA, a legally incorporated private organization whose role is to govern a community through its documents and covenants, and you will also need to understand the nuances of multi-party negotiations.

Instructions

Each problem begins with an overview of the legal principles involved in the matter. The topics of the problems are fairly common business dealings. After reading the legal principles for each problem in this chapter, you will be ready to apply those principles to the practice problems below using the TABLE method. The limited legal information you are given in the areas of negotiating salaries, non-disclosure agreements, business acquisitions, and HOAs should not be interpreted as a primer on those areas of the law. Rather, the information is included here solely to use as a basis for negotiating the various problems. As an alternative, or in addition to negotiating these problems with the limited information about the law provided here, you may wish to research the law in your state, or another state, and negotiate the problem using that research.

Each problem contains general information followed by confidential information in which each negotiator will choose a bargaining position on key issues. While the general information will be known by both sides, your bargaining position is confidential, although you may disclose it, or some of it, during the negotiation session if you choose to do so. Following the section on confidential information, you are given guidelines and suggestions as to how to approach the negotiations using the TABLE method.

After reviewing the information, you should complete the Tactical Planning Worksheet (provided in Appendix A or Appendix A-1). Be sure to include your bargaining positions on your worksheets. After completing a Tactical Planning Worksheet for each problem, you and your counterpart are ready to conduct a negotiation in which you attempt to reach an agreement. While there is no time limit set for each problem, you should be able to complete the initial negotiations for each problem within 30 minutes.

After you complete each negotiation, you and your negotiating counterpart should exchange planning worksheets so that you can analyze the bargaining positions you and your counterpart planned for the negotiation. Finally, you should complete the Post Negotiation Self-Reflection Worksheet (found in Appendix B).

For further explanation of the methodology for negotiating the problems, please refer to the Authors' Notes in Chapter 1, Introduction.

Laws Relevant to Salary Offers

There are federal, state, and local laws that are relevant to salary offers. When negotiating salary offers, it is important to research the applicability of the various laws. Discussed below are a select few of those laws that may be helpful for negotiating the problems in this chapter.

Federal Laws Relevant to Salary Offers

There are numerous federal laws regarding employment that are relevant to salary offers. For example, Title VII of the Civil Rights Act of 1964 (Title VII) makes it illegal to discriminate against a job applicant or an employee because of the person's race, color, religion, national origin, or sex (including pregnancy).[1] Title VII was amended by the Lilly Ledbetter Fair Pay Act in 2009 (Lily Ledbetter Act).[2] Since the enactment of the Lily Ledbetter Act an employee may bring a legal action for pay discrimination under Title VII after the last pay violation, as opposed to only by the required time after the initial pay disparity. The Lily Ledbetter Act provides that pay discrimination can occur when a pay decision is made, when an employee is subject to that decision, or at any time that an employee is injured by it, and that regardless of when the discrimination began, each paycheck that contains discriminatory compensation is a separate violation.

Case law interpreting Title VII is also critical for understanding the federal laws in this area. For example, the United States Supreme Court, in *Price Waterhouse v. Hopkins,* found that Title VII's prohibition on the basis of sex prohibits employers from discriminating on the basis of the employer's stereotype of the person's respective gender or gender stereotyping.[3] Recently, both the U.S. Court of Appeals for the Second and Seventh Circuits have found that Title VII's prohibition of discrimination on the basis of sex prohibits discrimination on the basis of sexual orientation.[4]

Other relevant anti-discrimination federal laws include Title I of the Americans with Disabilities Act of 1990 (ADA), which makes it illegal to discriminate against a qualified person with a disability and the Genetic Information Nondiscrimination Act of 2008 (GINA), which makes it illegal to discriminate against applicants or employees because of genetic information. Another example is the Age Discrimination in Employment Act of 1967 (ADEA), which protects persons who are 40 or older from discrimination because of their age.[5]

These federal anti-discrimination laws apply to employers with more than 15 employees (more than 20 employees for age discrimination).[6] They apply to numerous types of work situations, including hiring, promotions, wages, and benefits. Prospective employers and applicants should be cognizant that these anti-discrimination protections apply even before an applicant has an offer.[7] Thus, for example, employers should ensure that their questions during the salary offer negotiations, while seemingly innocuous, are in fact compliant with such laws. Along those lines, prospective employees should be mindful in their answers to questions to not inadvertently respond with information that could lead to discussions that would be protected, such as not to chill further discussions.

The Equal Pay Act of 1963 (EPA), another relevant federal law, targets gender discrimination in pay. This law requires employers to pay men and women employees working at the same establishment equal wages "for equal work" on jobs that require "equal skill, effort, and responsibility, and which are performed under similar working conditions."[8] The EPA, however, permits unequal pay for equal work under one of four exceptions: (1) a seniority system; (2) a merit system; (3) a system that measures earnings by quantity or quality of production; or (4) a differential based on any other factor other than sex.[9]

There is extensive case law regarding when various types of jobs meet or do not meet the "equal work" requirement in the EPA. Generally, to initiate a case under the EPA, an employee must show that a coworker of the opposite sex received greater compensation despite performing substantially equal work. The case law interpreting what qualifies as substantially equal work varies, with some courts using a very narrow interpretation while others use a slightly broader interpretation.

State and Local Laws Relevant to Salary Offers

In addition to the federal laws, almost all states have adopted laws that prohibit forms of discrimination against a job applicant or employee.[10] These laws prohibit discrimination in employment based on various factors, such as race, gender, age, marital status, national origin, religion, or disability. While several of these state laws track the language in the federal laws, many offer additional protections against employment-related discrimination.

These state laws vary widely with some having few protections against employment discrimination and other states significantly expanding on the protections in the federal laws. Alabama provides an example of a state on the less protective end of the spectrum. While Alabama has a statute prohibiting age discrimination (over age 40), it has no state law prohibiting discrimination in employment because of sex, race, disability, or other factors, and any such claims would have to be addressed by federal law when and if it applies to an employer.[11] Similarly, Georgia has a statute prohibiting discrimination for public workers, but has no state law prohibiting employment discrimination for private employees.[12]

Other states have statutes that expand on the federal laws by covering employers with fewer than 15 employees or by expressly proscribing various types of discrimination. For example, the Connecticut anti-discrimination in employment statute applies to employers with three or more employees (other than religious organizations).[13]

Moreover, the Connecticut statute expressly prohibits discrimination on the basis of race, color, religious creed, age, sex, gender identity or expression, marital status, national origin, ancestry, present or past history of mental disability, intellectual disability, learning disability or physical disability, sexual orientation, civil union status, pregnancy, criminal conviction alone, or medical marijuana.[14]

Also, on the broader protection side of the spectrum is Oregon, which has a non-discrimination statute that applies to employers with one or more employees and prohibits discrimination on the basis of various factors including race, religion, color, sex, sexual orientation, gender identity, national origin, marital and familial status, disability, expunged juvenile record, pregnancy, childbirth, and related medical conditions, and victims of domestic violence or sexual crimes.[15] In addition to Oregon, several other states' anti-discrimination in employment laws apply to employers with more than one employee. Those states include Arizona, Hawaii, Michigan, Minnesota, Montana, New Jersey, North Dakota, and Vermont.[16]

Despite the existence of federal and state anti-discrimination and equal pay statutes, substantial pay gaps based on gender, race, and ethnicity persist in the United States. The gender pay gap is typically measured by comparing women's median annual earnings to those of men. According to the most recent data, in 2024, women earned an average of 85% of what men earned when analyzing median hourly wages for both full-time and part-time employees.[17] While the pay gap narrowed slightly in 2024, progress in closing the gender pay gap had slowed in prior recent years. In fact, 2023 marked the first time in two decades that the national gender wage gap widened, with women earning just 82.7 cents for every dollar earned by men, down from 84 cents in 2022.[18] Projections now suggest that, at the current rate, it will take more than four decades for women to reach pay equity with men.[19] The wage gap is even wider for women of color.[20]

Educational attainment has not eliminated these disparities. Women now outnumber men among college graduates and are more likely to hold advanced degrees, yet women are paid less than men at every education level.[21] For example, in 2024, women with a college degree earned $37.89 per hour on average, compared to $50.01 for men, a gap of over $25,000 in annual earnings for full-time workers.[22] Occupational segregation, caregiving responsibilities, and societal expectations remain significant contributors to these gaps, alongside persistent discrimination.

In order to reduce the pay gap, some states and local governments have enacted laws that go beyond previous measures. For example, the Washington Equal Pay and Opportunities Act, originally updated in 2018, continues to prohibit pay discrimination based on gender and includes provisions for wage transparency. As of July 1, 2025, the law expanded to provide protections to cover all classes protected under the Washington Law Against Discrimination, including age, race, disability, sexual orientation, and more.[23] Employers must provide pay information in job postings, and recent amendments clarify remedies and compliance procedures.

In 2017, Puerto Rico signed the Puerto Rico Act No.16 (Puerto Rico Equal Pay Act).[24] This law expands upon the Federal Equal Pay Act in a similar manner to the laws enacted in Washington State. Puerto Rico's provisions in some respects go even further. The Puerto Rico Equal Pay Act prevents employers from even asking about the employees' former wages unless directly volunteered or after a salary has been negotiated and included in an offer letter. This shifts the balance of power and information to the potential or current employee allowing the employee to enter into the negotiations without fear that their previous salaries will affect their future wages. The Puerto Rico law also includes provisions for victims of pay discrimination including double compensatory damages and back pay penalties for violations.[25]

The state of Vermont's new pay transparency law, effective July 1, 2025, requires employers with five or more employees to disclose salary ranges in job postings.[26] Vermont has one of the smallest gender pay gaps among U.S. states, at 11%. Additionally, the law also prevents employers from conducting interviews based on the prospective employee's previous salary.[27]

Restrictions on requiring pay history disclosure appears to be a legislative trend. In addition to the states discussed above, other states have also recently passed laws regarding pay history. For example, California's salary history ban, first enacted in 2017 and clarified by subsequent legislation, prohibits employers from asking about an applicant's salary history and requires disclosure of pay scales upon reasonable request.[28] The law remains in force. In Delaware, an employer may only ask about pay history once an employee has accepted the job offer.[29] Massachusetts passed the "Act Relative to Salary Range Transparency" in July 2024, with salary range disclosure requirements set to take effect on October 29, 2025. Employers with at least 100 employees must also submit EEO-1 reports to the state.[30] In Oregon, an employer may not question or request an applicant's pay history and Oregon prohibits wage disparities for comparable work across protected classes.[31] In addition to these various state laws, several local governments have also enacted laws dealing with pay history. For example, New York City provides that employers may not ask for an applicant's prior salary.[32] In Philadelphia, an employer cannot ask an applicant's pay history or use prior salary to set the salary for a new employee.[33]

Strategies for Employers Negotiations of Salary

Often, experts tend to suggest strategies only for employees in negotiating salaries. However, employers are also in need of strategies for salary negotiations because they have much at stake as well. Employers may have put great time and effort into recruiting potential employees and they do not want to run the risk of losing those employees due to failed salary negotiations. According to a recent survey by Glassdoor, 54% of employees do not negotiate their salary.[34] In addition, some employers advertise jobs as non-negotiable, thus trying to alleviate the stressful salary negotiation. However, for many employers it is expected and anticipated that they will negotiate salary with a job candidate.

An employer walks a fine line when negotiating salary. While the employer wants to negotiate the best deal for his company, he does not want to alienate his future employee by taking an overly aggressive position during salary negotiations. It will be a hollow victory for the employer if he gets the deal he wants, but the negotiations have put a strain on the employer-employee relationship, making it difficult for them to work together in the future. In order to avoid such a result, there are certain strategies the employer should implement for a positive negotiation that will help maintain a good working relationship in the future. The following strategies are helpful for the employer engaging in negotiating salaries.[35]

Research Comparable Market Rate Salaries: Before sitting down to negotiate, the employer should conduct research to determine the going rate for the job he is offering. For some entry-level jobs, that rate may be easy to find. There are many salary comparison sites, such as Indeed's Salary Tool, or Salary.com, that collect data from thousands of employers for specific jobs. The Employer is able to narrow his search by location and company. One downside is that many of these sites rely on self-reporting, so the sites' accuracy is only as good as those who are reporting. Yet with thousands of reports, it is easy to glean some meaningful market salary ranges for a particular job. Furthermore, AI tools may be particularly helpful in providing more information on comparable salary structures for the industry.

Make Salary Offers Precise: Employers should consider offering prospective employees precise salary offers rather than round numbers (*e.g.*, "we can offer $121,250" rather than "we can offer $120,000"), because a specific number signals that the employer was very deliberate and careful in arriving at the salary offer number. In order for this to be helpful, the employer should have objective criteria supporting the specific number.

Use Recruiters to Identify Candidates: For certain positions, it may be beneficial for the employer to contact a recruiter. Of course, using a third-party recruiter will result in extra cost, but if a position is somewhat unique or the employer needs more assistance in recruiting, an outside recruiter may be helpful. Once the outside recruiter has identified potential employees and the employer decides on the candidate he wishes to hire, the salary negotiation may run more smoothly thanks to the help of the recruiter. The recruiter will be able to set the stage for the employee and employer as to expectations based on the job and experience of the employee, and the salary discussions may be streamlined due to this outside help.

Carefully Examine a Candidate's Past Work History: Before salary negotiations begin, an employer should take time to review the work history of the candidate. Specifically, make sure references are checked and resumes verified. While some employers leave this task to after salary negotiations, it is helpful to learn as much about the employees' past job history for discussion during salary negotiations. For example, with the candidate's permission, the employer may contact one of the candidate's references who reveals that the candidate prefers to work from home instead of in the office. Of course, the candidate may have revealed this fact himself either at the interview or the salary discussion stage. However, by learning this fact before the negotiations, the employer can factor in how this flexibility in job location may impact salary. If the job requires more in office time, the employer agreeing to allow home office work time may prove a benefit to the candidate that is more important than a salary debate.

Prevent Discriminatory Questions: Part of any tactical planning is the preparation of questions. In negotiating salary offers, employers should be mindful to avoid asking questions that violate or imply violating anti-discrimination laws. For example, an employer should not ask the employee if there is "any situation at home" that will require them to take more time off than is usual for a job of this nature. This type of question could violate both federal and state anti-discrimination laws because it could solicit information on the prospective employee's marital status or family obligations. Another example of a possible discriminatory question may be asking for the employee's salary history. As noted above, various laws prevent employers from inquiring about their prospective employee's past salary.

Be Prepared to Discuss Benefits: As noted above, an employer should realize that many employees value other benefits alongside money. Therefore, an employer should be prepared to discuss and, if within the framework of their company, offer other benefits to employees in addition to or in lieu of a higher salary. Some of these benefits include health benefits, vacation time, flexible schedules, and the aforementioned ability to work remotely. Thus, when the employer begins the negotiating process, he may wish to discuss the entire benefits package with the candidate, and not just money. This is especially important if the employer is somewhat limited in the salary range. If the employer can determine other motivating factors for the employee besides compensation, he will be able to prioritize other parts of a compensation package to keep the negotiations on track.

Be Professional: It should be obvious that the employer should maintain a high level of professionalism during negotiations. The employer should be a role model for the candidate. The employer should recognize that she is a representative of the company. Even if the candidate's demands seem unreasonable, the employer should maintain a calm demeanor and always try to re-focus negotiations that get off track. Professionalism is not simply about good manners. An employer also conveys professionalism by being prepared to discuss all aspects of job compensation, communicating offers and requirements clearly, and having the ability to extend the best offer the company can give.

Knowing When to Let Go and Having Alternatives: In preparing for the salary negotiation, the employer should have planned the minimum acceptable level to make the deal. If the employer reaches that point, and there is no agreement to be made, he must be prepared to walk away. However, before walking away, the employer should try to assess the candidate's other options. A candidate who eagerly shuts down the negotiation likely has many other employment options available, while a candidate who seems to try to reach for a deal may have limited options. If it appears a candidate has limited options, the employer may want to take a break in salary negotiations. Suggesting that the candidate think over the last proposal and get back to the employer in a day or two may result in a better outcome for the employer. This approach not only allows a candidate time to reflect on the offer, but also shows the candidate that the employer is not overly eager to make a deal. However, it should be made clear to the candidate that a day or two delay is not an invitation for the candidate to restart the salary negotiations.

As in any negotiation, determining the minimum acceptable level will also relate to the alternatives available to the employer. In the case of a salary negotiation, the employer should hopefully have other job candidates lined up in case the salary negotiation fails. The comfort of having other candidates available will allow the employer to walk away more easily.

The more frequently an employer is involved in hiring, the better he will understand the best ways to communicate with candidates for successful outcomes in salary negotiations. However, it is important not to lose sight of the fact that each salary negotiation is unique, and as with any negotiation, preparation is key for an employer to have a successful salary negotiation with a candidate. The better the employer is prepared, the more likely the negotiation will run smoothly, and the employer will be able to maintain a positive relationship with his future employee.

Strategies for Employees Negotiations of Salary

There is no shortage of strategy advice for employees negotiating salaries. Most often, salary negotiations are separate from job offers. Although employers may discuss salary in general during the interview process, often the real salary negotiations take place either during the offer stage or in a separate meeting a short time after the offer has been made. In a single stage process, a prospective employer offers the candidate a job and then discusses salary with the candidate. The prospective employer may offer the candidate the job with a set salary, indicating the job is non-negotiable, or begin salary discussions concurrently with the job offer. In a two-stage process, an employer may offer the prospective candidate the job and delay salary discussions if and until the candidate accepts the job. Therefore, a prospective employee should be prepared for both scenarios. The following strategies are helpful for employees engaging in salary negotiations.[36]

Research: Prospective employees should always be prepared to discuss salary, and should do their research to find out as much as they can about the salary structure generally for the industry in which they are seeking a job and specifically for the company in which they are interviewing. As noted in strategies for the employer, there are various websites, including AI tools, that provide helpful information about comparable salaries for various positions.

List Priorities and Prepare Your Offers: In preparing to negotiate salary, a candidate should also include in his ideal salary package including non-monetary items such as vacation time, health coverage, retirement plans, and flex time. The list may be lengthy and will vary depending on the job and industry. A sales position may entail negotiations relating to travel while a corporate office position may be all about the corner office. Once the candidate has made the list and prioritized his items, he is ready to prepare his highest realistic salary goal and his minimum acceptable level.

Delay Salary Negotiations Until After Receiving a Job Offer: It may be tempting to try to negotiate salary during the initial interview before getting a job offer. After all, if a job candidate discovers that the prospective employer is not willing to negotiate salary, or the employer proposes a salary that is nowhere near acceptable, why should the candidate waste his time and continue to interview? However, if the candidate has done thorough research before the interview, he should have some knowledge as to whether the company's salary is within an acceptable range. If not, the candidate should simply pass on the interview. Furthermore, even though the candidate has prepared to discuss salary offers before the interview, if the candidate initiates a salary discussion early on in the interview process, it is almost a sure-fire way not to get an offer. The prospective employer will likely interpret a rigorous approach to discussing salary prior to the offer as premature and wonder if the candidate has any affinity for working with the company beyond getting paid.

Be Enthusiastic: As a prospective employee, an employer looks to see your motivation for the job which can translate to a higher salary offer. Once the candidate has been given an offer, it is important to not only be confident about your ability but to convey that you are excited to be given the opportunity to work for the employer. This enthusiasm ties in with a candidate's likeability factor.

Convince Them of Your Worth: It is always important in any negotiation to set forth objective criteria as to why you are making an offer. A salary offer is no different. A salary request should always be coupled with the reasons why you are worth that number.

Collaboration Not Competition: Receiving a job offer and its subsequent salary negotiation begins as an arm's length discussion. Except if you are being hired by family or a friend, you likely have had no prior relationship with your potential employer before salary negotiations. However, if you ultimately accept the job, this relationship has the potential of becoming an arm-open relationship, in a business sense. Therefore, the candidate should do everything possible to keep the negotiations friendly and respectful. Even though you want to advocate for your salary request, if you ultimately take the job, this discussion is just a first in a series of future negotiations. How you set the tone during this negotiation may set a precedent for future negotiations.

Walk Away Politely and Respectfully: If discussions do not produce your desired salary and you have decided to decline the job because your alternative is preferable to the offer on the table, your exit strategy is important. Although this job may not have worked out for you, you never know in the future if your paths may cross again with this employer. Therefore, it is always desirable to keep the door open, especially within the same industry. If the negotiations do not result in your employment, you should express your thanks for the offer.

PROBLEM 7-1: SALARY

GENERAL INFORMATION: *Assume for purposes of this negotiation that the Vermont laws discussed above apply.*

Maria is a 28-year-old who is building a strong reputation in the marketing industry, having been involved in several successful national campaigns and has a popular online presence. She holds a master's degree in marketing from a top university and speaks frequently at professional conferences and is a guest on various business-oriented podcasts. After receiving her master's degree, Maria took a job with a small marketing firm, but now seeks to move on to better advance her career. Her former manager understood her need for advancement and told her although he does not want her to leave, his company does not have the resources to make her an offer that would be competitive with offers she would likely receive from other companies. She gave her former manager a requested 60 day notice one month ago. In the past month, she has had several companies actively recruiting her, but has narrowed her search down to two prospective employers: Company 1 and Company 2.

Jackson from Company 1 has offered Maria a position with a starting salary of $150,000. Company 1 is a well-established firm with a strong reputation in the marketing industry and a robust client portfolio. Company 1 has been slow to adapt to the online community and focuses its business mainly on established well-known companies. Jackson has indicated that the company is open to negotiating the salary, bonus structure, and other terms of employment. The initial offer includes the option to work remotely up to three days per week, requires occasional travel to client sites (estimated at 10% of the year), and provides two weeks of paid vacation annually. Jackson has provided Maria with an employment agreement for her review.

Company 2 is a dynamic start-up in the marketing sector. Naomi from Company 2 offered Maria a lower base salary of $120,000. While the company is newer to the industry, it has demonstrated rapid growth and offers significant potential for advancement, including the possibility of moving Maria into a management role within one to two years. Company 2 also advocates for its employees to have an online presence and has indicated to Maria that they may support funding her own podcast if their budget allows it. Company 2's offer includes the option for fully remote work, but travel to industry events and client meetings could total up to 25% of the year. There is no vacation policy at Company 2, but the company has a personal day policy that allows employees to take up to 10 days off per year for any reason with pay.

Company 1 has interviewed 35 candidates for this position, but Maria is widely considered their top choice. While Jackson believes there are other qualified candidates, he recognizes Maria's unique qualifications and is motivated to secure her acceptance. Both Maria and Jackson are aware that the typical starting salary for a candidate of Maria's caliber in this field is between $100,000 and $170,000, with highly sought-after candidates sometimes commanding even higher compensation packages.

Maria prefers the stability and reputation of Company 1 but is attracted by the advancement potential, online focus, and flexibility offered by Company 2. After reviewing Company 1's employment agreement, Maria called Jackson to express her interest in the position and to discuss the salary, bonus provisions, remote work arrangements, travel expectations, and vacation time. Jackson responded that he has flexibility on these points and scheduled a meeting to negotiate.

The compensation and benefits provisions from Company 1's offer are excerpted below:

Compensation and Benefits (Excerpt from Company 1's Offer)

1. As full compensation for all services provided, the employee shall be paid at the rate of $150,000 per year. Such payments shall be subject to such normal statutory deductions by the Employer. Bonuses may be awarded at the discretion of the employer.
2. The salary mentioned in paragraph (1) shall be reviewed on an annual basis.
3. The employee may work remotely up to three days per week, subject to business needs and supervisor approval.
4. The employee will be required to travel to client sites as necessary, estimated at 10% of the year.
5. The employee is entitled to two weeks (10 business days) of paid vacation annually, in addition to company holidays.

CONFIDENTIAL INFORMATION

Both Jackson and Maria will prepare confidential planning worksheets for the upcoming negotiation. These worksheets will include their bargaining positions on the following issues:

A. For Jackson: the maximum salary and non-monetary benefits he is willing to offer.

B. For Maria: the minimum salary and non-monetary benefits she is willing to accept.

C. For both: proposed bonus provisions, remote work arrangements, travel expectations, and vacation time.

TACTICAL PLANNING

In planning the negotiation, both the employee and employer should carefully consider the balance of power. An employer typically has more power than a prospective employee, in that the employer makes the hiring decision and typically has a number of candidates to choose from. However, be aware of situations, such as this problem, where the prospective employee is a highly recruited candidate for the job, and thus, the employee's uniqueness may prove to reallocate some of the power.

Refer to Chapter 2 to guide you through the steps in preparing your Tactical Planning Worksheet (Appendix A) for this problem. Be sure to refer to the strategy guidelines for Employers and Employees discussed in this chapter and the information contained in the general information and confidential information above for this problem.

ARRANGING THE NEGOTIATION

For purposes of this negotiation, you may assume the negotiation will take place in-person, at Jackson's office.

BARGAINING

In a traditional salary negotiation, the employer and employee should begin with some ice-breaking. In this instance, it is important for the parties to establish a rapport not only to set the tone for a positive negotiation but also to establish a foundation for a future working relationship.

As the parties move to bargaining, the parties are benefitted from the fact that the opening offer has already been made prior to the negotiation, because Jackson has offered Maria $150,000 as a starting salary. At this point, either Jackson or Maria should acknowledge this offer as the starting point, and both parties should be prepared to exchange offers and counteroffers on salary, bonus, remote work flexibility, travel requirements, and vacation time. Both parties will likely have questions, and those questions should be interspersed throughout the negotiation in order for each party to gain information and perhaps adjust the goals they have outlined on their planning worksheets.

LETTING GO OR RESOLVING & EXECUTING THE AGREEMENT

As the bargaining phase concludes, there are likely three possible outcomes: (1) Maria and Jackson reach a mutually acceptable agreement; (2) they do not reach an agreement and Jackson and Maria decide to part ways; or (3) final offers are made and Jackson and/or Maria decide to think it over and come back with a decision a short time in the future.

It is unlikely the negotiation would continue beyond this session. However, one scenario where the negotiations may continue is if Maria and Jackson came to a tentative agreement on an issue, but Jackson was unable to complete the deal because he did not have the authority. For example, if Jackson did not have the authority to change the terms of the vacation policy, he may have to consult with the company's lawyers and obtain approval to make the agreed changes with Maria. However, if the company lawyers do not give their approval, negotiations may need to continue, or this may be a deal breaker.

If Maria and Jackson come to terms on the salary and benefits, the employment agreement will reflect those changes. At this point, Maria and Jackson will sign the agreement and, hopefully, this will be the start of a great working relationship.

ETHICS AND EQUITY

Both Maria and Jackson are aware of the salary range for this position in this field. Therefore, neither Maria nor Jackson should make a claim that the range is higher or lower. However, Maria should be aware that employers may not be forthcoming as to the highest salary they can offer. Just like a settlement negotiation in a litigation context, an employer likely does not want to offer his highest authority initially when negotiating salary offers. However, Jackson should be careful not to misrepresent that the salary he can offer is the highest if it is not. As in any negotiation, this type of lie can not only derail the negotiation, but, if discovered, can also set up future problems not only to his credibility but also to that of the company.

Maria should also be mindful of not overselling her value, and in the course of doing so, make misrepresentations as well. Unfortunately, it is somewhat typical for job candidates to inflate the number of salary offers they have been offered, in an effort to raise the stakes in the present negotiation. Playing the "I've got better offers game" may backfire. For example, in this case, Maria does have a legitimate other offer, and she may wish to use that offer as a negotiating point. However, if she should misrepresent that she has other additional offers from other companies, her lie may be quickly discovered, as many industries are like small communities, and shared information is not uncommon. Even if Maria does not reveal the names of the companies that gave her these made-up offers, Jackson may be well aware that her alleged salary offers do not sound legitimate, given the current market in that industry, Further, if Maria oversells herself, she may find Jackson withdrawing his offer, and she has now eliminated her number one choice for a job.

Jackson, as an employer, should also be mindful of recent laws that do not allow an employer to ask a candidate about salary history. If he attempts to violate these laws, he would not only be engaging in unethical behavior, but also positioning his company to be the subject of a lawsuit. It is expected that Jackson would also act ethically and not discriminate against Maria during salary negotiations based on such factors as race, gender, age, marital status, national origin, religion, or disability. It is difficult to determine during a negotiation if discriminatory conduct is occurring, However, if proven after the fact, Jackson could be in violation of numerous state and federal laws.

TACTICAL PLANNING WORKSHEET REVEAL

After concluding the negotiations, you and your counterpart should exchange your individual Tactical Planning Worksheets so that you both can see the bargaining positions you had planned to use during the negotiation. You should compare the two worksheets and see how far apart you were initially. Also, you should analyze whether and why you strayed from your worksheet, especially in the areas of offers and counteroffers. What positive aspects from your counterpart's worksheet do you wish you had included in yours?

POST-NEGOTIATION SELF-REFLECTION WORKSHEET

At the conclusion of the reveal session for this problem, be sure to complete the Post-Negotiation Self-Reflection Worksheet (found in Appendix B). Your Post-Negotiation Self-Reflection Worksheet should be completed individually and optimally within a short period of time after the Tactical Planning Worksheet reveal, while the negotiation session is fresh in your mind.

Laws Relevant to Non-Disclosure Agreements

Non-disclosure agreements (NDAs) are contracts designed to protect confidential information across many industries, with particularly widespread use in technology sectors where intellectual property forms the core of competitive advantage. Estimates suggest that between 33 and 57% of U.S. workers operate under NDAs or similar confidentiality restrictions, with prevalence exceeding 70% in computer and mathematical occupations.[37] These agreements are most frequently deployed to safeguard trade secrets, secure proprietary technical specifications, protect product development roadmaps, and maintain confidentiality during mergers and acquisitions.

Federal Laws Relevant to Trade Secrets

Most of the laws governing NDAs are state laws. There is, however, an important federal law providing federal protection for intellectual property deemed trade secrets. The federal Defend Trade Secrets Act (DTSA) is similar in many ways to the Uniform Trade Secrets Act (UTSA), which was adopted by 47 states. The UTSA aims to harmonize the protection of trade secrets across states by providing a consistent legal framework. It defines trade secrets and provides remedies for misappropriation, thereby reducing legal uncertainties. The DTSA provides a federal claim for trade secret misappropriation. DTSA allows an opportunity for employers to litigate trade secret misappropriation in federal courts and provides them an alternative to state laws on misappropriation of trade secrets. The DTSA provides protection for misappropriation of financial, scientific, business, economic, technical, or engineering information in the form of "patterns, plans, compilations, program devices, formulas, designs, prototypes, methods, techniques, processes, procedures, programs, or codes, whether tangible or intangible, and whether or how stored, compiled, or memorialized physically, electronically, graphically, photographically, or in writing" as long as reasonable measures are taken to protect the secrecy of the information and the employer can prove that economic value is derived from that secrecy.[38] The DTSA establishes federal protections for confidential business information that derives independent economic value from secrecy, provided owners implement "reasonable measures" to maintain confidentiality. Thus, under the DTSA a trade secret must be information that the owner has taken reasonable measures to keep secret and that derives independent economic value from not being generally known or readily ascertainable.

Enforceability of NDAs

While NDAs serve as critical tools for protecting sensitive information, their validity and scope are influenced by a complex interplay of federal and state laws. Recent legislative developments, such as the Speak Out Act of 2022, have introduced limitations on the enforceability of NDAs, particularly in cases involving workplace misconduct.[39] While NDAs remain critical tools for safeguarding trade secrets and proprietary data, this evolving legal landscape underscores the importance of carefully drafting NDAs to ensure they are enforceable and do not infringe upon employees' rights.

NDAs in the technology industry are generally enforceable when they are designed to protect legitimate business interests, such as trade secrets, confidential information, and proprietary data. NDAs are more likely to be challenged if they are overly broad, lack clear definitions, or impose unreasonable restrictions. The information must be specific enough to separate the trade secret from general knowledge in the trade.[40]

Tech companies report attempted trade secret theft annually, with inadequate NDAs contributing to large percentages of successful breaches. By combining precise contractual language with technical safeguards, organizations can leverage NDAs as dynamic tools for innovation protection rather than static legal formalities.

NDA cases in the technology area are often contested in court filings. High profile tech NDA cases may serve as a guide to understanding the types of issues involved in NDAs that lead to litigation. For example, in *Oculus vs. ZeniMax*, a Dallas jury awarded ZeniMax Media $200 million after finding that Oculus co-founder Palmer Luckey violated a non-disclosure agreement and Oculus recovered an additional $300 million for other claims.[41] Critical evidence showed Oculus co-founder Palmer Luckey using ZeniMax's latency-reduction code without authorization, despite signing a confidentiality agreement. The verdict underscored that NDAs remain enforceable even when trade secret claims fail, provided the agreement contains clear use restrictions.

The absence of an NDA or proper NDA due diligence and compliance leaves tech companies more vulnerable. For example, Waymo LLC alleged that former Waymo engineer Anthony Levandowski downloaded 14,000 files containing LiDAR schematics and sensor designs before founding autonomous trucking startup Otto, later acquired by Uber.[42] The case highlights the need to have NDAs in place and for proper NDA compliance and due diligence.

PROBLEM 7-2: NON-DISCLOSURE AGREEMENT

GENERAL INFORMATION: *Assume for purposes of this negotiation that California law governs the employment relationship and the enforceability of any non-disclosure agreements.*

Austin is a senior software engineer being recruited by Gener Data Solution's hiring manager, Zelda. Gener Data Solutions (Gener) is a mid-sized technology company specializing in cloud-based analytics platforms. Gener requires all employees to sign a non-disclosure agreement (NDA) protecting the company's proprietary technology, and confidential business strategies. This NDA is a standard part of Gener's recruitment for positions involving access to sensitive information, especially given the company's ongoing development of advanced analytics products and its competitive position in the industry.

The NDA presented to Austin states that, in consideration of the employment opportunity, he agrees not to disclose any confidential or proprietary information of Gener at any time during his employment or for a period of two years after his employment ends. The agreement specifically covers trade secrets such as source code, proprietary algorithms, client data pipelines, pricing models, business strategies, product roadmaps, and any other information designated as confidential by Gener. Austin also agrees not to use any of this information for his own benefit or for the benefit of any third party, except as necessary in the ordinary course of his duties for Gener. Upon the conclusion of his employment, he must promptly return all materials containing confidential information. The NDA further provides that Gener may seek injunctive relief if Austin breaches any of its provisions, and that the agreement's terms are severable, meaning the rest of the agreement remains enforceable even if one part is found invalid.

As part of the offer, Gener proposes a base salary of $158,000 per year, 0.5% equity in the company vested over four years, a hybrid work schedule of three days in-office and two days remote, and an annual performance bonus of up to 15% of base salary. Austin, however, is interested in negotiating the terms. He requests a higher base salary of $170,000, 0.75% equity, and the option for full remote work. He also expresses concern that the NDA's two-year post-employment restriction may be overly broad and could limit his future career opportunities in the analytics sector. Austin asks for a shorter NDA duration and a clearer definition of what constitutes "proprietary systems" to avoid ambiguity. Austin has concerns about the scope and duration of the NDA. He has worked on similar technologies in the past and does not want to risk unintentional exposure to future claims of misappropriation. He also wants clarity on how the NDA might affect his ability to showcase non-sensitive work in a portfolio or transition to future employment in the tech field.

Zelda insists that the NDA is non-negotiable due to recent incidents of information leaks at similar companies, but that some of the terms may be clarified and more fully explained. She offers a $20,000 signing bonus if Austin accepts the original terms of the NDA without any changes. She is willing to negotiate the salary but tells Austin that if he pushes for a higher base salary, the equity portion of the offer may be reduced. The negotiation centers on balancing Austin's compensation and work flexibility requests with Gener's need to protect its trade secrets and maintain a competitive edge in the market. The proposed NDA from Gener is below:

NON-DISCLOSURE AGREEMENT

This Non-Disclosure Agreement ("Agreement") is entered into as of the date below, by and between Gener Data Solutions ("Employer"), a company specializing in cloud-based analytics platforms, and Austin ("Employee"), in consideration of the employment opportunity provided by Employer.

1. Term of Agreement

This Agreement is effective upon execution by both parties and remains in effect throughout the term of Employee's employment and for two (2) years following termination of employment, regardless of the reason for termination.

2. Nature of Agreement

This Agreement does not constitute a contract of employment for a specific term. It is limited to the subject matter of non-disclosure of confidential information as described herein.

3. Definition of Confidential Information

"Confidential Information" means all non-public information, whether written, oral, electronic, or otherwise, disclosed to or accessed by Employee during the hiring process or employment, including but not limited to: (A) Source code, proprietary algorithms, and software designs developed or used by Gener; (B) Client data pipelines and architectures; (C) Product roadmaps, unreleased features, and development plans; (D) Pricing models, business strategies, and financial information; (E) Client lists, contracts, and contact information; (F) Any other technical, financial, or business information designated as confidential by Gener. Confidential Information excludes information that (i) is or becomes publicly available through no fault of Employee, (ii) is lawfully obtained from a third party without restriction, or (iii) is independently developed by Employee without reference to Gener's confidential information.

4. Covenant Not to Disclose

Employee agrees that at no time during employment, or for two (2) years after termination, will Employee directly or indirectly disclose to any person, firm, or corporation any Confidential Information of Employer, except as required in the ordinary course of Employee's duties for Employer.

5. Use of Confidential Information

Employee agrees not to use any Confidential Information for Employee's own benefit or for the benefit of any third party, except as required or necessary for performing duties for Gener.

6. Return or Destruction of Materials

Upon termination of employment or upon request by Employer, Employee shall promptly return or destroy all documents, records, or materials (including electronic files) containing Confidential Information, and certify such return or destruction to Employer.

7. Injunctive Relief and Remedies

Employee recognizes and acknowledges that any breach of this Agreement would cause irreparable harm to Employer, for which monetary damages may be inadequate. Employer shall be entitled to seek injunctive relief and any other remedies available at law or equity to enforce this Agreement.

8. Severability

If any provision of this Agreement is determined to be illegal or unenforceable, the remaining provisions shall remain in full force and effect.

9. Governing Law

This Agreement shall be governed by and construed in accordance with the laws of the State of California.

10. Acknowledgement

Employee acknowledges that this Agreement is a condition of employment with Gener Data Solutions, given the sensitive nature of the company's proprietary technology, client relationships, and competitive position in the analytics industry.

Austin called Zelda to express his continued interest in the role, but asked to discuss the salary, bonus structure, equity, and especially the NDA terms before accepting the position. Zelda agreed to set up a meeting to discuss Austin's concerns.

CONFIDENTIAL INFORMATION

Both Austin and Zelda will prepare Tactical Planning Worksheets for the upcoming negotiation. Each party's planning worksheet is confidential. It includes bargaining positions on the issues involved in the negotiation in the role of the Employee (Austin) or the Employer (Gener). This information should not be shared with the other party prior to the negotiation. For purposes of this problem, in addition to the other components of your Tactical Planning Worksheet, your planning worksheet needs to include your bargaining position on these issues:

A) For Gener (Employer): The maximum salary, bonus, equity, and non-monetary benefits the company is willing to offer to Austin.

B) For Austin (Employee): The minimum salary, bonus, equity, and non-monetary benefits he is willing to accept.

C) For Austin and Gener: The permissible scope, duration, terms, and limitations of the non-disclosure agreement.

TACTICAL PLANNING

Refer to Chapter 2 to guide you through the steps in preparing your Tactical Planning Worksheet (Appendix A) for this problem. Be sure to refer to the strategy guidelines for Employers and Employees discussed in this chapter and the information contained in the general information and confidential information above for this problem.

ARRANGING THE NEGOTIATION

Assume the negotiation takes place in Gener's offices, though in practice, it could occur via telephone, video conference, or other appropriate means.

BARGAINING

After a brief ice-breaking and agenda setting discussion, the parties should begin negotiating the terms of Austin's employment agreement and NDA. Each parties' worksheets should reflect their goals, and they should set forth their offers, counteroffers, and concessions. They should also be prepared to make reasonable adjustments to their positions based on new information that emerges during negotiation.

LETTING GO OR RESOLVING & EXECUTING THE AGREEMENT

If Austin and Zelda come to terms on the employment terms and the NDA, both the employment agreement and the NDA will reflect those changes. At this point, the parties will sign the agreements.

ETHICS AND EQUITY

NDAs are common in technology and other industries where employees have access to trade secrets, proprietary technology, product roadmaps, and client lists. The agreement must balance the employer's right to protect sensitive information with the employee's right to use general skills and knowledge in future employment. The parties should avoid unethical tactics, such as exaggerating the risk or downplaying the sensitivity of the information.

TACTICAL PLANNING WORKSHEET REVEAL

After negotiations, exchange Tactical Planning Worksheets to compare initial bargaining positions and analyze any deviations during negotiation.

POST-NEGOTIATION SELF-REFLECTION WORKSHEET

Complete the Post-Negotiation Self-Reflection Worksheet (found in Appendix B) soon after the reveal session, while the negotiation session is fresh in your mind.

Laws Relevant to Small Business Acquisitions

Acquiring a small business such as a bakery involves navigating a complex web of legal requirements and potential pitfalls that extend beyond standard business acquisitions. The process necessitates thorough legal due diligence, compliance with food-specific regulations, and obtaining numerous licenses and permits at federal, state, and local levels. Buyers must carefully examine the target bakery's legal documentation, regulatory compliance history, and potential liabilities while understanding the unique legal obligations associated with food service businesses. From verifying proper food handling certifications to examining equipment leases and supplier contracts, each element warrants meticulous scrutiny to avoid costly post-acquisition surprises or liabilities. Additionally, state-level regulations, particularly those governing ingredients, labeling, packaging, and kitchen operations must be understood even if a bakery operates in just one location, as these laws can affect products sold across state lines, thereby implicating interstate commerce regulations.

Legal due diligence is a critical first step in acquiring a bakery business. It involves a comprehensive investigation of the target company's legal, operational, and financial standing prior to finalizing the acquisition. This review should uncover potential issues that could financially or operationally impact the acquiring company's post-acquisition operations. The scope of legal due diligence encompasses everything from intellectual property to pending litigation, with the aim of ensuring everything is in order. During the due diligence process for a bakery acquisition, buyers should review several key documents including premises and equipment leases and confirm their transferability, inspect equipment condition—particularly high-value assets such as industrial ovens and refrigeration units—and evaluate financial records especially supplier and customer contracts to assess the bakery's sustainability and profit potential.

In addition, operating a bakery requires various licenses and permits, all of which must be verified, confirmed, and transferred during the acquisition process. These typically include: a business license, issued by state or municipal authorities, (usually between $50 and $200);[43] an Employer Identification Number (EIN), assigned by the IRS;[44] a food service license (ranging from $100 to $1,000);[45] food handler's permits, certifying employees have completed approved food safety training (typically $5 to $30 per person); a building health permit, confirming compliance with sanitation and health and safety regulations (costs varying from $50 to $1,000);[46] a certificate of occupancy, issued post-inspection of the premises to ensure compliance with building codes (typically around $100);[47] a resale permit, allowing wholesale purchasing without sales tax (typically between $0 and $50);[48] a dumpster placement permit, required for proper food waste disposal (about $10 to $100 per week); a sign permit for exterior signage ($20 to $50); and a "Doing Business As" (DBA) registration, if operating under a different name than the legal business name ($5 to $50).[49] According to the U.S. Small Business Administration (SBA), states and local governments regulate a broader range of small business activities than the federal government, making it essential to research state, county, and city regulations specific to the bakery's location.

Beyond standard business regulations, bakeries face additional scrutiny regarding food safety. The U.S. Food and Drug Administration (FDA) enforces regulations covering food production, ingredient safety, and labeling requirements.[50] When acquiring a bakery, buyers must verify compliance with these standards, including prior inspection reports, to avoid liability for past violations. Additionally, several states have recently enacted or are considering legislation restricting specific ingredients such as food additives in food products. For example, California's AB 418, enacted in 2024, prohibits the use of brominated vegetable oil, potassium bromate, propylparaben, and Red No. 3 in food manufactured or sold in California after January 1, 2027.[51] Illinois has introduced similar ingredient ban legislation, and other states such as New York, New Jersey, and Pennsylvania are considering similar restrictions. Companies selling products in these jurisdictions must comply even without a physical presence there.

State regulations for bakeries can vary significantly. In Florida, bakery businesses must choose between two types of food service licenses: a seating license for bakeries that include seating for customers to dine in, and a non-seating license for bakeries without customer seating. The Florida Department of Business and Professional Regulation requires bakery owners to create an online account, complete a plan review, apply for the appropriate license, pay applicable fees, and pass a licensing inspection.[52] In Maryland, bakeries must obtain a business license controlled by city or county authorities, a certificate of occupancy for physical bakery locations, a food handler's license (also known as a food service license), a seller's permit for sales tax collection, and a catering business license if offering catering services.[53]

In sum, acquiring a bakery involves navigating a more intricate legal landscape than standard business purchases, requiring comprehensive due diligence and detailed attention to evolving food laws. Given the patchwork of federal, state, and local requirements, including novel ingredient bans and sanitation standards, working with legal and industry professionals is essential to facilitate a successful and compliant transaction.

PROBLEM 7-3: ACQUIRING A SMALL BAKERY BUSINESS

GENERAL INFORMATION: *Assume for purposes of this negotiation that the transaction is governed by the laws of California, a hotspot for vegan culinary innovation and a large consumer base interested in sustainable and ethical eating.*

George Martinez, 68, founder of Best Frisco Bakery in San Francisco, seeks to sell his 15-year-old business for $2.4 million due to his worsening health conditions. The bakery's assets include $350,000 in kitchen equipment and appliances, the 1,200-square-foot bakery property valued at $1.7 million (with $120,000 in needed structural repairs), and $150,000 in cash reserves. The bakery has averaged a 10% profit, which nets $100,000, over the last 3 years. The bakery has no outstanding debt or liabilities. It currently holds a business license, food service license, health permit, and certificate of occupancy. Its food handlers are certified, and the bakery has consistently passed local food inspections. Four years ago, George launched Veronica's Very Vegan Treats as a tribute to his late wife, a lifelong vegan who developed the recipes. While the vegan line historically accounts for 10% of revenue, George would like any buyer to continue offering these items as long as they remain profitable. He will transfer the recipes without requiring an NDA or confidentiality agreement.

Sophia Clark, 38, a pastry chef at a high-end San Francisco restaurant, wishes to leave her current job and open her own bakery. She is interested in purchasing George's bakery. Sophia has $2.3 million in financing but faces investor pressure to secure George's bakery or purchase another bakery before the holiday season. She has had preliminary discussions with George, but they have not agreed on any terms or conditions. The major issues they have identified from their discussions are as follows.

> ***Vegan Line:*** Sophia is unsure if she wants to continue the vegan line, which has minimal profitability. If she does continue it, she wants the ability to substitute ingredients if necessary, as some vegan ingredients are difficult and expensive to source. However, any ingredient substitutions would maintain the vegan designation. It is very important to George that Veronica's Very Vegan Treats remain on the menu. However, he does not expect Sophia to continue the vegan line if it is not profitable. Therefore, he will agree that Sophia may discontinue the line if it is unprofitable for two consecutive quarters. He is willing to be somewhat flexible on ingredient substitutions.
>
> ***Purchase Price:*** Sophia believes the $2.4 million selling price is high due to the building's structural issues, which will cost $120,000 to repair. In addition, the fire inspector has cited the bakery for fire code violations that will cost $40,000 to fix before the next inspection in six months. Due to these costs, Sophia believes the price should be reduced by 15%. George, however, offers to cover 30% of the repair and fire code update costs with no price reduction.
>
> ***Staff Retention:*** George prioritizes job security for his staff of five employees, including two bakers trained in Veronica's vegan recipes. Sophia plans

to automate inventory management, potentially eliminating two positions. However, she has no experience with vegan bakery items and is willing to negotiate keeping at least one of George's employees to make those items if the vegan line is part of the deal.

Redevelopment: Last year, the city commission approved a site across from the bakery for a luxury hotel, which will host many business conventions and special events. The hotel is expected to take two years to complete, with construction beginning in six months. The completed hotel will likely raise the bakery's property value and greatly increase foot traffic. However, road closures and traffic re-routing during construction may temporarily decrease customer visits.

Both Sophia and George have alternatives if their negotiation fails. George can keep the bakery, with his son running it until the hotel is completed. At that time, George will have a clearer picture of the bakery's value and viability. However, George's health is deteriorating, and he is concerned he may not live to see the hotel's completion. He also prefers that the bakery not become an issue in his estate. While George and his son have a close relationship, his son has changed jobs frequently and has little bakery experience, which may require George to be more involved than he wants or is able.

If Sophia does not purchase George's bakery, she may lease a smaller space or partner with another bakery, though neither option offers Best Frisco Bakery's prime location. Both face time constraints: George must repair the structural damage and complete fire code updates within six months, while Sophia's financing expires in 90 days.

George and Sophia have agreed to meet again to try and resolve the remaining issues and finalize the sale of the bakery.

CONFIDENTIAL INFORMATION

Both George and Sophia should prepare tactical planning worksheets for their upcoming negotiation. Each party's planning worksheet is confidential. It includes bargaining positions on the issues involved in the negotiation for George (the seller) or Sophia (the buyer). The information should not be shared with the other party prior to the negotiation. For purposes of this problem in addition to the other components of the tactical planning worksheet, your planning worksheet needs to include your bargaining position on these issues:

A. For George: the minimum sale price he is willing to accept, given his deteriorating health, his desire for a timely and uncomplicated exit, and his wish to honor his late wife's legacy through the continuation of Veronica's Very Vegan Treats. He must also weigh his willingness to accept non-monetary terms such as his concerns about his son's limited experience should the sale fall through, and the bakery remain in the family. George is also motivated to avoid the bakery becoming a burden for his estate.

B. For Sophia: the maximum price she can pay, factoring in the needed repairs and fire code updates, her openness to continuing the vegan line only if it remains profitable and with the flexibility to substitute ingredients, and the pressure from her investors to close a deal quickly. She must also consider her alternatives if the purchase fails, such as leasing a smaller space or partnering with another bakery, though neither offers the prime location of Best Frisco Bakery.

TACTICAL PLANNING

Refer to Chapter 2 to guide you through the steps in preparing your Tactical Planning Worksheet (Appendix A) for this problem. Consider the information contained in the general information and confidential information above and the applicable law.

ARRANGING THE NEGOTIATION

For purposes of this negotiation, you may assume you may assume the negotiation will take place in person.

BARGAINING

They should begin the negotiation by building rapport and acknowledging their shared interests in a smooth transition and the ongoing success of the business. The discussion should proceed by addressing the major issues: purchase price and repair responsibilities, the future of Veronica's Very Vegan Treats, staff retention, and the implications of zoning and redevelopment. During bargaining, both parties should be prepared to exchange offers and counteroffers on both monetary terms, such as price and allocation of repair costs, and non-monetary terms, including menu offerings and employee retention. They should ask clarifying questions to uncover deeper interests, such as George's health timeline and Sophia's investor deadlines, and be willing to adjust their goals as new information emerges.

LETTING GO OR RESOLVING & EXECUTING THE AGREEMENT

There are several possible outcomes to this negotiation. The parties may reach a full agreement with mutually acceptable terms, a partial agreement requiring further discussion, or no agreement, in which case George's son would run the bakery and Sophia would pursue alternative options. If an agreement is reached, all terms should be documented in writing, including the final price, repair responsibilities, conditions for the vegan line, staff employment, and contingencies related to the hotel development.

ETHICS AND EQUITY

Both parties should act honestly and transparently about their constraints and intentions. They should avoid misrepresenting facts or capabilities and maintain professionalism to preserve their reputations and relationships with the community. Special care should be taken to ensure that the negotiation process does not damage relationships, especially since the bakery has a longstanding presence in the neighborhood.

TACTICAL PLANNING WORKSHEET REVEAL

After negotiations, you and your counterpart should exchange their individual Tactical Planning Worksheets to compare initial positions and reflect on the negotiation process. Also, you should analyze any deviations from the original plans and identify positive strategies used by your counterpart.

POST-NEGOTIATION SELF-REFLECTION WORKSHEET

Each party should complete a self-reflection worksheet individually shortly after the negotiation session (found in Appendix B). Reflect on whether your goals were met, and what strategies were effective or ineffective.

Laws Relevant to Homeowners' Associations

A Homeowners' Association (HOA) is a private, legally incorporated organization that governs a housing community, collects dues, and establishes rules for its residents. HOAs are primarily found in the United States, Canada, and the Philippines, though they exist in other countries as well. They typically oversee subdivisions, planned communities, condominium buildings, and other residential areas where residents share common spaces or amenities.

Homeowners' Associations are prevalent across the United States, with approximately 370,000 such organizations governing residential communities with over 77 million residents.[54] These private entities significantly impact property ownership rights, community standards, and property values in planned neighborhoods, condominiums, and other common-interest developments.

HOAs are typically formed by real estate developers to market, manage, and sell homes within a residential subdivision. Initially, the developer controls the HOA, but this control is eventually transferred to the homeowners after a predetermined number of lots are sold. At this point, the homeowners themselves become responsible for the management and maintenance of the HOA. The primary mission of these associations is to maintain the quality of the community and protect property values within it.

Membership in an HOA is typically mandatory for property owners within the association's jurisdiction, making it a condition of purchasing a home in the community.[55] This arrangement creates a binding legal relationship between property owners and the association, with both parties having specific rights and responsibilities. HOAs operate through a formalized governance structure to ensure consistent management of community affairs and maintenance of shared assets.

Homeowners' associations are run by a board of directors or governors, typically elected by the community's residents.[56] These boards are responsible for enforcing the association's rules, overseeing financial matters, and making decisions that affect the community as a whole. The board might consist of volunteers from the community who are elected to serve specified terms. The governance structure ensures that residents have representation in decisions affecting their community while maintaining the association's objectives.

Every homeowners' association operates according to a set of governing documents that establish its authority, structure, and rules. These documents typically include Articles of Incorporation, Bylaws, and the Declaration of Covenants, Conditions, and Restrictions (CC&Rs).[57] The Articles of Incorporation legally establish the association as a corporate entity, usually as a non-profit organization. Bylaws detail the internal rules for governing the association, including procedures for meetings, elections, and board operations.

The CC&Rs are particularly important as they establish the specific rules and restrictions that apply to properties within the association's jurisdiction. These might include architectural guidelines, maintenance requirements, use restrictions, and other regulations designed to maintain community standards. The CC&Rs, along with other governing documents, must align with relevant state and local municipal laws and are legally enforceable through courts if necessary.

One of the most significant aspects of living in an HOA-governed community is the requirement to pay regular dues or fees. These dues or fees can be collected monthly, quarterly, or annually and vary widely based on the community's location, included amenities, and specific needs. The funds collected through these fees are primarily used to maintain common areas and facilities such as swimming pools, fitness centers, clubhouses, landscaping, trash collection, and security services. These associations can impose regular dues as well as special assessments for major projects or unexpected expenses. If homeowners fail to pay these dues or assessments, HOAs typically have the authority to charge late fees, impose fines, and place liens on properties. In extreme cases of non-payment, some HOAs even have the power to foreclose liens on properties despite on-time mortgage payments, though this power varies by state and is often subject to limitations.[58] The specific procedures and limitations for assessment collection and enforcement are typically detailed in both state laws and the association's governing documents.

The legal framework governing homeowners' associations is multifaceted, combining state-specific legislation, federal laws, and the association's own governing documents. This complex legal structure establishes the boundaries within which HOAs must operate, ensuring accountability while providing the authority needed to fulfill their mission of community maintenance and property value preservation.

HOA regulations vary significantly from state to state, with some states having extensive laws governing their formation and operation while others provide minimal oversight. States such as Florida have developed comprehensive bodies of HOA law that address numerous aspects of association governance and homeowner rights.[59] Other states have more limited HOA regulations, providing less specific guidance on association operations.

While state laws provide the primary regulatory framework for HOAs, several federal statutes also impact their operations. These federal laws typically address broader social issues and civil rights rather than the specific mechanics of association governance. For instance, HOAs must comply with the Fair Housing Act, which prohibits discrimination in housing based on protected characteristics such as race, color, religion, national origin, sex, disability, and familial status.[60] Federal laws supersede any conflicting provisions in an HOA's governing documents, ensuring that basic civil liberties are protected even within privately governed communities.

Homeowners' associations possess significant legal powers to fulfill their mission of maintaining community standards and protecting property values. However, these powers are balanced by homeowner rights and legal limitations designed to prevent overreach. Understanding this balance is crucial for both association boards and residents of HOA-governed communities.

HOAs have broad authority to regulate property appearance and use within their jurisdiction. They can create and enforce rules regarding exterior modifications, landscaping, parking, noise levels, and other factors affecting community aesthetics and quality of life. When homeowners violate these rules, associations can issue warnings, impose fines, restrict access to amenities, or pursue other enforcement actions as permitted by their governing documents and state law.

While HOAs possess significant authority, homeowners also have important rights within these communities. Most states require HOAs to maintain transparency by providing access to financial records, meeting minutes, and other association documents. Homeowners typically have the right to be notified of and participate in association meetings, vote in board elections, and propose amendments to governing documents. These participatory rights ensure that residents have a voice in the governance of their community.

A homeowner has the legal right to sue their homeowners' association if they are injured due to the HOA's failure to properly maintain common areas, such as tripping on an exposed wire in a shared space. HOAs are responsible for ensuring that common areas are safe and well-maintained, a duty often outlined in their governing documents and reinforced by state law. To succeed in such a lawsuit, the homeowner generally must demonstrate that the HOA knew or should have known about the hazardous condition and failed to remedy it, resulting in the injury. This involves proving that the HOA breached its duty of care, that the breach directly caused the injury, and that the homeowner suffered actual damages, such as medical expenses, lost wages, or pain and suffering.

However, there are important limitations and considerations when suing an HOA. In some cases, if the homeowner's own negligence contributed to the injury—such as ignoring warning signs or acting recklessly—the amount of compensation may be reduced under comparative negligence rules. Additionally, many states and HOA governing documents require homeowners to notify the association of the hazard and sometimes to pursue alternative dispute resolution, such as mediation, before filing a lawsuit. If the HOA had contracted out maintenance to a third party, liability might be shared or shifted, though the HOA could still be held responsible for inadequate oversight. Some states also provide limited immunity to HOA board members if they acted in good faith, though this does not shield the HOA itself from liability. Furthermore, homeowners must act within the statute of limitations, typically two to four years, or risk losing the right to sue.

It is also important to understand that suing an HOA is, in effect, like suing oneself and one's neighbors. Any damages awarded to the injured homeowner are typically paid out of the HOA's insurance or reserve funds, which are funded by the dues collected from all members, including the plaintiff. This means that a successful lawsuit could ultimately lead to increased dues or special assessments for the entire community. Therefore, while homeowners have the right to seek compensation for legitimate injuries, it is often in everyone's best interest to resolve disputes with the HOA cooperatively whenever possible.

PROBLEM 7-4: HOMEOWNERS' ASSOCIATION

GENERAL INFORMATION: *Assume for purposes of this negotiation that the transaction is governed by the laws of Florida.*

On December 15 of this year, Silas Buckner, a homeowner in the Juniper Homeowners' Association (HOA) community in Orlando, Florida, tripped over an exposed coaxial cable in a grassy area adjacent to a hedge. This area is commonly used by residents as a shortcut to access the neighborhood pickleball courts, bypassing the longer sidewalk route. At the time of the incident, Silas was checking his phone for directions to a pickleball tournament while using the shortcut. The cable, installed by Connectable Cable Co. ("Connectable"), had become partially exposed due to soil erosion caused by frequent foot traffic along the shortcut. The shortcut saves residents approximately seven minutes compared to the designated sidewalk path.

Since the construction of the pickleball courts, the HOA installed a sign stating "Pickleball Courts this way" with an arrow directing residents along the sidewalk. However, the HOA was aware that many residents continued to use the grassy shortcut through the hedge, despite the signage. In the first week of November at least five homeowners, including Silas, had complained to the HOA about the exposed cable. In response, the HOA emailed residents twice in November, warning against using the shortcut and citing safety concerns. Despite these warnings, the HOA took no physical steps to block access to the shortcut, even though they knew it remained popular. The exposed cable was visible from the sidewalk.

Also in the first week of November the HOA submitted a repair request to Connectable. However, Connectable deprioritized the repair due to a backlog caused by a recent storm that damaged infrastructure throughout the area. On November 20, a Connectable technician inspected the site, noted the cable's instability, but marked it as "low risk." The technician spray-painted an orange circle around the cable to indicate its location for a follow-up repair crew, but no further action was taken before Silas's accident.

The HOA is currently negotiating the renewal of its liability insurance contract. Any damages paid by the insurance company on behalf of the HOA in this incident could significantly raise the cost of the HOA's policy, resulting in higher assessments and fees for all homeowners or possibly requiring the HOA to seek a new insurance carrier. At the same time, Connectable has recently faced financial difficulties that have been publicized in the media. Any substantial damages paid in this case would further strain Connectable's finances, potentially harming its reputation and limiting its ability to secure future business contracts.

As a result of the incident, Silas sustained a fractured wrist and a torn ligament, both requiring surgery and ongoing physical therapy. His medical bills total $40,000. Silas also claims $20,000 in lost wages, as he was unable to work remotely during his recovery. He has filed a lawsuit against the HOA, seeking damages for his injuries, lost wages, and pain and suffering. The HOA through its insurance company has impleaded Connectable as a third-party defendant, alleging that Connectable was negligent in failing to repair the cable in a timely manner.

Although Silas wants to recover damages for his injury and believes both the HOA and Connectable were at fault, he is uncomfortable suing the HOA, as any judgment would ultimately be paid by his neighbors through their increased liability insurance rates and dues. He also dislikes the adversarial nature of a lawsuit, which could require some of his neighbors to be deposed or testify if the case goes to trial. Additionally, Silas's close friend is an HOA board member and has told Silas that the Board strongly believes the accident was entirely Silas's fault and that the HOA should not be held responsible. Silas is concerned that the lawsuit may affect his friendship with his friend on the Board and his relationships with other neighbors. Despite his strong belief that the HOA and Connectable should pay his damages, Silas's Attorney is willing to meet with attorneys from both the insurance company for the HOA and Connectable to attempt to settle the matter out of court.

CONFIDENTIAL INFORMATION

Silas Buckner (Homeowner/Plaintiff), Juniper Homeowners' Association (HOA/Defendant), and Connectable Cable Co. (Third-Party Defendant) should prepare tactical planning worksheets for the upcoming negotiation. For this problem they should use the multi-party Tactical Planning Worksheet found in Appendix A-1. Each party's planning worksheet is confidential. It includes bargaining positions on the issues involved in the negotiation. This information should not be shared with any of the other parties prior to the negotiation. Each worksheet should address the following issues, tailored to the facts and interests in this dispute:

A) For Silas Buckner: The minimum amount of monetary compensation Silas is willing to accept for medical expenses, lost wages, and pain and suffering. His willingness to accept a structured settlement, partial payment, or non-monetary remedies (such as HOA safety improvements or public acknowledgment of responsibility). His concerns about the impact of the lawsuit on neighbor relationships and his desire to minimize adversarial proceedings.

B) For Juniper HOA: The maximum amount the HOA is willing to contribute to a settlement without causing a significant increase in insurance premiums or assessments. Non-monetary remedies the HOA is willing to offer (*e.g.*, improved safety measures, public communication to residents). Strategies to minimize negative publicity and maintain community relationships. The extent to which the HOA will seek to shift liability or financial responsibility to Connectable Cable Co.

C) For Connectable Cable Co.: The maximum amount Connectable is willing to pay toward settlement given its financial and reputational constraints. Willingness to accept partial responsibility or to propose alternative solutions (such as expedited repairs, future service discounts to the HOA). Concerns about reputation, future business, and avoiding precedent for similar claims.

TACTICAL PLANNING

All parties should carefully consider the balance of power and underlying interests. For example, Silas is motivated to resolve the dispute without harming community relationships; the HOA is concerned about insurance costs and community harmony; Connectable is focused on financial survival and reputation management. Refer to the general information, confidential information, and the applicable laws to prepare your Tactical Planning Worksheet.

ARRANGING THE NEGOTIATION

For this scenario, assume the Attorneys from all three parties will meet in person for this negotiation at the HOA's community meeting room.

BARGAINING

After agenda setting and ice-breaking, the parties should begin the negotiation session. All parties should be prepared to exchange offers and counteroffers, including both monetary and non-monetary terms. Ask questions to uncover underlying interests and adjust goals as needed. Furthermore, during the negotiation in a multi-party suit, some of the parties may wish to meet separately. For example, in this negotiation, the HOA and Connectable's attorneys may wish to confer without the presence of the attorney for Silas in order to come up with a joint settlement plan.

LETTING GO OR RESOLVING & EXECUTING THE AGREEMENT

There are many possible outcomes to this negotiation but some of the likely outcomes are: 1) a settlement with agreed-upon contributions from the HOA and Connectable, and commitments to safety improvements; 2) no agreement, resulting in continued litigation; 3) a tentative agreement pending approval by insurance carriers or HOA board; 4) a partial agreement on some issues and a desire among the parties to meet again to resolve the remaining issues.

If a settlement is reached, document the agreement in writing, including payment terms and any non-monetary commitments (*e.g.*, cable burial, signage, or resident communications).

ETHICS AND EQUITY

All parties should act honestly and avoid misrepresenting facts or authority. The HOA and Connectable must be transparent about their financial and insurance constraints. Silas should accurately represent his damages and concerns. Parties should avoid threats or actions that could damage relationships beyond repair, especially Silas and the HOA, as that relationship will continue after the litigation concludes, and its repercussions could affect the neighborhood.

TACTICAL PLANNING WORKSHEET REVEAL

After negotiations, parties should exchange their individual Tactical Planning Worksheets to compare initial positions and reflect on the negotiation process. Because this is a multi-party negotiation, the reveal should also address whether alliances, if any, were beneficial. Also, the parties should analyze any deviations from their original plan and identify positive strategies used by other parties.

POST-NEGOTIATION SELF-REFLECTION WORKSHEET

At the conclusion of the reveal session, each party should complete a self-reflection worksheet individually (found in Appendix B). Reflect on whether your goals were met, what strategies were effective or ineffective, and how the negotiation process affected relationships and future interactions within the community.

CHAPTER 8

Negotiating Family Relationships

"So you can achieve your goal of making me happy, I'll let you give me everything I want."

In this chapter, you will practice negotiating within the context of family relationships using the TABLE method. The chapter explores a range of family-related negotiations, including negotiating prenuptial agreements and addressing issues of lack of capacity and undue influence in the context of a will contest.

The scenarios in this chapter will require you to consider the complex and often sensitive issues inherent in family relationships. For example, when negotiating a prenuptial agreement, you will need to think about the financial terms, such as asset division, spousal support, and inheritance rights, and also the emotional implications for the couple. Negotiating a prenuptial agreement often involves balancing transparency and trust, while also respecting each person's concerns and expectations for the future. For the problems involving will contests, you will consider the sensitive issues of lack of capacity and undue influence. In these situations, you must analyze the dynamics of power and vulnerability, identify potential conflicts of interest, and ensure that all parties' voices are fairly represented. You will need to consider the interests and priorities of multiple family members, navigate longstanding relationships, and find solutions that preserve family harmony while addressing practical concerns.

Negotiating within families presents unique challenges. Emotional histories, ongoing relationships, and the potential for long-term consequences make these negotiations distinct from those in business settings. In order to successfully negotiate the problems in this chapter you will need to develop strategies that foster open communication to achieve agreements that respect both individual needs and family bonds.

Instructions

Each problem in this chapter begins with an overview of the legal principles involved in the matter. The topics of the problems relate to negotiations in the family context. After reading the brief overview of the relevant laws for each problem in this chapter, you will be ready to apply those principles to the practice problems below using the TABLE method. The limited legal information you are given in the areas of prenuptial agreements, testamentary capacity, and undue influence is included here solely to use as a basis for negotiating the various problems.

As in Chapter 7, each problem in this chapter contains general information followed by confidential information in which each negotiator will choose a bargaining position on key issues. While the general information will be known by both sides, your bargaining position is confidential, although you may disclose it, or some of it, during the negotiation session if you choose to do so. Following the section on confidential information, you are given guidelines and suggestions as to how to approach the negotiations using the TABLE method. The format for negotiating these problems is the same format as provided in Chapter 7. However, since you are now experienced in applying the TABLE method you are not walked through the entire TABLE method strategy for the problems on testamentary capacity and undue influence.

After reviewing the information, you should complete the Tactical Planning Worksheet (provided in Appendix A or, for Problem 8-5, Appendix A-1). Be sure to include your bargaining positions on your worksheets. After completing a Tactical Planning Worksheet for each problem, you and your counterpart are ready to conduct a negotiation in which you attempt to reach an agreement. You should be able to complete the initial negotiations for each problem in this chapter within 30 minutes.

After you complete each negotiation, you and your negotiating counterpart should exchange planning worksheets so that you can analyze the bargaining positions you and your counterpart planned for the negotiation. Finally, you should complete the Post Negotiation Self-Reflection Worksheet (found in Appendix B).

For further explanation of the methodology for negotiating the problems, please refer to the Authors' Notes in Chapter 1, Introduction.

Laws Relevant to Prenuptial Agreements

The four simple words "I want a prenup," spoken by one future spouse to the other, often strikes fear in the recipient and has a dramatic effect. Many future spouses when hearing these words are immediately offended and respond with a resounding "No." After the "No" often comes proclamations of "If you loved me, you wouldn't want a prenup" or "You don't think our marriage is going to last." These statements by a future spouse are often spoken due to a lack of knowledge and understanding about the purpose and benefits of a prenuptial agreement and the positive role it can play for both spouses in a marriage. These fears are often based on preconceived myths that surround prenuptial agreements, mainly that these agreements are used by the wealthy to deprive a future spouse of receiving any assets from the marriage. However, today's prenuptial agreements, if negotiated properly, can be an effective way for both spouses to manage and direct their lives together.

This chapter allows for practicing the TABLE method in its entirety, from soup to nuts, for negotiating a prenuptial agreement. A prenuptial agreement (prenup), also referred to as a premarital or antenuptial agreement, is a contract between a couple contemplating marriage that allows the couple to define and convey their expectations, especially with regard to their finances and property for the upcoming marriage, and to determine their legal rights during the marriage and in the event of divorce and at death. A prenup serves as a handy vehicle for applying the principles of TABLE for several reasons. First, it involves a clear example of an arms-open negotiation, where the parties have prior a close relationship and are intent on maintaining that relationship after the negotiations are complete. Second, negotiating a prenuptial agreement generally requires the parties to confront various difficult and sometimes emotionally fraught issues including death or ill health. This chapter demonstrates how using the TABLE method alleviates some of the stress involved in such sensitive negotiations. Finally, and perhaps most importantly, a prenuptial agreement demonstrates in starkest terms the power of negotiations. Negotiating a prenuptial agreement allows the couple to determine many of their own terms for their upcoming marital relationship, instead of leaving the terms to the default provisions of state laws. This chapter describes some general legal principles regarding prenuptial agreements. Recall that this book, however, is not intended to provide legal advice. Rather, the general legal principles included in this chapter are for use in practicing negotiation skills through the problems. Also, note that the statutes and cases cited are subject to revision, and local rules may somewhat vary the analysis.

If a couple decides not to have a prenup, they are choosing to have state laws governing marriage determine the terms and conditions of their marriage. In effect, a couple marrying without a prenup enters into a contract whose terms are determined by an automatic default state legal system.[1] Often the couple contemplating marriage without a prenup is not even aware of the parameters of their state's default contractual laws regarding marriage. To illustrate this, Exhibit 8-A sets forth what a Fictional No-Prenup Marital Contract could look like based on an unknown underlying state law. Notice the Fictional No-Prenup Marital Contract is extremely unpredictable in its application, partly because the couple's married legal relationship would generally be subject to the laws of the state, or foreign country, where the married couple ultimately wind up residing as such laws may exist at the time. In a highly mobile society, this unpredictability often provides an impetus for the couple to negotiate the terms of their marriage themselves, instead of leaving the terms of their marriage to the vagaries of the various state law systems. Before a couple enters into a marriage, with or without negotiating a prenup, they should have some awareness of the contractual nature of a marriage and the legal consequences of entering into the marital relationship. Moreover, a couple contemplating negotiating a prenup should familiarize themselves with the likely default laws that would apply if they do not enter into a prenup, so they have some understanding of what they would obtain, or give up, if they enter into a negotiated prenuptial agreement.

Overview of Different Default Legal Systems Absent a Prenup

The laws governing spousal rights and obligations vary tremendously from country to country and, within the United States, from state to state. As seen from the Fictional No-Prenup Marital Contract in Exhibit 8-A, without a prenuptial agreement the laws that apply to marital property division, support, or distribution will generally be the laws of the state where the couple eventually reside, which may not be the state where they got married. For example, a couple who flies to Las Vegas for their wedding, but who live their entire marriage in Florida will be subject to the laws of Florida in the case of divorce or death. Moreover, even if a couple gets married in the state where they have been living, absent a prenuptial agreement, they cannot simply rely on that state's laws. For example, a couple who marries in Florida where they live at the time but then move to California and live there would generally be subject to the laws of California in the case of divorce or death.[2]

Common Law States and Community Property States

The United States has two general legal systems of marital property ownership: (1) common law and (2) community property. The vast majority of U.S. states (41 of the 50) are common law states. These common law states derived their legal system of marital property from the English common law legal system. The remaining nine states are community property states. Those states are Arizona, California, Idaho, Louisiana, Nevada, New Mexico, Texas, Washington, and Wisconsin.[3] Although only nine of the fifty U.S. states are community property states, two of those states (California and Texas) are particularly populous states. Accordingly, approximately one-third of the U.S. population resides under a community property regime. The community property regime derives from the civil law system and came to the U.S. primarily by way of French and Spanish settlers.

Common Law States

In the forty-one common law states, marital status alone does not affect ownership of property earned during an ongoing intact marriage. Rather, during the marriage, in common law states, each spouse is the separate owner of all he or she earns during the marriage and the person whose sole name appears on the title of property (*e.g.*, name on deed to a vacation house or the title to a car), is deemed the owner of that property even if that person is married.[4] Assume Sam and Sally are married and reside in a common law state. Sam receives a substantial holiday bonus at work. As he is leaving his office, he notices a car sale at the dealership next door. He sees a little sports car, purchases it with his bonus check, and puts the title to the car solely in his name. In a common law state, Sam is deemed the sole owner of the car during their marriage. Also, in common law states, each spouse is the separate owner of all he or she earns during the marriage. In the event of a divorce, however, ownership and title do not control division of property in a common law state. This separate title-based ownership system only applies during the ongoing marriage. If the couple divorces in a common law state, the state's divorce laws generally determine the ownership of the property. Also, upon death, the common law states generally provide rights to the surviving spouse beyond his or her separate property.

Common Law States—Equitable Distribution upon Divorce

The laws for dividing property at divorce in common law states vary from state to state, but they all use the general notion of *equitable distribution*, whereby the courts have authority to divide property equitably between the spouses getting divorced. While all of the common law states use *equitable distribution* for divorce, the common law states apply two very different systems for equitable distribution, namely, the *all property* and the *dual property* systems. As the name implies, under the *all property* system, used in a few common law states, upon divorce, the court divides any property owned by either spouse. That is, in *all property* equitable distribution jurisdictions, the divorce courts take into account all of the property of the two spouses, regardless of when or how it was acquired or which spouse held title to the property, and attempt to divide that total equitably between the spouses. By contrast, under the *dual property* system, property is categorized as either *non-marital property* or *marital property* and only *marital property* is subject to equitable distribution.[5] Generally, in *dual property* states, property acquired prior to the marriage by either spouse and property acquired by gift or inheritance by either spouse, is deemed *non-marital* property and is not subject to equitable distribution. On the other hand, property purchased or earned during the marriage is *marital property* to be divided equitably upon divorce. In some of the dual property states, however, *non-marital* property could still be divided between the couple, if the court finds that fairness (equity) requires it.

The underlying nuances for equitable distribution are complex and vary significantly among the common law states. For example, under the dual property system of equitable distribution, questions often arise as to when property is actually *marital property* and when it is *non-marital property*. In some dual property states, for example, potential future earnings tied to professional licenses (*e.g.*, medical licenses) or educational degrees are deemed marital property.[6] In other dual property states, such professional licenses are not deemed marital property. Also, although the property one of the spouses had before the marriage is usually not considered marital property, some pre-marital property could be considered marital property. For example, when marital earnings were used to improve or repair the pre-marital property, or to pay debts on the property, or even if the couple lived in or otherwise used the pre-marital property during their marriage, such property, or a portion of it, could be considered marital property.[7] In addition, non-marital property could become marital property by commingling the property in a way such that it cannot be distinguished from other marital property. For example, if a wife received an inheritance of $500,000 from her mother, and instead of keeping the amount in a separate account, deposited it in a joint account with her husband or combined it with marital funds to purchase property or pay marital debts or expenses, the inheritance could become marital property. The percentage of the pre-marital property deemed to be marital property and subject to division varies by state and would ultimately be determined by a court. Issues also arise in determining whether property is marital or non-marital, for property obtained after the couple separates but before divorce. For example, in some states a married couple continue to accumulate marital property until they divorce, but in other states a separation stops the accumulation of marital property.[8]

The equitable distribution system is also somewhat difficult to predict because the system is intended to divide the marital property fairly (*equitably*), which may, but may not, be equally between the couple. Courts often take several factors into consideration in making the determination as to the equitable distribution. The factors may include the:

- Length of the marriage;
- Age, health, and mental fitness of each party;
- Standard of living established during the marriage;
- Future earning power of the parties;
- Financial condition of each party;
- Contributions to the marriage of each party;

- Needs of the children (if any) and;
- Any other factor the court may feel is relevant.[9]

Common Law States—Surviving Spouse's Rights upon Death

When one of the spouses dies in a common law state, absent a prenuptial agreement, the state's intricate rules regarding a surviving spouse's rights to the other's property at death would apply. All common law states allow a spouse to leave his or her property by validly executed will to the other. Without a valid will, the state's laws regarding dying without a will (referred to as dying intestate) apply. Surviving spouses have favored status in most states when their spouse dies intestate. In many states, if the children of the decedent and of the surviving spouse are children of both, the surviving spouse of an intestate estate inherits the entire estate.

Issues arise, however, when a spouse would prefer to leave some or all of his or her property at death to someone other than the surviving spouse. What happens, for example, when a spouse chooses to leave some, or all, of her property to her children from a prior marriage or to her parents instead of to her surviving spouse? All U.S. common law states, except for Georgia, provide that a spouse who was disinherited or who was not satisfied with the property distribution in their deceased spouse's estate plan can choose to receive a surviving spouse's elective share of the deceased spouse's property as provided by state law. The state laws vary as to what percentage or portion (*e.g.*, 50%, one-third, 30%, etc.) a surviving spouse might be entitled to, and which assets are included in determining the decedent's estate for spousal elective share purposes. In addition to the right to claim a spousal elective share (sometimes referred to as a forced share), a surviving spouse in many common law states also has significant other rights upon death of a spouse. For example, a surviving spouse could claim a share of the deceased spouse's estate as a pretermitted spouse when the deceased spouse had written a will before marrying the surviving spouse. In addition, surviving spouses often have rights to homestead (usually the right to remain for life in the family home), certain exempt property, and family allowance under state laws. The laws governing these various rights differ from state to state.

Often couples enter into a marriage with children from a prior relationship. These couples may mistakenly believe that they can ensure their children's interests in their estates simply by drafting a will. Absent a prenuptial agreement, however, the state's default laws on death may provide a very different result. For example, assume Alice, a financial analyst, has two children from her prior marriage. She marries Bob, who has not been previously married and has no children. Bob has a steady job as an accountant and is financially independent. After the marriage, Alice and Bob agree, but do not put the agreement in writing, that if Alice should die her property should go to her two children. Alice writes a will leaving her property to her children. At Alice's death, despite Alice's faith in him and despite Alice's will, Bob could change his mind about Alice's children and legally take his spousal elective share of her estate, as provided under state law. The amount Bob could obtain as a spousal elective share varies from state to state but could be as much as half of Alice's estate, which she planned would go to her children.

Community Property States

There are numerous differences among the community property states, but some generalizations are available. Generally, the nine community property states agree that a spouse's *separate property* includes: (1) property owned prior to the marriage and (2) property acquired during the marriage by gift or inheritance. Similarly, *community* property states commonly define "community property" as a catchall of all property acquired during the marriage that is *not* separate property.[10]

Significant consequences flow from this categorization. In a community property state, upon marriage each spouse acquires an ownership interest in one-half of the property the other spouse earns during the marriage, regardless of how the property is nominally titled. For example, if one spouse earns an annual salary of $200,000, the other spouse is deemed to own one-half of those earnings, $100,000, by virtue of the marriage.

Similarly, property purchased with marital earnings is community property and owned one-half each. For example, assume Sam and Sally, the couple we met before, were married in and resided in a community property state. Sam still wants that little sports car. He purchases it with his bonus from work and puts title to the car in his sole name. In a community property state, since the purchase was after they were married and from his earnings, Sam and Sally are deemed one-half owners each automatically, even though Sam alone paid for it and only Sam's name is on the title.

The theory often used to explain the community property regime is the partnership theory of marriage. The partnership theory recognizes that the economic success of a partnership is due to the efforts and contributions of both partners in the partnership, whether or not both are earning wages.[11] Even if one spouse is not earning wages, that spouse's non-monetary contributions are just as significant to the success of the partnership as the wage-earning spouse's contributions. For example, Morgan is a stay at home parent whose primary responsibility is care of the children and managing the household. Her spouse, Dylan, works in an engineering firm. The partnership theory of community property deems each spouse's efforts as contributing equally to the economic success of the partnership. In its best light, the community property regime allows the spouses the flexibility to determine their roles in the marriage in ways that are optimal to the success of the family, even when such a division might otherwise be economically detrimental to one of the spouses (*e.g.*, the one taking a break from a career).

Community Property States—Division of Property on Divorce

Generally, the various community property states provide that upon divorce each spouse keeps his or her *separate* property but divide *community property.* Where the community property states differ, however, is in how they divide the *community* property upon divorce. In some community property states upon divorce, the *community property* is split equally, such that each spouse obtains one-half.[12] In other community property states upon divorce, instead of splitting the *community property* one-half each, the courts in those states divide the community property based on *equitable division*. Thus, in those community property states there could be an unequal disposition of the community property, if the court determines that an unequal split of the community property is equitable.[13]

Death—Community Property States

The death of a spouse ends the marriage and therefore the community. Generally, in community property states at death a spouse can dispose of (1) his or her separate property and (2) one-half of the community property. Recall that in a community property state immediately upon the marriage each spouse acquires an ownership interest in one-half of the marital property.[14] Because a surviving spouse in a community property state was already recognized as a partner in the marriage by virtue of obtaining his or her one-half of the community property, the surviving spouse does not also have any rights to elect against the deceased spouse's will.

Moving from Community Property States to Common Law States

Spouses who acquired property while living in a community property state (*e.g.*, California) might later move to a common law state (*e.g.*, Florida). Even though the couple is moving to a common law state, some of their property may retain its community property status.[15] Several common law states have enacted statutes based on the Uniform Disposition of Community Property Rights at Death Act. Generally, these statutes serve to maintain each spouse's legal rights in the property that was community property before the couple moved to a common law state. The idea behind these statutes is that most persons who move from one state to another do so for reasons that have nothing to do with the community property system or common law system (*e.g.*, they move for job opportunities or family reasons) and they did not intend to change the community property characteristics of their previously acquired properties when they moved. Generally, these statutes presume that property purchased during marriage while a spouse was resident in a community property state remains community property even though the spouses move to a separate property state. If a spouse in such a separate property state owned such original community property at death, one-half of such community property would generally be distributed pursuant to the decedent's will or the laws of intestacy. The other one-half of the original community property would be deemed to be the property of the surviving spouse. There are instances, however, in which property loses its community property status.

Moving from Common Law States to Community Property States

A move from a common law state (*e.g.*, New York) to a community property state (*e.g.*, Arizona) may create significant issues for a surviving spouse. Unlike common law states, the community property states do not give the surviving spouse the right to a spousal elective share at death. A couple who spent most of their marriage in a common law state and only a couple of months or years in a community property state may have little community property. At death, the surviving spouse in that scenario would have little community property and yet no right to take against the deceased spouse's will.

Other Issues Involving Community Property

While earned income is considered community property, the nine community property states differ in their rules on many other significant issues, some of which are noted below. The following discussion is helpful in two ways: (1) if a couple decides not to negotiate a prenup they should recognize that these issues would be addressed by their states' default law in instances of divorce or death and (2) if the couple decides to negotiate a prenup they could look at these topics and determine if and how they want to agree on their resolution.

> ***Income from Separate Property:*** There are two different rules among the community property states for whether income, such as dividends, interest, or rent, derived during the marriage from otherwise separate property remains separate or is deemed community. For example, assume one of the spouses had owned stock prior to the marriage and that separate property stock generated dividends during the marriage. Some community property states would treat the dividend income that was generated during the marriage from that separate property as still generally deemed separate. By contrast, if the spouses resided in other community property states, the dividend income that arose during the marriage from that separate property is treated as community property.
>
> ***Comingled Property:*** In a community property state, there is a strong presumption that property acquired during a marriage is community and is owned one-half each. On the other hand, if one spouse has separate prop-

erty prior to the marriage and sells that property during the marriage the proceeds from the sale of the separate property would continue to be separate as long as the spouse does not combine the proceeds with community property. Issues arise, however, when separate and community property are combined, commonly referred to as comingled property. The community property states have developed varying laws for determining when property is deemed comingled and the consequences of such characterization.

Debt Payments on Separate Property: If separate property was burdened with a debt and community property was used to pay down the debt, many community property states provide that the separate property remains separate, but that the community property used to pay the debt must be reimbursed. Other community property states, however, would not deem the property as remaining separate, but instead apportion the property pursuant to their state laws.

Life Insurance Proceeds: When community property is used to pay premiums on a life insurance contract purchased before the marriage, in some community property states the proceeds of the life insurance policy would remain separate, but the community would be entitled to reimbursement for the amount paid as premiums.[16] In other community property states, the insurance policy proceeds would be divided pro rata based on the allocation of monies used to pay the premiums. If the life insurance policy is a term life policy, many of the community property states characterize the proceeds by focusing on whether the premiums for the most recent term were paid from community or separate funds.

Creditors: The community property states differ on when creditors can reach community property. In some community property states a creditor of one spouse can reach the community property, even if the debt was incurred by one of the spouses prior to the marriage. Separate property is generally, however, not subject to the creditors of the other spouse. In some states, debts incurred during the marriage are presumed to be community debt.[17]

Personal Injury Recovery: In some community property states the amounts recovered from a claim or judgment for a personal injury sustained during the marriage are deemed separate property except for amounts designated to compensate for lost earnings. In other community property states, the amounts received in satisfaction of a claim or judgment from a personal injury is community property, if the injury occurred during the marriage.

Management: Generally, during an ongoing marriage, each spouse has equal rights to manage, control, and dispose of the community property. In some community property states, however, gifts of community property (other than to the other spouse) require the other spouse's consent.[18]

Alimony and Spousal Support in Common Law and Community Property States

Both community property and common law states could award alimony or maintenance. Generally, the law of the state where the couple resides determines the type of alimony available to the parties. Several states have structured their laws on alimony in part on the Uniform Marriage and Divorce Act (UMDA). Generally, under the UMDA alimony awards are in the amounts and for the periods of time the court deems appropriate and fair after considering all relevant factors including:

- The financial resources of the spouse requesting the support;
- The time the requesting spouse needs to obtain education or job training in order to find employment;
- The standard of living during the marriage;
- The age, health, and mental fitness of the spouse seeking the amount;
- The length of the marriage and;
- The ability of the other spouse to make the maintenance payments.[19]

Courts have great flexibility in applying these factors. Moreover, while equitable distribution of property and alimony are distinct concepts, in some states the courts combine the concepts. For example, where the equitable distribution of marital property results in a fairly sizeable estate for each party, the courts might decide that each is adequately self-sufficient and that there is no need for an award of alimony or maintenance.

Prenuptial Agreements

After reading through the overview of the state default laws and discovering that they are not well tailored to their marriage goals, a couple might decide to enter into a prenuptial agreement.

Enforceability of Prenuptial Agreements

Prenuptial agreements are enforceable in every state and rarely set aside by a court. In the early days of prenuptial agreements, when they were not as common, the courts often held them invalid under the theory that most prenups were simply tools the rich used to take advantage of a less financially secure spouse. It was believed that the wealthier spouse was able to coerce his partner into signing a prenup and that these agreements effectively promoted divorce. However, today, with full recognition of prenups by all states, prenups are looked upon more favorably, as a planning mechanism for the couple, not only if they divorce but also in the event of death of a spouse.

However, prenups are not impenetrable and are subject to being set aside under several of the principles. Generally, a prenup is subject to being set aside for the following reasons.[20]

No fair and reasonable financial disclosure: Without full disclosure of each of the party's income, assets, and liabilities, the agreement is subject to being set aside by a court.[21] False information or misleading information will not constitute proper disclosure.

Not properly drafted or executed: A prenup must be in writing and signed by both parties. It is best for the parties to hire separate attorneys to draft their prenup, so as to avoid a future claim by a spouse that there was a lack of independent advice or a conflict of interest.

Illegal or invalid provisions or provisions against public policy: Provisions that are illegal or against public policy should not be included in a prenuptial agreement. For example, a provision in the agreement stating that the couple will not accurately report their earnings in order to avoid their income tax obligations would be illegal and unenforceable. A provision that would be against public policy would be a prenuptial agreement provision that restricts child support, custody, or visitation rights.

Time pressure: Both parties should have time to properly consider and review a prenuptial agreement. A prenuptial agreement signed right before walking down the aisle is subject to being set aside for duress. A spouse may be able to make an argument that her spouse pressured her to sign the prenup or he would cancel the wedding. However, if the parties were represented by separate counsel who had advised their clients thoroughly as to the contents of the agreement, the last-minute signing may not have much effect in invalidating the agreement.

Unconscionable: If the prenuptial agreement basically allows one spouse to prosper while the other spouse suffers great harm, the agreement may be set aside as unconscionable. Generally, finding a prenup agreement is unconscionable is difficult, since the agreement is entered into in part for the purpose of spouses giving up certain rights. However, even if the initial agreement was permissible, a court may consider a material change in circumstance after the agreement is entered into that may cause unanticipated economic hardship to a party. In this circumstance, a court may set aside certain provisions or the entire agreement.

Benefits of Prenuptial Agreements

A prenup may be beneficial for many couples depending on their circumstances. For example, for spouses who contemplate that they might move to another state, or another country, with a different set of laws, a prenuptial agreement provides some certainty against changes in the marital laws of the place where they are residing and the places where they may move. Additionally, couples may want to have a prenuptial agreement, if they happen to fall into any of these following common scenarios.

1) One or both of the future spouses have children from prior relationships and want to provide for them;
2) The future spouses have assets acquired prior to their marriage or anticipated through inheritance;
3) A business partnership or company agreement requires a future spouse to have a prenuptial agreement in place so the business can maintain business confidences during divorce actions;
4) A future spouse already has substantial retirement benefits, stock options, profit sharing, or other employee benefits;
5) One of the future spouse's has significant outstanding debt;
6) One or both of the future spouses have been so traumatized by drawn-out divorce proceedings (either their own or a family member's) that only a thoughtfully negotiated prenuptial agreement with their prospective spouse will ease their concerns about entering into a marriage;
7) A family trust requires a future spouse to have a prenuptial agreement in place as a condition to receiving the benefits from that trust; and
8) A future spouse expects to become, or is already, involved in a family-owned business or already has a business.

While most of these common scenarios are straightforward, both the family trust and the family-owned business as an impetus for a prenup require more explanation. While the newly engaged couple may not want to consider the possibility of divorce or death, their parents may be well aware of the risks. Parents (on one or both sides) may insist on setting up some financial protection for their child before the wedding. Even if the parents are excited about the upcoming marriage and thrilled to be welcoming their future son or daughter-in-law into their family, they may be wise enough to know that life sometimes does not always go as planned or hoped.

Parents who worry about the possibility that their child might divorce may decide that they should not simply leave that child an inheritance outright through their wills.[22] The parents might instead set up a family trust for that child with prenuptial requirements included in the trust document.[23] The parents could, for example, set up a family trust naming their child as the trust beneficiary but provide that the beneficiary could obtain trust assets only if he or she has a prenuptial agreement in place. The family trust could contain language such as the following:

> Notwithstanding the foregoing distribution provisions, if a beneficiary under the trust marries after the trust is established or is married when the trust is established, the Trustee shall not distribute income or principal from the trust to or for the benefit of the beneficiary until the Trustee is provided a copy of a valid prenuptial, postnuptial, or similar agreement whereby the spouse or intended spouse has waived rights to income and principal from the beneficiary's trust.

Notice that this example prenuptial-agreement-trust-clause is not very strict. In this example, the trust document only requires that the marital agreement contain language waiving the spouse's interest, if any, in the family trust property itself. It does not require the agreement to have the spouse waive rights to the trust beneficiary's non-trust property. If the parents prefer, they could tailor the family trust language to say that the trust beneficiary only benefits from the family trust if the beneficiary shows the trustee a copy of a broadly worded prenuptial agreement where the trust beneficiary's spouse has waived *all rights*. The family trust could even include a sample prenuptial agreement and provide that the beneficiary's prenuptial agreement should substantially conform to the sample. A middle ground might have the family trust provide that the trust beneficiary show the trustee that the spouse has waived rights to the trust and waived rights to elect against the trust beneficiary's estate.

This approach of having a family trust with an embedded prenuptial agreement requirement may seem somewhat elaborate. It is becoming more popular, however, because parents are increasingly finding that can no longer rely on the family trust system alone to protect their children's inheritance in the event their children get divorced. In the past, parents focusing on estate planning thought that as long as they did not include their prospective son or daughter-in-law as a trust beneficiary, their children's beneficial interests in the family trust could not be reached by a former son or daughter-in-law in cases of divorce. Until fairly recently, this assumption may have been correct. In the past, if a family trust did not name the children's spouses as beneficiaries, and the trust document gave the trustee discretion on when and how to distribute trust assets to a trust beneficiary, the beneficiary's interest in the family trust while the assets were still in the trust,[24] would, in most states, have been protected from the beneficiary's creditors, including the beneficiary's former spouse's claims. Recently, however, the laws surrounding a former spouse's access to family trusts at divorce have become much murkier, even in states with laws once viewed as designed to protect such discretionary beneficial trust interests.[25]

Moreover, if a state uses an *all property* approach to equitable distribution, then the beneficiary's interest in the trust could be subject to division. Some courts may count the beneficiary's interest in the trust as the beneficiary's property, even if that beneficiary's interest in the trust is dependent on the discretion of a trustee. Even states that use a *dual property* approach may look at the beneficiary's interest in the family trust in determining how to divide property upon divorce of that beneficiary. While most states using the *dual property* system for equitable distribution continue to treat inherited wealth as separate and not subject to equitable division during divorce, courts may look at assets in a family trust in deciding how to divide marital non-trust assets.

A family trust with a prenuptial agreement requirement serves several purposes. First, it increases the likelihood that upon a divorce the trust beneficiary will be able to keep the trust assets. Second, it may help to protect the parents and their estate plans from being dragged into their child's messy divorce litigation. Even if a former daughter or son-in-law could not ultimately reach assets in the family trust under state law, absent a prenuptial agreement waiver, a divorce court might issue subpoenas for the parent's estate planning documents or otherwise try to delve into the parents' assets during a divorce. Finally, perhaps the most important benefit of the prenuptial requirement being embedded in the parent's trust is that it allows the about-to-be-married child to raise the topic of a prenuptial agreement with his or her fiancé and blame the idea on the folks.

Another impetus for a prenup includes protecting a family business. Parents and other owners of a closely held business may want to protect disruption of an ongoing business by insisting that any equity owners have prenuptial agreements in place. Although a buy-sell agreement itself would probably give the company a right of first refusal in cases of involuntary stock transfers (such as in a divorce), the added feature of the prenup might help to prevent involving the company in divorce litigation.

The above list of scenarios for prenups is not exhaustive. There are, of course, numerous other reasons why couples may wish to negotiate a prenup, including simply facilitating open discussions and nurturing healthy communications.

Standard Coverage of a Prenup

Prenuptial agreements can be relatively simple or quite complex but generally include provisions for determining each other's rights in the event of divorce, separation, or death. See Exhibit 8-B for a sample prenuptial agreement. In their prenup, the couple could agree not to seek a share in each other's property in those events or to only seek a share that is different from the one they could claim under their state's default rules. For example, the agreement could provide that certain property, such as a future spouse's pre-marital home or business will remain separate even if the couple divorced. They may agree that income or appreciation on separate property should stay separate or alternatively that income or appreciation should be deemed marital. They might agree to keep separate all life insurance proceeds, even if the premiums were paid by marital earnings. They may wish to borrow the community property concept that one-half of all marital earnings belong to each spouse, regardless of who earns the property or how it is titled.

With regard to death, the prenuptial agreement could cover property passing by will, property passing if a spouse dies without a will (intestate), or property passing in other ways, including by trust or by rights of survivorship. A future spouse could agree to waive rights to spousal elective share, intestate share, pretermitted share, homestead, exempt property, and family allowance. Waivers of these death-type rights are more common when one or both of the future spouses have children from a prior relationship. A spouse who wants to preserve property for children of the first marriage may ask the other spouse to waive some or all of these rights.

In addition to handling property division at death or divorce, the future spouses could in most states waive or determine support in their prenuptial agreement. They could, for example, waive any rights to such support, particularly if both spouses are capable of and expect to continue working. Alternatively, the future spouses could agree to certain support, especially if one spouse might not be earning income for some years.

It is important to note that state laws vary on what they permit to be included in prenups and how they must be executed. The Uniform Premarital and Marital Property Act ("Act")[26] has been adopted in a majority of states in whole or in part. Its purpose is to bring "clarity and consistency" to the prenuptial agreements made between couples that modify or waive rights at death or divorce. The Act recognizes that prenuptial agreements may contain many different legal terms and formats, and since courts will strive to enforce them, it is beneficial to have some uniformity. The Act defines certain legal terms and provides what is generally permitted and prohibited in such agreements.

Other Provisions in a Prenuptial Agreement

In addition to the standard provisions, couples may wish to tailor their prenup to address their particular goals and objectives. These additional provisions, such as lifestyle provisions, may be outside the scope of typical contracts and, accordingly, they may be subject to more scrutiny by a court and harder to enforce.

Lifestyle Provisions in Prenuptial Agreements

Prenuptial agreements are very effective in solidifying a couple's expectations concerning issues such as the allocation of finances, inheritance, and business-related interests. However, couples may also find it tempting to include conduct requirements for their married life through a prenuptial agreement. They may think, "As long as we're drafting this document, let's put everything we can think of that may become a problem in our marriage. Then we will know exactly what is expected of each other." This kind of sentiment is probably the reason behind so-called lifestyle provisions in prenuptial agreements. These provisions are meant to control behavior. Some of these lifestyle provisions may be unenforceable in court, but some couples believe that by putting the provisions in writing, the effect will be that a future spouse may, at least, stop and think before engaging in the specific conduct. Some typical lifestyle provisions include the following.

> ***Infidelity Provisions:*** A very popular lifestyle provision, the infidelity provision, requires a spouse to pay a fine or other penalty if unfaithful.[27] Reportedly, actor Catherine Zeta-Jones has such a clause in her prenuptial agreement with her husband and fellow actor Michael Douglas, providing a $5 million dollar bonus to her for each time he is unfaithful.[28] These provisions are usually included in circumstances where a future spouse has a known history of infidelity.
>
> ***Weight Provisions:*** Prenuptial agreements have been known to contain provisions assessing monetary penalties if a spouse gains weight during the marriage. Some agreements penalize the spouse based on the amount of the

gain (*e.g.*, over 10 lbs.). Other provisions seek to have the spouse maintain a certain maximum weight and penalizes weight gain over that amount (*e.g.*, 120 lbs.). The weight limit provisions may even specify the dates and times for the weigh-ins. Hopefully, a spouse will not have to weigh-in immediately following Thanksgiving dinner.

In-law Provision: Prenuptial agreements may attempt to limit or restrict the time a couple spends with their in-laws. For example, a provision may bar a mother-in-law from sleepovers. Another provision might limit a couple's visits with their in-laws to no more than two consecutive days. Presumably, in-law jokes are still permitted. Similar provisions may also limit the time a future spouse could spend with certain family or friends.

Drug Testing Provision: For a spouse with a known or suspected drug problem, the random drug testing clause is a common addition to the prenuptial agreement. Typically, if the test is positive, a monetary penalty is imposed. The sample collecting procedure is usually left up the couple.

Social Media Provisions: Rapidly gaining popularity, social media provisions typically restrict spouses from disparaging each other on social media. Other social media provisions restrict posting of nude or unflattering photos of a spouse or forbid posting anything about the spouse without prior approval by the spouse.[29]

Baby Payout Provision: In this type of provision, a baby boom means a big payout for one of the spouses. This clause provides a monetary reward for each child born. Beyoncé and Jay-Z presumably had such a clause. In the event of divorce, Beyoncé would allegedly collect five million dollars for each child born of the marriage.[30] While this clause sounds like child support, determining child custody and support issues are decided by a judge and prohibited in prenuptial agreements. These provisions are typically meant to promote procreation, but the monetary incentive may not accomplish the goal and may in fact backfire. For example, if one spouse wants more children and the other spouse thinks one is enough because the payout is just too expensive, would that spouse stop "trying" to procreate? It would be better for the couple to have a discussion about having children before marriage, and hopefully they will both put forth the necessary effort.

No Children Provision: The no children provision is the opposite of a pay per child provision. In this provision, the couple agrees not to have children. Enforcing this clause is difficult if not impossible.[31] Parents are legally responsible for the welfare of their children whether they "wanted" the child or not. Trying to assess a penalty for having a child may violate public policy.[32] Furthermore, it does not quite create a Hallmark memory for the child. While it is disheartening for a child to find out he or she was not wanted, it is devastating for the child to find out that mom or dad has to pay a penalty for the child being born. If one party truly desires not to have children, and the other does, the couple should sit down and discuss the matter thoroughly before deciding to get married. A prenup may not be the appropriate vehicle to address the issue of their issue.

Religious Provisions: Couples may wish to put in the prenuptial agreement a provision about their religious practices or the practices of their children. This may be especially desirable in marriages of mixed faiths, or in marriages where one spouse is more devout in their religious practice than the other. For example, in a marriage where one spouse is Jewish and the other spouse is Christian, the couple may include a clause that their children will be raised in the Jewish faith. In that clause would be an explanation as to what "being raised in the Jewish faith" would entail. Specifically, the couple may agree that the children will attend temple services or religious school. While adults may include in a prenuptial agreement what religious holidays they wish to celebrate, such restrictions on children are typically unenforceable. Courts have deemed such provisions as imposing an unconstitutional restraint on the religious freedom of the child, reasoning that a preference for a certain religion is too restrictive on a child's right to choose how or if they want to engage in religious practice.[33]

Pet Provisions: Pets are considered by many couples as members of the family. As such, it is easy to see that a dispute as to where their "child" may reside after a divorce is a real concern. Although prenuptial agreements cannot decide custody and child support for human children, a couple can decide what to do about their animal child in case of divorce through a clause in the prenuptial agreement. Without a couple deciding custody of their pet in their prenuptial agreement, a court would likely award the pet to a spouse along the same terms as other property (*e.g.*, one spouse gets the dog and the other spouse gets the smart TV). Furthermore, a pet could get caught up in a contentious divorce and the battle over custody could turn ugly. It may not be wise for couples to leave Fido's future up to a judge or to battle over their pet's future at the time of a divorce. Instead, it is best for the couple to decide their pet's future themselves while they are in a loving relationship.

In drafting a pet prenuptial agreement provision, the couple should determine with whom the pet will live, and who will pay for the medical and food costs associated with the pet. It is possible to have a shared custody clause, in which the couple agrees not only to split the costs associated with the pet, but also for the pet to be a part-time resident of both homes in case of divorce.

The prenuptial agreement clause works best if the couple owns the pet before marriage because it will be easier to decide that specific pet's fate should the couple divorce. However, if the couple anticipates obtaining a pet after marriage, the couple could draft a clause concerning any future pets.

Caution on Lifestyle Provisions

When negotiating a prenup, it may be tempting to include some of these lifestyle provisions. However, a couple should consider whether they really want to live their married life monitoring their spouse's conduct and enforcing penalties or rewards as set forth in the prenuptial agreement. The couple should talk about these issues and decide before marriage if their lifestyles are compatible.

Attorney's Fees in Prenuptial

Once a couple has agreed upon the terms in a prenuptial agreement, they are hopeful that in the event of divorce, the agreement will be enforced, and divorce proceedings will be a formality rather than a battle. In order to ensure that the agreement is enforced and unchallenged, some couples include a clause, which uses payment of attorney's fees as a disincentive for challenging the agreement. One method would be to have a clause stating that any party challenging the prenup will have to pay both spouses' attorney's fees. Another less restrictive clause would reward a spouse who successfully wins a challenge to a prenup by having the losing spouse pay the winning spouse's attorney's fees.

While state law will dictate whether such provisions are enforceable, generally the losing spouse pays provisions are likely to be upheld. However, an agreement that restricts either party from challenging the prenuptial agreement by punishing the challenger is likely to be found by a court to be a restraint on a party's due process right of access to the courts.

Mediation or Arbitration Provisions

As with many negotiations, couples may choose to limit or avoid courts as much as possible by having their divorce resolved through mediation or binding arbitration. Although often used interchangeably, mediation and binding arbitration are not the same procedure. In mediation, parties jointly hire a neutral third party, called a mediator, to hear their dispute.[34] The mediator then offers recommendations on how the parties may resolve the dispute. However, the parties can ultimately decide whether to follow the mediator's recommendations or not, and then proceed to court to finalize the divorce. In binding arbitration, a neutral third party called an arbitrator, hears the parties' dispute, and then makes a binding decision as to the resolution of the divorce, much like a judge would do in a court of law.

There are benefits to including a mediation or arbitration clause. First, these procedures allow the parties to decide on a mediator and arbitrator, whereas a judge is randomly assigned to their case. Second, the costs associated with hiring mediators and arbitrators are usually much less than those associated with a lengthy court battle. Third, an effective mediator or arbitrator will be skilled at hearing both sides of a dispute, making efficient use of time, and keeping the peace. A court proceeding is often a formalized, time-consuming process whereby the judge has little time to sort through a myriad of issues. In fact, many courts recommend or require a couple to go through mediation before the court renders a final decision.

These alternative systems may even be combined. A couple may choose to include both mediation and arbitration in their prenuptial agreement. For example, a couple may have a clause agreeing to first go to mediation, and if that process does not work, to then go to binding arbitration. Of course, while mediation or arbitration may be a more efficient process, there is no guarantee that the process will run smoothly or that the mediator or arbitrator will be as skilled as a judge. These alternative dispute resolution provisions in prenuptial agreements are typically upheld as providing the couple alternatives to lengthy court proceedings.

Sunset and Escalator Provisions

One reason a couple may be eager to have a prenuptial agreement is because of a nagging doubt that their marriage may not last "until death do them part." Couples might believe, however, that if their marriage lasts a certain number of years (*e.g.*, 5 or 10 years) the prenuptial agreement would no longer be necessary. A sunset clause is basically an expiration date for the prenuptial agreement. Chris Rock reportedly had such a clause in his prenuptial agreement with his spouse, Malaak Compton Rock.[35] Under the terms of their sunset clause, their prenuptial agreement would "sunset" on the couple's 18th wedding anniversary, but unfortunately, they did not ride off into the sunset on a road of marital bliss. After 20 years of marriage, Chris filed for divorce. Both Chris and Malaak agreed the prenuptial agreement was no longer valid due to the sunset clause. Subsequently, Malaak sought a division of Chris Rock's purportedly $70 million net worth. Malaak alleged she had given up her career to care for their children and that he should pay her a significant amount of that $70 million so that she can maintain her lifestyle. The battle led to a messy tabloid divorce.

Chris Rock's divorce is not typical of the outcome of having a sunset provision. In the best of cases, the sunset clause terminates the prenuptial agreement but the long-term marriage is stable and the couple stays married. In other cases, the sunset clause could have the perverse effect of accelerating divorce. For example, a sunset clause effective in year five of the marriage may encourage a divorce in year four so that the prenuptial agreement is still valid.

There are many variations on sunset provisions. Some provisions, frequently called escalator provisions, do not offer a complete sunset of the agreement but reward a spouse for staying in the marriage over time.[36] Perhaps a better name for these provisions would be sunrise provisions, because they provide monetary rewards or, or a greater division of assets, at designated years in the marriage.

Sunset provisions and their variations are attempts to reward longevity in a marriage. Unfortunately, they often encourage ending the marriage before the sunset date. It would be better for a couple to review their prenuptial agreement at various times during the marriage, or, if or when, circumstances change in their marriage to see if the prenup they entered into still reflects their wishes. A prenuptial agreement can always be amended or revoked by agreement of the couple. Placing a random time frame for altering or revoking the agreement is artificial. The sunset clause often becomes a total eclipse of the marriage.

Companion Documents

Couples negotiating prenups may realize that in addition to the prenup they want to execute additional documents to round out their marital or estate planning goals. Often the process of negotiating the prenup serves as the impetus for couples to also enter into related, or companion agreements.

Trust Created by Fiancé

The previous discussion on trusts focused on trusts created by parents, grandparents, or other family members of the couple planning to wed. In other words, those were trusts created by a third party (*e.g.*, the parents or grandparents). This section mentions trusts created by one of the two prospective spouses themselves. Before going any further, it helps to clarify that if a prospective spouse puts premarital assets into a trust and names himself or herself a trust beneficiary, that trust is generally referred to as a self-settled trust. In the vast majority of states, such a self-settled trust does not provide any more creditor protection (from future creditors including former spouses upon divorce), than not having the assets in a trust.[37] This section is not referring to such self-settled trusts. Rather, it discusses the possibility of one of the future spouses setting up a trust for the benefit of other people.

A future spouse may want to create a trust prior to the wedding with his or her own pre-marital assets and name third parties as beneficiaries. For example, a future spouse with children from a prior relationship may want to set up a trust with some separate assets prior to the wedding for the benefit of his or her children. This trust could be revocable or irrevocable. If the person setting up the trust (settlor) can change his or her mind about the trust (that is, if the trust is revocable) then, the assets could still count during equitable distribution particularly if the state uses an "'all property' approach."[38] Even if the state does not use the *all property* approach, the assets in the revocable trust could be subject to equitable distribution to the extent they were comingled with marital funds. Setting up such a revocable trust, however, might help to create discipline in keeping the assets in the trust separate from marital assets. To reduce the risk that the assets in the trust for the children could be reached during a divorce, it helps to combine the trust with a prenuptial agreement whereby the new spouse waives any right to assets in the pre-marital children's trust.

Wills, Health Care Proxies, and Durable Powers of Attorney

In the process of negotiating their prenups, prospective spouses should consider the benefits of also executing needed companion documents such as wills, health care proxies, and durable powers of attorney. It is important that there is consistency and clarity among these related documents.

PRENUPTIAL AGREEMENT PROBLEMS

INSTRUCTIONS: After reading the legal principles and strategies in this chapter, you are now ready to apply those principles and strategies in negotiating practice problems using the TABLE method. Below are three problems involving couples negotiating prenuptial agreements. Each problem contains general information followed by confidential information in which each negotiator will choose a bargaining position on key issues. While the general information will be known by both sides, your bargaining position is confidential, although you may disclose it, or some of it, during the negotiation session if you choose to do so. Following the confidential information, you are given guidelines and suggestions as to how to approach the negotiations using the TABLE method.

After reviewing the information, you should complete the Tactical Planning Worksheet for the problem (Appendix A). For completing the worksheet, you are given the state in which the problem takes place to use as the basis for your legal research. Also, be sure to include your bargaining positions on your worksheets. After completing a Tactical Planning Worksheet for each problem, you and your counterpart are ready to conduct a negotiation in which you attempt to reach an agreement. While there is no time limit set for each problem, you should be able to complete the initial negotiations for each problem within 30 minutes.

After you complete each negotiation, you and your negotiating counterpart should exchange planning worksheets so that you can analyze the bargaining positions you and your counterpart planned for the negotiation. Finally, you should complete the Post Negotiation Self-Reflection Worksheet (Appendix B).

For further explanation of the methodology for negotiating the problems, please refer to the Authors' Notes in Chapter 1, Introduction.

OVERVIEW OF PROBLEMS 8-1, 8-2, AND 8-3

PROBLEM 8-1 is a two-person negotiation in which an engaged couple is attempting to negotiate the preliminary terms for their prenuptial agreement.

PROBLEM 8-2 is a two-person negotiation based on the same parties and facts as Problem 8-1. However, you are asked to apply a different jurisdiction's laws than in Problem 8-1.

PROBLEM 8-3 is a two-person negotiation involving attorneys negotiating on behalf of the engaged couple.

8-1

GENERAL INFORMATION: *Assume for this problem that the couple resides in a common law, all property equitable distribution state for purposes of divorce. Also, assume that the state's law provides that at death the surviving spouse would be entitled to elect one-third of all the decedent's estate.*

Isabella and Jake are engaged to be married. They are in their late 20s, both currently employed, and it is the first marriage for both. He earns $90,000 per year as a software engineer, and she earns $110,000 as a financial analyst. They have no children from prior relationships. They have a dog that they adopted from an animal rescue group six months ago. Jake currently rents an apartment for $2,000 per month. Isabella lives in a condo valued at $500,000. She inherited the condo from her grandmother several years ago debt free. The condo maintenance fee is $150 per month, and the utilities are $250 per month. Carrying costs for the condo (real property taxes and insurance) are $4,000 per year. Jake plans to move into Isabella's condo after their wedding. In addition, Jake and Isabella have the following major assets:

Isabella	Jake
$75,000 in stock	$50,000 in stock
Engagement ring valued at $20,000	

Jake is expecting an inheritance of $1,000,000 from his grandfather. His grandfather is 90 years old and in poor health. Neither Jake nor Isabella has student loan debt or other debt.

Jake and Isabella have fully disclosed their assets to each other. Jake and Isabella both hope to have one child. Jake has expressed a preference to take a few years off from work when they have their child. Isabella prefers to continue working after the child is born because she is in line for a series of promotions at her job and is concerned that she would lose the opportunity for promotion if she takes time off.

Jake's parents and Isabella's parents are both divorced. They both witnessed the stress and emotional toll placed on their respective families during the divorce process. Neither of their parents had a prenuptial agreement and thus their respective divorces were time consuming and involved lengthy court proceedings. While Jake and Isabella believe their marriage will not end in divorce, they have decided to discuss entering into a prenuptial agreement, which will allow them to plan the distribution of their assets and property in the event of divorce or death. Although, they believe that a prenuptial agreement is best to protect them in case their marriage is short term, they do not want the prenuptial agreement to last forever. Therefore, they have preliminarily decided to include a sunset clause in the prenuptial agreement and wish to negotiate the specifics of that clause.

They hope to be able to negotiate the preliminary terms of their prenuptial agreement before hiring lawyers. After they have reached consensus on the major issues, they have agreed to obtain separate lawyers to formalize the agreement and to work out any remaining issues. They also want to make sure that the agreement complies with the law and has full legal effect.

CONFIDENTIAL INFORMATION

The information contained in your planning worksheet is confidential. It includes your bargaining positions on the issues involved in the negotiations. This information should not be shared with the other party prior to the negotiation. For purposes of this problem, your planning worksheet should include your bargaining position on each of these issues:

A. The custody of the dog

B. The ownership (title) and disposition of the condominium

C. Jake's inheritance from his grandfather

D. Division of assets during and post marriage

E. Division of expenses during marriage

F. Time off from outside employment after birth of a child

G. The sunset clause

Although Jake and Isabella agreed to "discuss" the matter, they are realistically attempting to negotiate a prenuptial agreement.

TACTICAL PLANNING

Use the Tactical Planning Worksheet (Appendix A) to plan for the negotiation.

ARRANGING THE NEGOTIATION

Jake and Isabella would need to arrange the logistics for negotiating their prenuptial agreement. They would need to decide where and when to meet and how much time to allocate to their initial discussion. For purposes of this negotiation, you can assume that Jake and Isabella have chosen an in-person, informal, setting such as his apartment or her condominium for the initial discussion.

BARGAINING

Jake and Isabella, as an engaged couple, do not require traditional ice-breaking for their negotiation. It would seem somewhat awkward for Jake to begin the negotiation by asking ice-breaking questions such as, "How about that football game last night," or "We have been having some hot weather lately." However, they should avoid the temptation to jump right in with the first offers. Instead, they should spend some time communicating their hope that a prenuptial agreement will further strengthen their relationship and that their goal is to have a prenuptial agreement that is mutually beneficial.

Jake and Isabella should also make full use of their planning worksheet during the bargaining phase. However, neither of them should feel the other is "hiding" something on the worksheet for several reasons. First, in an arms-open negotiation such as this, engaged couples should feel that they are participating in an open discussion and there is no secret hidden agenda in the worksheets. Second, in the prenuptial agreement arena, as noted above, full disclosure is required for the agreement to be enforceable. If a partner appears to be hiding the worksheet, the other partner may interpret this conduct as attempting to hide assets.

Once the couple begins the process of exchanging offers, counteroffers, and concessions, it may be tempting for Jake or Isabella to quickly reject each other's proposals without due consideration under the belief that "no holds barred" responses will move the negotiations along. However, they may find that this approach can derail this negotiation in the same manner as any other negotiations. For example, if Jake or Isabella act dismissively in rejecting an offer, this behavior may quickly dissolve their collaborative approach.

In addition, the couple should stay calm, as the more emotional they get, the less likely they will be able to agree on matters. They should try not to interrupt each other and really listen to concerns expressed by the other. As in any other negotiation, they should feel free to ask questions, especially about their partner's concerns or objections. Jake and Isabella should also keep in mind that this is a collaborative process, not an adversarial one. In other words, they should think of this negotiation as if they are putting together a business, the business of husband and wife. They should not think of this negotiation as attempting to settle a lawsuit, as in husband v. wife. Further, just because they are engaged does not obviate the need for each of them to provide objective criteria to support their offers, counteroffers, and concessions. Providing the reasons and explanations supporting their offers will only encourage reciprocal communication and facilitate working toward solutions.

LETTING GO OR RESOLVING AND EXECUTING THE AGREEMENT

If Jake and Isabella come to an agreement on all or major issues, they should make an informal list of the terms they have agreed upon while it is fresh on their minds. They should next make an appointment to see their separate attorneys to formalize the agreement soon.

Although unlikely, if their negotiation has been a failure and they are deadlocked on all issues, it may be time for them to end the negotiation. This may occur after one discussion, or several discussions. It is best if Jake and Isabella try and work out your differences and take as much time as necessary to do so, but at some point, these negotiations may become non-productive and even destructive, especially if they begin to argue more than discuss. It should be their top priority to preserve their relationship.

If Jake and Isabella are deadlocked and believe further discussion on remaining issues would be more harmful than helpful, they may want to meet, together, with an attorney or a mediator to try and work out the remaining issues and formalize the agreement. They should end the negotiation by making a list of what is agreed upon, if anything, what is disputed and their positions on these disputed issues, and a list of questions have for their attorneys. Their meeting with the attorney or mediator should be a collaborative approach to resolving the issues on the table, hopefully in a productive and amicable manner. If they do come to a basic agreement with the attorney or mediator, they should then consult separate attorneys to formalize the agreement as noted below.

If consulting with an attorney or mediator does not help to resolve their issues, they will need to consider the alternatives they have outlined in their planning worksheet. Most likely, their worksheets reflect two alternatives: 1) forgoing the prenuptial agreement and getting married or 2) forgoing the marriage for lack of a prenuptial agreement. While these alternatives seem quite drastic, if the prenuptial agreement is of utmost importance to either of them, and they are unable to come to an agreement, they will need to choose their best alternative.

Jake and Isabella should hire separate attorneys to execute the final agreement. Hiring an attorney to formalize the prenuptial agreement is required in some states, but, even if not required, it is important to have the expertise of an attorney to make sure the agreement complies with the law. Also, each party hiring their own attorney is evidence that this agreement was entered into independently and without coercion or outside influence from the other party. Having each party meet with an attorney will also be beneficial in that each will have the opportunity to ask questions of their attorney about the agreement and obtain the attorney's legal opinion about the terms preliminarily agreed upon. However, certainly by Jake and Isabella doing the initial negotiation, the visit to their attorneys will be much easier and less stressful than if they had begun the process of negotiating the prenup at their respective attorneys' offices.

Hopefully, their attorneys will hammer out the details, provide advice, and draft an agreement that will be acceptable to both parties. Once the agreement is formalized, Jake and Isabella can put the agreement away along with any stress endured with the process and continue planning their wedding.

ETHICS AND EQUITY

In this very arms-open relationship, one would expect the couple to act ethically and equitably in negotiating their prenuptial agreement. However, the manner in which they relate to each other has probably already been established, and thus each may believe they can predict if they will receive fair treatment from their spouse to be. However, the purpose of this book is not to psychoanalyze their relationship, but to offer guidance in negotiating skills. The couple should keep in mind that if the past history of their relationship involves instances of dishonesty, they must be particularly diligent in pursuing honesty in prenup negotiations. Honesty is a key ingredient in drafting a prenuptial agreement, in that these agreements require proper disclosure of assets from both parties to be enforced. However, some couples may be tempted not to disclose all of their assets or to undervalue their assets, especially if the couple have unequal assets. Even though they will pledge their love to their fiancé, money is a different issue for some and they may want to maintain control of a portion of their assets and hide it from their spouse. Whatever the reasons behind non-disclosure, parties who fail to fairly and reasonably disclose their finances, will likely be discovered and any protection they sought from a prenup could be lost. In essence, the nondisclosure may result in their worst fear. During divorce proceedings, all the hidden assets will likely be uncovered and when revealed, the prenuptial agreement may be set aside, leaving a court to decide how the assets would be the distributed.

Couples should also make a great effort to treat each other equitably during this negotiating process. For example, if the couple's dynamic is for one of them to take control and make all decisions, that person should take a step back from their usual course of conduct in the negotiations. Because this is a negotiation, and the terms of the prenup must be mutually acceptable and agreed upon willingly by both parties, any suggestion to a court that one party was bullied into accepting terms may result in that agreement not being enforced due to coercion or duress.

TACTICAL PLANNING WORKSHEET REVEAL

After concluding the negotiations, you and your counterpart should exchange your individual Tactical Planning Worksheets so that you both can see the bargaining positions you had planned to use during the negotiation. You should compare the two worksheets and see how far apart you were initially. Also, you should analyze whether and why you strayed from your worksheet, especially in the areas of offers and counteroffers. What positive aspects from your counterpart's worksheet do you wish you had included in yours?

POST-NEGOTIATION SELF-REFLECTION WORKSHEET

At the conclusion of the reveal session for this problem, be sure to complete the Post-Negotiation Self-Reflection Worksheet (found in Appendix B). Your Post-Negotiation Self-Reflection Worksheet should be completed individually and optimally within a short period of time after the Tactical Planning Worksheet reveal, while the negotiation session is fresh in your mind.

8-2. For this negotiation, assume the same facts and parties as in Problem 8-1. For this problem, however, assume that the couple resides in a common law, *dual property* equitable distribution state. Also, assume that the state's law for this problem provides that at death the surviving spouse is entitled to one-third of all the decedent's estate.

How would this change the negotiation strategy for each party?

8-3. GENERAL INFORMATION: *Assume for this problem that the couple resides in a community property state that divides community property equally.*

Carl and Sharon are engaged to be married. They both have been married previously. Carl is 66 years old and has one child from his previous marriage. Sharon is 65 years old and has two children from her previous marriage. They both recently retired. They wish to enter into a prenuptial agreement. Carl wants to keep their assets separate and share the expenses jointly during their marriage. Sharon believes that Carl should pay all of the expenses while they are married, and that there should be some distribution of Carl's assets to her upon his death since he is much wealthier than Sharon. However, they both agree that they want to leave some of their assets to their children.

Carl and Sharon currently live in separate apartments. Sharon rents her apartment and Carl owns his apartment. Sharon's lease is up in two months. At that time, they plan to marry and live in Carl's apartment. They have agreed that if Carl should predecease Sharon, Sharon will remain in the apartment until her death if she wishes. Sharon has long-term health care coverage, at a cost of $7,000 per year in premiums. If she becomes incapacitated, she will be able to use her insurance to take care of her health needs. At Sharon's death, the apartment would pass to Carl's children. Carl and Sharon also have the following assets:

Carl	Sharon
Stock funds valued at $6,000,000	Stock funds valued at $1,000,000
Apartment valued at $1,200,000	

Carl and Sharon have decided to have their respective attorneys work out the details and draft the prenuptial agreement. Therefore, you and your partner will assume the role of the attorneys who will negotiate the prenuptial agreement on behalf of their clients.

CONFIDENTIAL INFORMATION

You should assume that you have met with your client prior to the negotiation and have determined their bargaining positions on the following issues.

The bargaining positions on these issues are confidential and should not be shared with the other party prior to the negotiation. Please include your client's bargaining position on each of these issues on your planning worksheet.

A. Their alternatives if they do not agree on a prenuptial agreement
B. Division of expenses including upkeep expenses associated with Carl's apartment
C. Division of assets

TACTICAL PLANNING

The attorneys should complete the Tactical Planning Worksheet (Appendix A) based on the attorney's discussion with the client prior to the negotiation as noted in the Confidential Information above.

ARRANGING THE NEGOTIATION

In arranging the negotiation, it is possible that the fiancés, given their experience with previous marriages, will want to attend and participate in the negotiation along with the attorneys. This is an exceptionally bad idea. In general, clients attending negotiations with their attorneys may cause disruption making the negotiation process more difficult. In the case of fiancés attending a prenuptial agreement negotiation with the attorneys, the potential for a disastrous result is high. The attorneys will want to be strong advocates for their clients, yet the fiancé/client may be caught between wanting to get the best result for himself and worrying about hurting the person he loves. The attorneys will be placed in extremely sensitive positions. Therefore, in arranging the negotiation, it is important to reassure the client that the attorneys should handle the prenuptial discussions but will keep them informed of all the details throughout the process. In any negotiation, attorneys are ethically bound to keep clients reasonably informed about their case, so this is a requirement and not a special accommodation.

After having, hopefully, convinced the fiancés to allow the attorneys to handle to negotiation, the next step is to arrange where and when the negotiation will take place. Since this is a more formalized negotiation involving attorneys, the first negotiation meeting may likely be in person, in a setting such as in an office conference room. However, it is possible to use alternative formats, such as the phone or videoconferencing, to start the negotiation. The format will likely depend on the accessibility and convenience of the attorneys.

The negotiation should be scheduled promptly. Many couples wait until shortly before the wedding, some even days before the wedding, to consult attorneys to negotiate prenups. Perhaps it is a reluctance to initiate what they perceive will be a tedious and stressful event that disrupts the joyous wedding planning, or they believe that the negotiating and drafting of the agreement is a simple procedure, which can be accomplished in a few hours, like the wedding rehearsal.

In the case of a second marriage as with Sharon and Carl, they may not be having a grand ceremony with months of planning and will want to marry without delay. However, a prenuptial agreement drafted hastily due to time constraints gives ammunition to a party to have it set aside later down the road. Attorneys and clients should be reminded that the more time the attorneys have to negotiate and draft the agreement before the wedding, the more time they will have to work out potential roadblocks. Generally, attorneys should have at least six months prior to the wedding to negotiate and execute a prenup. Therefore, as soon as they are retained, they should get down to the business of negotiating the prenup. Attorneys should also feel comfortable rejecting potential clients who have not allocated sufficient time before the wedding for the attorneys to thoroughly negotiate and draft a prenuptial agreement.

BARGAINING

In a formalized setting, there will be a need for ice-breaking and setting the agenda. It is important for the attorneys to establish a rapport that will facilitate a productive negotiation. Also, setting the agenda, especially as to the time allotted for the initial negotiation, will be helpful in that attorneys may be bound by other obligations or appointments that will limit the amount of available time to negotiate. If the attorneys learn of these time constraints at the beginning of the negotiation, they can better allocate their time for discussion. If there is no discussion as to a time allotment, the attorney may suddenly jump up from the table and say, "I gotta go." This sudden exit may harm the rapport established, as the other attorney may find this conduct unprofessional or simply just a trick or tactic.

It is also important for the attorneys to make statements initially that they will strive to come to a fair and equitable agreement for their fiancé/clients. They should be sensitive to the fact that their clients entrusted many of their life decisions as a married couple to these attorneys and guard against letting negotiations get out of hand. Nothing would be more difficult than reporting to the fiancés that they were unable to work amicably with the attorney and negotiations broke down due to personality conflicts.

The attorneys should bring their tactical planning worksheets to the negotiation. Since they are negotiating in a representative capacity, they will likely need to refer to the worksheet when making offers, counteroffers, and concessions. They may also need to refer to research during the negotiation to support their objective criteria. Attorneys are advocates for their clients, and as such, have a duty of loyalty and confidentiality that will require them to protect information received from their clients.

LETTING GO OR RESOLVING AND EXECUTING THE AGREEMENT

Hopefully, the negotiation is successful, and the attorneys will arrive at a preliminary agreement. At this point, each attorney will need to take the agreement to their respective clients for final approval, since it is the client, not the attorney, who has the final authority to accept or reject all proposals. While the attorney should have preliminary approval to make and reject offers on behalf of clients during the negotiations, the final agreements must be approved by the client before it is put in contract form.

If the attorneys were unable to come to an agreement during the negotiation, they should adjourn and go back to their clients and discuss the next step. It may be likely there was agreement on some issues but not others. By discussing the outcome with their clients, attorneys can offer their advice as to what should occur from this point forward. Of course, it is important for the attorneys to remember that this is a couple, and if no mutually satisfactory agreement is reached, there will be a definite chill in the air when the couple discusses the outcome outside of the presence of their attorneys. In order to minimize the chilling effect, the attorneys should offer solutions to their clients consistent with their clients' goals but should also discuss alternatives with their clients. It is likely that clients will not get everything they want, as in most negotiations. However, the attorney should not bully the client into accepting the agreement by making a statement such as, "Well, if you don't sign, there goes your dreams of marrying your fiancé." Presenting an alternative in this way is not only insensitive but may allow the client to potentially raise the defense of coercion or duress if the client tries to set aside the agreement during a divorce proceeding in the future. Since no lawyer wants to become a witness or a defendant in a malpractice action, it is important to calmly and professionally discuss alternatives if the parties fail to reach an agreement.

If the fiancés agree to the proposed terms of the prenuptial agreement negotiated by their attorneys, the attorneys will then formalize the agreement and begin the drafting process. Once the attorneys have completed the drafting to their satisfaction, the attorneys will show the final draft form to their respective clients. The attorneys should draft the agreement using language that the couple can understand completely. The attorneys should also take the time to go over the agreement in its entirety with their clients to make sure there is no confusion.

Once the couple approves the prenuptial agreement, they should sign and witness the document with their attorneys present and as with any prenup, put it away for safekeeping along with your other "insurance" policies.

ETHICS AND EQUITY

As noted in Problem 8-1, parties must properly disclose their assets for the prenuptial agreement to be enforceable. In this case, since Carl and Sharon are represented by attorneys, their attorneys are ethically bound to require their clients to properly disclose assets and not offer advice to them on ways to conceal assets. If, in fact, an attorney aids a party in hiding assets, the attorney will not only be subject to discipline by the bar but could also be charged with fraud.

During the course of negotiations, their attorneys should advocate on their behalf but guard against creating animosity that may negatively impact the couple's relationship. The attorneys must try and strike a balance between advocating their clients' bargaining positions and preserving the couple's relationship. If they do reach an agreement for their clients, the attorneys will hopefully be able to report to the couple that these negotiations were collaborative, and the result is fair and balanced for both of them.

Attorneys must be sure that prenuptial agreements are not one sided. Prenuptial agreements that give one party everything and the other party nothing, may be set aside as unconscionable.

TACTICAL PLANNING WORKSHEET REVEAL

After concluding the negotiations, you and your counterpart should exchange your individual Tactical Planning Worksheets so that you both can see the bargaining positions you had planned to use during the negotiation. You should compare the two worksheets and see how far apart you were initially. Also, you should analyze whether and why you strayed from your worksheet, especially in the areas of offers and counteroffers. What positive aspects from your counterpart's worksheet do you wish you had included in yours?

POST-NEGOTIATION SELF-REFLECTION WORKSHEET

At the conclusion of the reveal session for this problem, be sure to complete the Post-Negotiation Self-Reflection Worksheet (found in Appendix B). Your Post-Negotiation Self-Reflection Worksheet should be completed individually and optimally within a short period of time after the Tactical Planning Worksheet reveal, while the negotiation session is fresh in your mind.

Laws Relevant to Testamentary Capacity and Undue Influence

Disputes over inheritance are among the most emotionally charged family negotiations, often arising from contested wills. Central to many of these disputes are claims of undue influence and lack of testamentary capacity; legal doctrines that frequently involve close family members, especially siblings; and navigating grief, loyalty, and long-standing rivalries. These disputes, while rooted in legal doctrine, are deeply personal, and negotiation often plays a critical role in resolving them outside the courtroom.

Parents often say they do not have a favorite child and claim to love their children equally. However, empirical studies suggest otherwise. Many parents do, in fact, have a favored child, whether consciously or not.[39] While parents may take this secret to their grave, it is sometimes revealed posthumously through a will that does not treat children equally by providing a larger inheritance to the favored child. This revelation can trigger a "Knives Out" scenario, where the disfavored siblings contest the will.[40] These contests frequently allege that the favored sibling exerted undue influence over the parent or that the parent lacked testamentary capacity at the time the will was executed. The challengers argue that without such influence or incapacity, the parent would have treated all siblings equally in death as they claimed to have done in life.

This section discusses negotiations involving will contests based on testamentary capacity and undue influence. Challenges to the validity of a will often involve claims that the person who made the will—referred to as the testator—either lacked the capacity to make the will or was unduly influenced into making the will. Claims based on undue influence often include allegations that the testator lacked capacity. However, claims of undue influence could also be brought independently of claims of lack of capacity. A person could have testamentary capacity and yet still be susceptible to undue influence by a third party such as a family member, friend, fiduciary, neighbor, or caregiver.

Generally, both lack of capacity and undue influence challenges are case law driven. State statutes do not generally address the underlying elements of such mental status challenges. Where states do have statutes regarding capacity and undue influence, the statutes are often limited to delineating which party—the will proponent or the will contestant—has the burden of proof. In most states, the proponent of the will must prove that the will was properly executed in accordance with the state's will formalities (*e.g.*, signature, witnesses, etc.), but the contestant of the will has the burden of establishing lack of capacity or undue influence. The states vary as to the evidentiary standard required for a successful contest with some states requiring clear and convincing evidence and others accepting the lesser preponderance of evidence standard.

Testamentary Capacity

Testamentary capacity is determined at the time when the will is executed, so subsequent incapacity is not determinative. Moreover, the standard for testamentary capacity is generally lower than that required to transact ordinary business, to make a deed, or to enter into a contract.

With some variation in phrasing, the states generally use a similar analysis for determining testamentary capacity. In many states, a testator is deemed to have testamentary capacity if the testator is able to comprehend four factors: (1) the nature and extent of his property; (2) the natural objects of his bounty (*e.g.*, the testator knows his children); (3) the disposition he wishes to make of his estate; and (4) the act of making a will. Some states refer to this analysis as a three-factor, or five-factor, rather than four-factor test, but the analysis is basically the same. For example, Florida appears to use a three-factor test. In Florida, testamentary capacity is referred to as the ability of the testator to understand in a general way (1) the nature and extent of the testator's property to be disposed of, (2) the testator's relation to those who would naturally claim a substantial benefit from the will (the natural objects of the testator's bounty), and (3) the practical effect of the will as executed.[41] Colorado appears to divide the factors into five factors such that testamentary capacity is found when the testator: (1) understood the nature of the act; (2) knew the extent of the testator's property; (3) understood the proposed testamentary disposition; (4) knew the natural objects of the testator's bounty; and (5) made a will that represented the testator's wishes.[42]

Regardless of the phrasing, the tests for capacity are very fact-intensive and there is an interplay among the factors. For example, if the testator seems to have a firm grasp of the individuals who would be the natural objects of his bounty and the testator leaves those persons the bulk of his property, evidence of the testator's failure to understand in a general way the extent of the testator's property might be given little weight. Conversely, a testator does not need to leave anything in the will to the natural objects of his bounty; he meets that particular factor of the testamentary capacity test if he simply knows the natural objects of his bounty at the time of will execution.

Undue Influence

The theory for invalidating a will based on undue influence is that the undue influence exerted on the testator destroyed the testator's free agency and substituted another person's volition for that of the testator. If a will contestant can show that a will, or a portion of a will, was the product of undue influence, that will, or portion, would be invalid, since it would not truly reflect the testator's wishes, but rather would be the product of another person's undue influence on the testator. Influence alone is not enough to invalidate a will, however. Rather, the influence exerted on the testator must be such that it replaces the testator's free agency with that of the influencer. Moreover, generalized influence is not enough; the influence must be aimed towards the creation of the will.

Because finding direct evidence of undue influence is often exceedingly difficult, most states, by case law, have developed factors that give rise to procedural presumptions of undue influence. The factors for raising a procedural presumption of undue influence, while not identical, are often similar from state to state. For example, in Arizona, a presumption of undue influence arises if the will beneficiary: (1) occupies a confidential relationship with the testator; (2) actively procures or prepares the execution of the will; and (3) is a principal beneficiary.[43] In Illinois, the presumption arises if the will beneficiary: (1) was in a confidential relationship with the testator and (2) there is clear and convincing evidence of suspicious circumstances.[44]

The Florida law of undue influence is similar. In Florida, a presumption of undue influence arises if the will contestant establishes that the will beneficiary: (1) was a substantial beneficiary; (2) occupied a confidential relationship with the testator; and (3) was actively involved in procuring the will. Generally, a substantial beneficiary is one who receives a substantial and unnatural devise. An unnatural devise may be found when the will beneficiary receives significantly more than the beneficiary would have received under intestacy in comparison to others in the same degree of relationship to the testator, or more than the amount the beneficiary would have received under a prior will of the testator. A confidential relationship between the beneficiary and the testator may be found from fiduciary relationships and from certain relationships of special trust and confidence, including relatives handling the testator's finances and daily needs, health professionals, and advisors. The Florida courts have provided the following nonexclusive list of criteria which are relevant to determining active procurement of the disputed will: (a) presence of the beneficiary at the execution of the will; (b) presence of the beneficiary on those occasions when the testator expressed a desire to make a will; (c) recommendation by the beneficiary of an attorney to draw the will; (d) knowledge of the contents of the will by the beneficiary prior to execution; (e) giving of instructions on preparation of the will by the beneficiary to the attorney drawing the will; (f) securing of witnesses to the will by the beneficiary; and (g) safekeeping of the will by the beneficiary subsequent to execution.[45]

A state's particular case laws would have to be analyzed very carefully to determine the applicable underlying elements for undue influence, to ascertain when a procedural presumption of undue influence arises, and to establish the effect of raising a procedural presumption. In Florida, for example, once the presumption of undue influence is raised the burden of proof shifts from the contestant of the will to the proponent of the will.[46] Thus, if the presumption of undue influence is raised, the proponent of the will would have to prove that the will was not the product of undue influence. In other states, however, even if the contestant raises the presumption of undue influence, the law might only shift the burden of production (as opposed to the burden of proof) to the will proponent.

Revocation

Generally, a will may be revoked by a subsequent validly executed will or codicil that expressly or impliedly revokes the prior will. In addition, a will may be revoked by the testator's physical act (*e.g.*, tearing, burning of the will).[47] In both cases—subsequent instrument or physical act—the revocation is only valid if the testator had intent to revoke. Accordingly, at the time of the revocation the testator must have capacity and be free of undue influence. Generally, if a will is deemed revoked, and there is no prior valid will that has not been revoked, distribution of the estate generally would be distributed under the applicable state's intestacy statutes.

There are significant advantages in negotiating to prevent litigating will contests based on undue influence or lack of testamentary capacity. First, such contests are often costly and fact intensive. Second, the parties may wish to preserve privacy for the deceased and the family. A will contest could provide unwanted publicity and could portray the family in a less than favorable light. Moreover, if the contest is an intra-family matter, the parties may prefer to avoid litigation in order to enhance the possibility of returning to family harmony.

TESTAMENTARY CAPACITY AND UNDUE INFLUENCE PROBLEMS

INSTRUCTIONS: After reading the introduction to will challenges based on lack of testamentary capacity and undue influence, you are now ready to try the following negotiating practice problems using the TABLE method. Below are two problems involving will contests. Each problem contains general information followed by confidential information in which each negotiator will choose a bargaining position on key issues. While the general information will be known by all sides, your bargaining position is confidential, although you may disclose it, or some of it, during the negotiation session if you choose to do so. Following the confidential information, you are given guidelines and suggestions as to how to approach the negotiations using the TABLE method.

After reviewing the information, for problem 8-4 you should complete the Tactical Planning Worksheet for the problem (Appendix A) and for problem 8-5 you should complete the multi-party Tactical Planning Worksheet (Appendix A-1). After completing a Tactical Planning Worksheet for each problem, you and your counterpart are ready to conduct a negotiation in which you attempt to reach an agreement. While there is no time limit set for each problem, you should be able to complete the initial negotiations for each problem within 30 minutes.

After you complete each negotiation, you and your negotiating counterpart(s) should exchange planning worksheets so that you can analyze the bargaining positions you and your counterpart(s) planned for the negotiation. Finally, you should complete the Post Negotiation Self-Reflection Worksheet (Appendix B).

For further explanation of the methodology for negotiating the problems, please refer to the Authors' Notes in Chapter 1, Introduction.

OVERVIEW OF PROBLEMS 8-4 AND 8-5

PROBLEM 8-4 is a two-person negotiation involving attorneys negotiating on behalf of a son and a daughter in a will contest over the testator's (their father's) will.

PROBLEM 8-5 is a multi-party will contest negotiation involving a daughter, a son, and an unrelated caretaker of the testator in a will contest over the testator's (father's) will.

8-4

GENERAL INFORMATION: *Assume for purposes of this negotiation that the decedent resided in Arizona and that the Arizona laws discussed above apply.*

Daniel passed away six months ago at age 90 from cancer. He is survived by his children Naomi and Sam. Seven months before his death, he executed a will leaving his entire $2.57 million estate to his daughter Naomi. Daniel had no prior wills. His estate consists of his house, valued at $900,000 with the remainder in securities and cash. Sam is now contesting his father's will.

Naomi had spent the last three years of Daniel's life as his full-time caregiver following his cancer diagnosis. She moved into Daniel's four-bedroom house after the lease was up on her apartment. Naomi told Sam she left her nursing job to manage Daniel's medical care although she told several co-workers several months before she left her job that she was planning to quit as she was burned out from her job, and wanted to just enjoy life for now. Naomi's husband, who had passed away suddenly four years ago, had left her an adequate inheritance. However, her financial advisor told her to find at least a part-time job, as he believed her current inheritance and savings would not allow her to maintain her standard of living beyond a few years.

During the three years she cared for her father, Naomi kept meticulous records of his care, documenting in detailed logs his daily medication, bath schedule, his oncology appointments (which she attended), and nightly checks of his oxygen levels. She also handled his financial matters including paying his bills and balancing his bank accounts. Neighbors rarely saw her leave the house, and when she did leave, she usually returned with groceries. Naomi's brother Sam, a financially stable engineer, lived 20 minutes away but visited sporadically. He frequently cancelled visits with his father, citing work demands. A text message he sent to Naomi stated, "You should handle all Dad's care because you're better at it and have nothing but free time." However, cell records later showed Sam attempted to call Daniel twenty times in the final six months that went unanswered and unreturned by Daniel or Naomi. Sam also attempted to stop by and visit his father ten times in the last six months of Daniel's life but was stopped at the front door by Naomi who told him their father was sleeping and not to disturb him. Sam left each time without pursuing the visit.

The contested will, drafted by Naomi's deceased husband's sister, who is a lawyer, includes a handwritten clause stating, "Sam's absence leaves no choice," although forensic analysis raises questions about whether Daniel penned those words. Two weeks before signing, Daniel had stopped high-dose opioids under his oncologist's advice, but pharmacy logs indicate he resumed low doses two days before signing the will. Naomi's attorneys emphasize her sacrifices in devoting her life to her father's care, and a journal entry where Daniel wrote, "Naomi's care is the only reason I'm still here." However, Sam's legal team points to a voice memo discovered on Daniel's phone where he mutters, "I want both kids provided for." In addition, Naomi's close friend was the notary during the will signing.

Financial complexities deepen the dispute. Sam contributed $28,000 toward in-home medical equipment early in Daniel's illness. Naomi faces scrutiny over a $30,000 Venmo transfer from Daniel's account to her bank account three weeks before the will's execution. Naomi contends her father authorized the Venmo transfer as a birthday gift to her. In addition, during a family meeting two years prior, Sam had persuaded Daniel to revoke a proposed $3,000 monthly stipend for Naomi, arguing a daughter should not profit from taking care of her own father, and that Naomi was being rewarded by living rent free with all her meals and incidental expenses covered.

The siblings' attorneys have decided to meet and try to negotiate a settlement before the case proceeds any further. Potential settlement options include granting Naomi the house in exchange for a portion of the liquid assets or factoring in Sam's early financial contributions against Naomi's caregiving costs. With a court ordered mediation scheduled in 10 days, both parties face pressure to determine what their father truly intended in his final days.

CONFIDENTIAL INFORMATION

Before beginning the negotiation, each negotiator should prepare a Tactical Planning Worksheet (found in Appendix A). Each party's Tactical Planning Worksheet is to be kept confidential. This information should not be shared with the other party prior to the negotiation.

For purposes of this problem, your planning worksheet should include your confidential bargaining position on these issues:

A. For Naomi (Daughter/Will Proponent): The maximum amount of the estate that she would concede to Sam.

B. For Sam (Son/Will Contestant): The minimum amount of the estate he would accept.

TACTICAL PLANNING WORKSHEET REVEAL

After concluding the negotiations, you and your counterpart should exchange your individual Tactical Planning Worksheets so that you both can see the bargaining positions you had planned to use during the negotiation. You should compare the two worksheets and see how far apart you were initially. Also, you should analyze whether and why you strayed from your worksheet, especially in the areas of offers and counteroffers. What positive aspects from your counterpart's worksheet do you wish you had included in yours?

POST-NEGOTIATION SELF-REFLECTION WORKSHEET

At the conclusion of the reveal session for this problem, be sure to complete the Post-Negotiation Self-Reflection Worksheet (found in Appendix B). Your Post-Negotiation Self-Reflection Worksheet should be completed individually and optimally within a short period of time after the Tactical Planning Worksheet reveal, while the negotiation session is fresh in your mind.

8-5—MULTI-PARTY

GENERAL INFORMATION: *Assume for purposes of this negotiation that the decedent resided in Florida and that the Florida laws discussed above apply.*

Tom, a widower, had properly executed a will five years ago, shortly after his second wife died ("2020 Will"). The 2020 Will, which had been drafted by Tom's long-time attorney and friend, devised Tom's entire estate to his only son, Bob. Tom also had a daughter, Alice, from Tom's previous marriage. Alice was ten years older than Bob. Unfortunately, when Alice turned 21 she had met and married an older man who was very controlling and who separated Alice from her father and Bob. Tom had warned Alice not to marry that man, but she was young and impetuous, and eloped. For many years, Alice was estranged from her family. Alice and her husband lived in Brazil during her marriage and Alice did not have much contact with either her father or her half-brother Bob during Alice's marriage.

Two years ago, Tom was diagnosed with terminal cancer. His doctors explained that Tom would need constant monitoring and assistance to administer his medical care. Tom was determined not to "die in a sterile hospital." Bob, who lived and worked 250 miles away from his father, asked Tom to move in with him. Tom did not, however, want to leave his old neighborhood. Tom reminded Bob that it was important to Tom that the family house stay occupied and that one day the family house would be Bob's house. Since Tom did not want to leave his house, Tom hired a nurse, Nancy, who moved into his house to assist him. Shortly after Nancy moved into the house, she started monitoring Tom's visitors and screening Tom's phone calls. When Bob tried to contact his father, Nancy would say he was too ill to talk. When Bob flew in to see his father, Nancy had given Tom so many sedatives that Tom was barely able to recognize his son. Tom became quite depressed, because he felt isolated.

Last year, Nancy started pestering Tom to revise his will, saying that she would have to leave Tom if she was not secure in the knowledge that she would be financially set after he died. Finally, at the beginning of this year, Tom agreed to execute a new will. When Tom tried contacting his long-time attorney, however, Tom found out that his long-time attorney had died. That same day, Nancy called an attorney friend of hers and asked him to rush over to the house. The attorney, who Tom had not met before, arrived and discussed the matter of a new will with Tom while Nancy was in the room. During the conversation with the new attorney, Tom insisted that the house had to go to Bob. When the attorney asked about the rest of Tom's property, Tom did not answer but Nancy said that Tom was only worried about the house going to Bob and the rest would go to her. Tom at that point had his eyes closed but the attorney thought that he was still awake. The next day, the attorney and his assistant, Jane, returned with a typed will. When the attorney arrived, Nancy ran and got the gardener, George, to come into the room to witness the signing. The attorney read the new will aloud in front of Tom, Nancy, George (the gardener), and Jane (the attorney's assistant). After reading the will, the attorney directed Tom to sign it. In his weakened state, Tom was only able to write his initials at the end of the will. After Tom initialed the will, Nancy, George, and Jane signed as witnesses. The attorney served as a notary for a self-proving affidavit. As the attorney was leaving, he handed the original of the new will ("Second Will") to Nancy. The Second Will contained a clause expressly revoking the 2020 will. The Second Will left Tom's house to Bob and the rest and residue of Tom's probate estate to Nancy. Bob was not notified of the Second Will.

One month after the signing of the Second Will, Alice came back into the country and went to see her father. Alice had just finalized her divorce and wanted to share the news of her divorce with her father and reconnect with him and end their long standing estrangement. Nancy had not been at the house on the day that Alice went to visit her father and Alice claims that her father was very relieved to hear about Alice's divorce and that he was also very happy to be reunited with his daughter.

Tom died the following week. At Tom's funeral, Alice hugged her half-brother, Bob, and told him that she was glad that they were going to equally share their father's estate. She also told Bob that on the day she had visited their father, he showed her the 2020 will which had left his estate entirely to Bob and that their father had said that he was revoking that will because he wanted his two beloved children to share his estate equally. Alice said that Tom then tore up the 2020 Will into many pieces in front of Alice and that as he did so he said "thank goodness you came back to me in time so you and Bob can share the estate and go back to being a family."

Assume that Tom had no debts and that Tom's assets consist of his house worth $1,000,000, securities in his name worth $2,000,000; a car worth $50,000; art work worth $25,000; household furnishings worth $30,000; and a bank account in his own name with cash of $60,000.

Nancy offers Tom's Second Will for probate. Bob (Tom's son) wants to contest the Second Will and wants to instead offer for probate the 2020 Will. Bob has a copy of the 2020 Will to produce and has a disinterested witness to testify regarding the 2020 Will. Bob did not find the original of the 2020 Will. Alice wants to challenge both the Second Will and the 2020 Will, because she would prefer for Tom to have died intestate, which would entitle her to one-half of the estate. All three parties (Nancy, Bob, and Alice) hire attorneys who agree to meet prior to filing suit to try to negotiate a resolution.

CONFIDENTIAL INFORMATION

Before beginning the negotiation, each negotiator should prepare the multi-party Tactical Planning Worksheet (found in Appendix A-1). Each party's Tactical Planning Worksheet is to be kept confidential. This information should not be shared with the other party prior to the negotiation.

For purposes of this problem, your planning worksheet should include your confidential bargaining position on these issues:

A. For Nancy (Nurse/Second Will Proponent): The maximum amount of the estate that she would concede.

B. For Bob (Son/Second Will Contestant and 2020 Will Proponent): The minimum amount of the estate he would accept.

C. For Alice (Daughter/Second Will Contestant and 2020 Will Contestant): The minimum amount of the estate she would accept.

TACTICAL PLANNING WORKSHEET REVEAL

After concluding the negotiations, you and your counterparts should exchange your individual Tactical Planning Worksheets so that you both can see the bargaining positions you had planned to use during the negotiation. You should compare the worksheets and see how far apart you were initially. Also, you should analyze whether and why you strayed from your worksheet, especially in the areas of offers and counteroffers. What positive aspects from your counterparts' worksheet do you wish you had included in yours?

POST-NEGOTIATION SELF-REFLECTION WORKSHEET

At the conclusion of the reveal session for this problem, be sure to complete the Post-Negotiation Self-Reflection Worksheet (found in Appendix B). Your Post-Negotiation Self-Reflection Worksheet should be completed individually and optimally within a short period of time after the Tactical Planning Worksheet reveal, while the negotiation session is fresh in your mind.

Exhibit 8-A

Fictional No-Prenup Marital Contract

This Agreement is made this day _______ of _______, 20____, by and between _______________, ("Spouse 1"), and _______________, ("Spouse 2"); who **by virtue of signing their marriage license and participating in their wedding ceremony today** *have entered into a legal binding relationship.*

RECITALS

1. By getting married the parties have entered into a legally binding relationship.
2. The Parties agree to the following:
   a. In the event of divorce or separation, the parties want the laws of the State where they happen to be domiciled or residing in at that time to apply to them, including its laws on spousal support, property division, and division of fees and costs relating to separation and divorce.
   b. At the time of the death of the first spouse to die, the parties want the laws of the State where they happen to be domiciled or residing in at the time to apply its laws to the distribution of that deceased spouse's property, whether or not that deceased spouse has written a Will or has children, and without taking into account the property or financial obligations of the surviving spouse.

IN CONSIDERATION of the parties getting married, the parties agree as follows:

1. **Property Rights.** In the event of the parties' separation, as defined under the State laws of whichever State the parties happen to be domiciled at the time, each party shall have the right to make such claims or demands of the other party for transfer, monetary award, equitable distribution award, equitable lien, or community property award, or division of any kind under any applicable statute or law of that applicable State that may govern the disposition of property upon separation or divorce, as such laws now exist or may hereafter be enacted or amended. Each party shall be entitled to receive the amount or value of property and be charged with the such debt, secured or unsecured, as determined by such law of that applicable State that may govern the disposition of marital or community property upon separation or divorce, as such laws now exist or may hereafter be enacted or amended.

2. **Spousal Support.** Each party has whatever rights he or she may have to receive alimony, maintenance, or spousal support from the other, including temporary, rehabilitative, indefinite and permanent, both periodic and lump sum, whether such right or claim results from common law, statutory law, or by way of equitable rights as may be applicable under the laws that now exist or may hereafter be enacted of the State where the couple happens to be domiciled.

PROPERTY RIGHTS UPON DEATH OF A PARTY

3. **Rights of Surviving Spouse.** Whether or not a spouse writes a will, the surviving spouse has the rights available under the laws of the State where the deceased spouse was domiciled or owned property at death, including all of his or her property rights, claims, and interests as a surviving spouse to the other party's property, including but not limited to, dower, curtesy, the right of election regarding the estate of the other or to renounce and take against the will of the other, interest in augmented estate, right to inheritance in the event of intestacy, family allowance, homestead rights, exempt property, and all other similar or related rights under applicable law, including the law of any state or foreign jurisdiction where the deceased spouse may be domiciled or own property at death, and further including any rights resulting from changes in law that may take effect after execution of this Agreement.

ATTORNEY'S FEES AND COSTS

4. **Fees and Costs Relating to Separation or Divorce or in Connection with the Administration of the Estate of a Deceased Party.** The parties acknowledge that, in the event of a marital separation, or upon the death of a party, they may each incur attorney's fees to represent their interests. Each party agrees that the State law where the parties reside shall govern whether each party is solely responsible for any such attorney's fees or costs incurred by him or her and any fees and costs incurred in connection with any suit for divorce, or that a party (or his or her estate) may incur in connection with the administration of the estate of a deceased party, or whether the party may also be responsible for some of the costs of the other party, including the other party's claim for any attorney's fees and costs associated with any future separation or divorce action, including, but not limited to, fees and costs awarded during the pendency of such action.

Signature of Spouse 1: NOT REQUIRED—DEEMED SIGNED BY VIRTUE OF MARRIAGE LICENSE AND PARTICIPATING IN MARRIAGE CEREMONY

Signature of Spouse 2: NOT REQUIRED—DEEMED SIGNED BY VIRTUE OF MARRIAGE LICENSE AND PARTICIPATING IN MARRIAGE CEREMONY

Exhibit 8-B

§ 50:57. Sample Prenuptial Agreement
8A Conn. Prac., Family Law & Prac. § 50:57 (3d ed.)

AGREEMENT

This Agreement in contemplation of marriage is made by and between _______________ [name of party 1] and _______________ [name of party 2], who will be referred to in this Agreement as the parties, as of [date of agreement].

WHEREAS, [name of party 1] and [name of party 2] are both single and legally free to marry each other; and

WHEREAS, each party recognizes that in the absence of an agreement such as this, certain interests, rights and claims may accrue to each of them in the property and interests of the other as a result of marriage to each other; and

WHEREAS, [[name of party 1]/[name of party 2]/the parties] [has/have] [a child/children] from a prior marriage for whom they desire to make appropriate arrangements through lifetime transfers and/or testamentary provisions; and

WHEREAS, the parties, to promote marital tranquility, desire to fix, limit, and determine by this Agreement the interest, rights, and claims that may accrue to each of them in the property and estate of the other by reason of their marriage or in the event of marital difficulties herein referred to, and to accept the provisions of this Agreement in lieu and in full discharge, settlement, and satisfaction, of any and all interests, rights, and claims that otherwise each might or could have under the law, in and to the property and estate of the other, both before and after the other's death.

NOW THEREFORE, in consideration of the anticipated marriage between the parties, and the mutual covenants and promises set forth herein, the parties agree as follows:

Article I. FINANCIAL DISCLOSURE

1.1 *[Name of party 1]* has disclosed to *[name of party 2]* the nature and extent of *[his/her]* assets and liabilities and the sources and amounts of *[his/her]* present income. Said disclosure included both earned and unearned income, whether or not the same is taxable for federal tax purposes. Such information is also set forth on Schedule *[designation of schedule]* attached hereto.

1.2 *[Name of party 2]* has disclosed to *[name of party 1]* the nature and extent of *[his/her]* assets and liabilities and the sources and amounts of *[his/her]* present income. Said disclosure included both earned and unearned income, whether or not the same is taxable for federal tax purposes. Such information is also set forth on Schedule *[designation of schedule]* attached hereto.

1.3 Each party has carefully examined the other's financial condition and position. Each party has had the opportunity to make further inquiries about the other's financial position, and each party acknowledges receipt of satisfactory information and responses to all such inquiries. Each party further acknowledges that he or she had ample time to conduct such inquiries prior to the execution of this Agreement.

1.4 Each party acknowledges that he or she has been fully informed as to the financial circumstances of the other party. The purpose of such financial disclosure is to enable each party, prior to entering into this Agreement, to fully understand the specific nature and extent of the assets, income and other property interests to which this Agreement applies.

Article 2. DEFINITION OF SEPARATE PROPERTY

2.1. Notwithstanding the contemplated marriage of the parties, and notwithstanding any periods of cohabitation prior to said marriage, each party agrees that the property described hereafter shall remain the separate property of the other party:

(1) All property, whether real or personal, belonging to the other party at the time of the signing of this Agreement; and

(2) All property acquired or to be acquired by the other party by gift, devise, bequest or inheritance, including gifts from one party to the other; and

(3) All property acquired by the other party in his or her separate name while living together outside the marital relationship; and

(4) Any recovery or claim arising from a personal injury suffered by the other party; and

(5) All interest, dividends, rents, profits or other income acquired from the aforestated separate property, or acquired from property purchased with separate property; and

(6) All appreciation in value of the aforestated separate property, whether attributable to market conditions or to the skills and efforts of the owner thereof or any other individuals or entities; and

(7) All proceeds (whether in money or in kind) from any sale, exchange or other transfer of separate property; and

(8) All insurance proceeds attributable to any loss, destruction or other damage to any separate property; and

(9) Any patents, trademarks, copyrights, licenses, licensing agreements or the like which either party holds at the time of this Agreement or subsequently acquires.

(10) All property purchased with the proceeds of the separate property or the interest, dividends, rents, profits or other income acquired from the aforestated separate property.

2.2. The parties specifically agree that the following events, without limitation, shall under no circumstances be evidence of any intention or agreement by either party to change their respective separate property interests into joint property, marital property or community property as those terms may be defined under the terms of the laws of any state which may have or acquire jurisdiction over either party:

(1) The filing of joint federal or state tax returns;

(2) The taking of title to other property, whether real or personal, in joint tenancy or in any other joint or common form;

(3) The designation of one party by the other as a beneficiary of his or her estate or as trustee or as any other form of a fiduciary;

(4) The commingling by one party of his or her separate funds or property with the separate funds or property of the other party, including the time, toil, and talent of either of the parties and the pledging of joint, separate, or community credit for the benefit of the other's separate estate;

(5) Any oral statement by either party;

(6) The use and payment of funds derived from said separate property or the interest, dividends, rents, profits or other income from property purchased with separate property for debts and obligations of the marriage or for the purchase of assets for either party or for the marital estate;

(7) Any written statement by either party other than any expressed written agreement changing separately owned property into jointly owned property or a written statement designating a particular piece of property as a gift to the other;

(8) The payment from the funds of either of any obligations, including but not limited to, the payment of mortgages, interest or real property taxes, repairs or improvements on a separately or jointly held residence;

(9) The joint occupation of a separately owned residence, even though designated as a homestead;

(10) The birth or adoption of one or more children to the parties of the marriage; and

(11) Any other event not included above.

Article 3. SEPARATE PROPERTY RIGHTS

3.1 All properties presently owned by [name of party 1], including those properties listed in Schedule [designation of schedule] and such property as defined in Article 2, are now [his/her] sole and separate property and shall remain the separate property of [name of party 1] together with all mutations, changes, increases, and appreciation in the value of said properties, and all of said properties shall be restored to [his/her] in the event the parties separate or in the event of a court ordered declaration of invalidity, annulment, or dissolution, or to [his/her] estate in the event of [his/her] death. [Name of party 2] does hereby waive and forever disclaim all marital and other rights in such property, and [name of party 2] agrees that [name of party 1] shall have the exclusive right to control and manage such property.

3.2 All properties presently owned by *[name of party 2]*, including those properties listed in Schedule *[designation of schedule]* and such property as defined in Article 2, are now *[his/her]* sole and separate property and shall remain the separate property of *[name of party 2]* together with all mutations, changes, increases, and appreciation in the value of said properties, and all of said properties shall be restored to *[him/her]* in the event the parties separate or in the event of a court ordered declaration of voidness, annulment, or dissolution, or to *[his/her]* estate in the event of *[his/her]* death. *[Name of party 1]* does hereby waive and forever disclaim all marital and other rights in such property, and *[name of party 1]* agrees that *[name of party 2]* shall have the exclusive right to control and manage such property.

3.3 Each party has the sole and exclusive right at all times to manage and control his or her separate property, the same as if he or she were unmarried.

3.4 Each party has the sole and exclusive right at all times to dispose of any part of his or her separate property by deed, will, or otherwise, on his or her sole signature, without any involvement or control by the other party, and the other party hereby ratifies and consents on his or her part to any such disposition.

3.5 Each party acknowledges that the right of the other to retain, manage and control his or her separate property as granted above extends not merely for the duration of the marriage, but additionally in the event the marriage ends by decree of dissolution, annulment or legal separation, including pendente lite proceedings, or at the death of either party.

3.6 Notwithstanding any other provision of this Agreement, either party may, only by appropriate, notarized written instrument, transfer, give, convey, devise, or bequeath any property to the other party. Neither party intends by this Agreement to limit or restrict in any way the right to receive any such transfer, gift, conveyance, devise, or bequest from the other, except as stated in this Agreement.

3.7 In the event one party voluntarily conveys to the other any interest in any property which is declared by this Agreement to be the separate property of such party, either by will or by instrument of conveyance or document of title signed by the transferring party, then the provisions of said will or instrument of conveyance or documents of title shall control over the provisions of this Agreement to the extent of any conflict between such documents regarding such property.

3.8 Each party acknowledges that no promises or other representations have been made by the other party or by any third person as to any future transfers of separate property.

3.9 Except as otherwise specifically provided in this Agreement, any property, funds or other assets now owned or hereafter acquired by the parties that are classified as the separate property of one of them can become the separate property of the other or the parties' joint property only by a written instrument executed and acknowledged with the same formalities as this Agreement by the party whose separate property is to be transferred or reclassified.

Article 4. INHERITANCES AND GIFTS DURING THE MARRIAGE

4.1 *[Name of party 1]* has a number of relatives who have apparently accumulated substantial wealth consisting of several million dollars. Due to the relationship and the love and affection between *[name of party 1]* and such individuals, it is anticipated that *[he/she]* will inherit substantial wealth from one or more of such individuals. It is further anticipated that *[name of party 1]* may receive substantial lifetime gifts from such individuals, that *[he/she]* is or may be designated, without *[his/her]* knowledge, as the beneficiary of one or more trusts, and/or that *[he/she]* is or may be, without *[his/her]* knowledge, a beneficiary of insurance on the life of one or more relatives. Any bequest, trust interest, inheritance, gift, insurance benefits or the like received by *[name of party 1]* prior to, during or after the marriage shall be *[his/her]* separate property free of any claim of *[name of party 2]*.

4.2 It is similarly anticipated that *[name of party 2]* may receive funds or assets during the marriage by way of gift, trust, inheritance, life insurance proceeds or the like. All such funds and assets shall be *[his/her]* separate property free and clear of any claim by *[name of party 1]*.

4.3 Each party has included in his or her financial disclosure any gifts, trust interest, inheritance or like benefits already received. Each has also included in his or her financial disclosure any gift, trust interest, inheritance, or similar benefit known to him or her which is absolutely vested at the present time. Apart from the disclosures already provided, both parties acknowledge that contingencies and circumstances beyond their control make it impossible to project or disclose at the present time the exact nature, amount, timing or other details of any gift, inheritance, trust interest, insurance proceeds or other similar benefits which he or she may receive in the future from any third party, and such impossibility shall not be a basis for any attack on this Agreement by separate legal proceeding or in any action for divorce, dissolution of marriage, legal separation or annulment.

Article 5. PROPERTY ACQUIRED JOINTLY DURING THE MARRIAGE

5.1 The parties contemplate that during the marriage they may jointly acquire a residence and other real and/or personal property.

5.2 In the absence of an express written agreement to the contrary, any jointly acquired property, whether real or personal, shall be owned by the parties in proportions equal to their respective contributions to the purchase price.

5.3 In the event jointly acquired real or personal property is financed through a mortgage or other loan, in the absence of any express written agreement to the contrary, it shall be owned by the parties in proportions equal to their respective contributions to the down payment.

5.4 All mortgage or loan payments, insurance, property taxes, maintenance expenses and other carrying charges and costs associated with the purchase, ownership, or upkeep of jointly owned property shall be paid by the parties in proportions equal to their respective ownership interests therein.

5.5 Upon any sale, exchange or other transfer of jointly owned property, each party shall be entitled to any resulting proceeds and shall be responsible for any resulting liability in proportions equal to their respective ownership interests therein.

5.6 Upon any termination of the marriage, whether by the death of one of the parties or by a judicial decree of annulment, legal separation or dissolution, the parties (and/or their respective estates) shall divide and distribute any jointly owned property in proportion to the parties' respective ownership interests therein.

5.7 Nothing contained herein shall preclude either party from transferring to the other, by will, deed or similar written instrument, his or her interest in any jointly owned property, nor shall anything contained in this Agreement constitute a waiver or rejection of such a transfer. Each party acknowledges that no representations or promises of any kind whatsoever have been made by the other or by any third person with respect to any such transfer or bequest.

5.8 In the event that either party transfers his or her interest in jointly owned property to the other, from and after the date of such transfer, the property in question shall be treated as the separate property of the recipient for purposes of this Agreement.

Article 6. INCOME AND EXPENSES DURING THE MARRIAGE

6.1 All earnings and accumulations resulting from the personal services, skills, efforts and work of *[name of party 1]*, together with all property acquired or further income derived therefrom shall be the separate property and income of *[name of party 1]*.

6.2 All the earnings and accumulations resulting from the personal services, skills, efforts and work of *[name of party 2]*, together with all property acquired or further income derived therefrom shall be the separate property and income of *[name of party 2]*.

6.3 During the marriage, each of the parties shall be responsible for the payment of his or her own personal expenses, including such items as clothing, medical and health care, separate travel and entertainment and the like. Neither party shall be obligated to make any contribution of any kind toward the living expenses or support of any child born to or adopted by the other prior to the marriage of *[name of party 1]* to *[name of party 2]*.

6.4 During the marriage, each party shall contribute equally to the parties' joint-living expenses, including groceries, joint travel and entertainment, and the utilities for the home(s) in which the parties reside.

6.5 Notwithstanding the foregoing, any funds expended by either party for the benefit of the other shall be presumed to be a gift, and not a payment for which reimbursement or repayment is later expected, unless the parties agree to the contrary in writing. The parties acknowledge that no promises or representations of any kind have been made by either party or by any third party as to any future gifts or other payments by either party on behalf of the other.

6.6 It is foreseeable that the parties may, from time to time, jointly occupy a residence solely owned by one of them, or may jointly use some other separately owned asset. It is the intent of this Article to create a joint obligation for the payment of operating expenses associated with such joint use. However, no such payment by the nonowner party shall create any right of ownership, right to reimbursement or other property right.

Article 7. PRESENT AND FUTURE LIABILITIES AND CREDIT

7.1 *[Name of party 2]* agrees that all liabilities, indebtedness, encumbrances, liens, debts, and obligations in *[his/her]* name, guaranteed by *[him/her]*, assessed against any property listed in Schedule *[designation of schedule]* of this Agreement, or for which *[he/she]* is otherwise liable (whether personal or contingent) are *[his/her]* sole liabilities and obligations, to be satisfied and paid solely from *[his/her]* separate estate and from which *[he/she]* will forever hold harmless, indemnify, and defend *[name of party 1]* from any claim.

7.2 *[Name of party 1]* agrees that all liabilities, indebtedness, encumbrances, liens, debts, and obligations in *[his/her]* name, guaranteed by *[him/her]*, assessed against *[his/her]* separate property listed in Schedule *[designation of schedule]* of this Agreement, or for which *[he/she]* is otherwise liable (whether personal or contingent) are *[his/her]* sole liabilities and obligations, to be satisfied and paid solely from *[his/her]* separate estate and from which *[he/she]* will forever hold harmless, indemnify, and defend *[name of party 2]* from any claim.

7.3 The parties agree that the property described in this Agreement as being the separate property of or belonging to the separate estate of *[name of party 1]* shall never be liable for the debts or obligations of *[name of party 2]*, except upon advance written agreement of the parties executed with the same formalities as this Agreement.

7.4 The parties agree that the property described in this Agreement as being the separate property of or belonging to the separate estate of *[name of party 2]* shall never be liable for the debts or obligations of *[name of party 1]*, except upon advance written agreement of the parties executed with the same formalities as this Agreement.

7.5 Notwithstanding the foregoing, either party may voluntarily elect to contribute toward the payment of a separate liability of the other. However, such payment shall not constitute an assumption of the liability by the contributing party nor shall such payment constitute an admission of responsibility for the liability by the contributing party. Both parties acknowledge that no promises or other representations have been made by either party or by any third person as to any future contributions of either toward the separate liabilities of the other. In addition, the payment of a liability by one party associated with separate property of the other party shall not constitute any degree of ownership in the separate property.

7.6 *[Name of party 1]* shall not have any authority to deal with the separate property or income or credit of *[name of party 2]* in any fashion with any third persons for any purposes, except by the prior written consent of *[name of party 2]*.

7.7 *[Name of party 2]* shall not have any authority to deal with the separate property, or income or credit of *[name of party 1]* in any fashion with any third persons for any purposes, except by the prior written consent of *[name of party 1]*.

7.8 The parties recognize the complexity of modern business credit transactions and each desires to allow the other to enter into such transactions without regard to his or her approval or joinder. If either party enters into a transaction wherein credit is extended to that party or that party becomes liable or obligated for the repayment, contingent or otherwise, of credit extended to any third party, whether or not the transaction is expressly denominated as a "separate-property" transaction, and unless a contrary intent is specifically and expressly stated, then that obligation will be satisfied by the party incurring it wholly from his or her separate property, and the party incurring the obligation will hold the other party harmless from that obligation and indemnify him or her if he or she is ever required for any reason to satisfy that obligation. The assets, if any, acquired through any such credit transaction will be and remain the separate property of the party obligating his or her separate property for the credit extended in acquiring the assets or resulting in the acquisition of the assets. Similarly, any business failure of one of the parties or any bankruptcy, reorganization, composition, arrangement, or other debtor/creditor action of or against a party will in no way affect the other party, and neither party is relying or will rely on the other party for any credits, accommodation, or indulgence in these regards.

Article 8. TAX LIABILITY

8.1 Any taxes, interest, or penalties that *[name of party 1]* may owe for income or gains received or accrued by *[his/her]* or that is otherwise attributable to *[his/her]* separate property or income as defined in this Agreement shall be *[his/her]* sole liabilities and obligations to be paid solely from *[his/her]* separate funds.

8.2 *[Name of party 1]* shall forever hold harmless, indemnify and defend *[name of party 2]* from any claims, liability and any and all tax liens that might hereafter arise through the filing of a joint return or the failure to file proper returns or to pay the required taxes with respect to *[his/her]* separate taxable income and/or gains as defined in this Agreement.

8.3 Any taxes, interest, or penalties that *[name of party 2]* may owe for income or gains received or accrued by *[him/her]* or that is otherwise attributable to *[his/her]* separate property or income as defined in this Agreement shall be *[his/her]* sole liabilities and obligations to be paid solely from *[his/her]* separate funds.

8.4 *[Name of party 2]* shall forever hold harmless, indemnify and defend *[name of party 1]* from any claims, liability, and any and all tax liens that might hereafter arise through the filing of a joint tax return or the failure to file proper returns or to pay the required taxes with respect to *[his/her]* separate taxable income and/or gains as defined in this Agreement.

8.5 The parties agree that if any tax liability arises from income or gains attributable to jointly held assets, each party shall pay the proportion of such liability which corresponds with his or her ownership share of said asset.

8.6 *[Name of party 2]* agrees to cooperate with *[name of party 1]*, and any tax accountants designated by *[him/her]*, in the preparation and filing of a joint tax return, in the event that *[name of party 1]* determines that such a filing method would result in a lower total tax to be paid by the parties. However, nothing contained herein shall obligate *[name of party 1]* to file a joint return if *[he/she]* prefers to file separately.

8.7 In determining the amount of tax to be paid by each party in the event that a joint return is filed, each party will pay his or her proportionate part of the joint aggregate income-tax liability of both parties based on the ratio that the net separate property taxable income of each party, computed as if he or she were a single person, bears to the aggregate net separate property income of both parties, with appropriate allowances for credits and other items (e.g. investment tax credits or recapture items) that are not reflected in the net taxable income.

8.8 *[Name of party 2]* and *[name of party 1]* each agree that upon the request of the other, he or she will consent to have gifts made by the other during his or her lifetime treated as made one-half by him or her for gift tax purposes, provided that any such gift is made during their marriage, and provided further that the total fair market value of such gifts by each completed in any calendar year qualifies under Section 2503(b) of the Internal Revenue Code (or any successor provision thereto) for the gift tax annual exclusion and is equal to or less than twice the amount of the said allowable annual exclusion. Moreover, should the Internal Revenue Code be amended to provide a limit on the dollar value of excludable annual gifts, the provisions of this Article 8 shall be void. The parties agree that they will make, execute, and file, upon the request of either of them or their respective personal representatives, whatever documents, including without limitation, gift tax returns, which are necessary in order to evidence such consent.

Article 9. WAIVER OF ESTATE RIGHTS

9.1 The parties understand that under the provisions of (state law/recite applicable estate law provisions) a surviving spouse has certain rights in and to the estate of the other, and that a surviving spouse may further be entitled to elect against the provisions of the Last Will and Testament of the other party. The parties further understand that similar rights may be conferred by the laws of the various other states in which the parties have resided in the past or may reside in the future. It is the intention of the parties that the rights of either, as a surviving spouse, shall be governed by the terms of this Agreement rather than by such statutes.

9.2 *[Name of party 2]* and *[name of party 1]* each renounces, waives, releases, and relinquishes any and all claims and rights which he or she may have or may hereafter acquire or possess to share in any capacity or to any extent in the estate of the other, whether arising by way of statutory allowance, set-off, distribution in intestacy, dower, curtesy, survivor or family allowance during administration, community property, quasi-community property, homestead interest, or election to take against any Last Will and Testament of the other; and each covenants and agrees that he or she will refrain from any action or proceeding that might change, impair, or abrogate any provision or the Last Will and Testament of the other.

9.3 The parties intend that the provisions of this Article shall constitute a waiver by each of them or the right of election granted to him or her by any statute and any rule or law of any jurisdiction, domestic or foreign, entitling a surviving spouse to all or any part of the estate or property of a deceased spouse or to any interest therein (including any income interest, dower, curtesy, community property, quasi-community property, homestead, or other marital interest of any kind whatsoever, real or personal, tangible or intangible) and of the set-off provided by law in any applicable jurisdiction, or in any other rule or law entitling a surviving spouse to all or any part of the estate or property of a deceased spouse.

9.4 Nothing contained in this Agreement shall be deemed to constitute a waiver by either of *[name of party 2]* or *[name of party 1]* of any devise or bequest to him or her actually contained in the Last Will and Testament of the other. Both *[name of party 1]* and *[name of party 2]* hereby acknowledge that no representations or promises of any kind whatsoever have been made by the other or any third person with respect to any such devise or bequest.

9.5 *[Name of party 1]* and *[name of party 2]* each hereby renounces, waives, releases, and relinquishes any and all right to act as an executor, administrator, or other fiduciary of the estate of the other unless appointed as such in the Last Will and Testament of the other.

Article 10. DISSOLUTION OF MARRIAGE

10.1 The parties are entering into this Agreement in anticipation of a long and happy marriage. Nevertheless, the parties acknowledge that differences may arise in the future and that the marriage may ultimately be terminated via an annulment, legal separation, dissolution or other judicial declaration during the lifetime of the parties. In the event of such an occurrence, it is the intention of the parties that their respective rights, duties, and entitlements be governed by the terms of this Agreement rather than by the laws of any state or nation which may have or subsequently acquire jurisdiction over the parties.

10.2 Following the marriage of *[name of party 1]* and *[name of party 2]*, if the parties should subsequently be divorced or legally separated from each other or should the marriage be annulled pursuant to a decree or order of any court or should they become separated pursuant to a separation agreement, for any reason whatsoever, including the fault of either party, *[name of party 1]* and *[name of party 2]* each hereby for himself or herself, and his or her heirs, distributees, executors, administrators, or assigns, waives, releases, relinquishes, and forever renounces any and all right in and to the income (including but not limited to the earnings from the investment thereof) or the property (including but not limited to the appreciation of such property) of the other, whether real or personal or partly real or partly personal of whatsoever nature and wheresoever located, to which he or she might be entitled by virtue of the marriage relationship under the laws of any jurisdiction.

10.3 Upon the filing by either party of a petition for divorce, dissolution of marriage, legal separation or annulment, the parties agree that it would be just, fair and equitable that the division of the property upon such termination shall restore to each party his or her separate property as defined herein along with any right to reimbursement as defined herein.

10.4 In the event of a divorce, dissolution of marriage, legal separation or annulment, the parties agree that jointly held personal property will be divided in kind, by value, in accordance with the proportionate ownership interests of the parties. In the event of any dispute over personal property, the parties will sell any commonly held personal property promptly, and the cash proceeds will be divided in accordance with the proportionate ownership interests of the parties. If there are no records reflecting such interest, the proceeds will be divided equally. Jointly held real estate will be sold and the proceeds be divided in accordance with the proportional ownership interest of the parties or the real estate will be valued at current market price and one party may buy the other party's ownership share. Gifts to both parties jointly, having a value in excess of $1,000 shall be divided equally by value.

10.5 The parties agree that prior to entry of any decree of divorce, dissolution of marriage, legal separation or annulment, they will execute a property settlement agreement setting aside to *[name of party 1]* all of the property described herein as being the separate property of *[name of party 1]*, or as belonging to the separate estate of *[name of party 1]* and setting aside to *[name of party 2]* all property described herein as being the separate property of *[name of party 2]*, or as belonging to the separate estate of *[name of party 2]*, and to divide any joint property as set forth in 10.4

above and to seek court approval of such property settlement agreement. The parties further agree that in any suit of divorce, dissolution, legal separation or annulment, neither party shall file any pleadings that request a division of property contrary to the provisions of this Agreement.

10.6 Each party hereby waives any right he or she might otherwise have or acquire to seek any alimony or spousal support from the other in any action for a divorce, dissolution of marriage, legal separation or annulment. The parties intend that this waiver shall apply to claims either might otherwise have for temporary or pendente lite alimony or spousal support during the pendency of the action as well as to claims for alimony or spousal support to be awarded in connection with any final judgment in such action. (Keep in mind that a provision of this type may not be upheld in its entirety, depending on the circumstances of the dependent spouse.)

10.7 In the event the waiver in the preceding paragraph is deemed ineffective or otherwise disregarded by a court of law for purposes of any claim for alimony or spousal support, whether during the pendency of any proceeding or in connection with any final judgment, it is the intention of the parties that the determination by the court as to the payment of alimony or spousal support be governed by the terms set forth herein.

(1) In determining the ability of *[name of party 1]* or *[name of party 2]* to pay such alimony or spousal support to the other, the court is to consider only the income from employment of *[name of party 1]* or *[name of party 2]* and the income from any joint assets to be divided between the parties pursuant to this Agreement.

(2) In making said determination as to the ability to pay, the court is not to consider the assets or net worth of the paying party, the income from any separate assets of the paying party as defined herein, any inheritance or trust interests of the paying party, any annuities to which the paying party is entitled, or any pension rights of the paying party.

(3) It is the intention of the parties that this paragraph 10.7 be given effect only if and to the extent that the waiver of alimony and spousal support set forth in paragraph 10.6 is disregarded or deemed ineffective by a court of law. The parties do not intend by this paragraph 10.7 to create or acknowledge the existence of any right or claim by either party to alimony or spousal support to be paid by the other.

10.8 In the event of any action between the parties for divorce, dissolution of marriage, legal separation or annulment, regardless of the jurisdiction in which the action is pending and regardless of the grounds upon which the action is based, neither party will request any determinations or seek any relief contrary to the terms of this Agreement.

10.9 In the event any decree of divorce, dissolution of marriage, legal separation or annulment containing an award to either party of any portion of the separate property of the other as defined herein, each party agrees to convey to the other any property which he or she may be awarded in such decree in contravention of this Agreement.

10.10 In the event of a subsequent action between the parties for divorce, dissolution of marriage, legal separation or annulment, each party shall pay his or her own accounting fees, attorney's fees, appraiser fees, and fees of expert witnesses of every kind and character and other expenses whether or not same are taxed as court costs, except that if either party unsuccessfully seeks to invalidate a portion or all of this Agreement or seeks to recover property in a manner which deviates from the terms of this Agreement, then such party shall be liable to the other party for all reasonable and necessary attorney's fees and costs incurred by the other party in successfully defending his or her rights under this Agreement.

Article 11. SEVERABILITY

If it should be determined that any provision, clause, section, or paragraph of this Agreement is invalid, is void or unenforceable for any reason, it shall be deemed severable from the remainder of the Agreement. It is the expressed intention of the parties that the remaining provisions, sections, clauses and paragraphs of this Agreement shall continue in full force and effect without being impaired or invalidated in any way and shall be considered valid and enforceable to the maximum extent possible since valid consideration exists for each and every portion of this Agreement independent from other portions of this Agreement. If a provision shall be deemed invalid due to its scope or breadth, it shall be deemed valid to the extent of the scope or breadth permitted by law. A finding by a court with jurisdiction to grant a divorce, dissolution of marriage, legal separation or annulment that any provision, clause, section or paragraph of this agreement is invalid, void or unenforceable, shall not effect an action between the parties based on the contract itself.

Article 12. AGREEMENT VOLUNTARY AND UNDERSTOOD

12.1 *[Name of party 1]* warrants and agrees that *[he/she]* executes and acknowledges this Agreement only after carefully reading same and after such reading and consultation with *[his/her]* attorney. *[He/She]* has fully considered and understands all of the terms and provisions hereof and their legal effect and ramifications. *[Name of party 1]* further acknowledges that *[he/*

she] believes it is in *[his/her]* best interest to sign, execute and deliver this instrument. *[Name of party 1]* further acknowledges that this Agreement is just, fair and equitable and that this Agreement is signed willingly, freely and voluntarily as *[his/her]* act and deed without reliance upon any representation of *[name of party 2]* or any of *[his/her]* agents, other than those expressly set out in this Agreement.

12.2 *[Name of party 2]* warrants and agrees that *[he/she]* executes and acknowledges this Agreement only after carefully reading same and after such reading and consultation with *[his/her]* attorney. *[He/She]* has fully considered and understands all of the terms and provisions hereof and their legal effect and ramifications. *[Name of party 2]* further acknowledges that *[he/she]* believes it is in *[his/her]* best interest to sign, execute and deliver this instrument. *[Name of party 2]* further acknowledges that this Agreement is just, fair and equitable and that this Agreement is signed willingly, freely and voluntarily as *[his/her]* act and deed without reliance upon any representation of *[name of party 1]* or any of *[his/her]* agents, other than those expressly set out in this Agreement.

12.3 Each party acknowledges that neither party has any reason to believe that the other did not fully understand the terms and effects of the agreement or that he or she did not freely and voluntarily execute the agreement. Each party acknowledges they have signed this Agreement in full knowledge and agreement that the terms contained herein are binding on each of them.

Article 13. CHANGES IN AGREEMENT

No change shall be made in any of the provisions of this Agreement except by an instrument in writing duly executed by the parties hereto.

Article 14. MODIFICATION AND WAIVER

A modification or waiver of any of the provisions of this Agreement shall be effective only if made in writing and executed with the same formality as this Agreement. The failure of either party to insist upon strict performance of any of the provisions of this Agreement shall not be construed as a waiver of any subsequent default of the same or similar nature.

Article 15. LEGAL COUNSEL; COUNSEL FEES

15.1 The parties hereto declare and acknowledge that each has had independent legal advice of his or her own selection. *[Name of party 1]* has been represented by *[name of counsel]* of *[address of counsel]*, *[name of county]*,

Connecticut; and *[name of party 2]* has been represented by *[name of counsel]* of *[address of counsel]*, *[name of county]*, Connecticut.

15.2 In the event that it shall be determined by a court of competent jurisdiction that either party shall have breached any of the provisions of this Agreement or of any court decree incorporating by reference or otherwise this Agreement or portions thereof, the offending party shall pay to the other party reasonable attorney's fees, court costs and other expenses incurred in the enforcement of the provisions of this Agreement and/or judgment or decree incorporating any or all of the provisions hereof.

15.3 Each of the parties shall be responsible for their respective counsel fees incurred in the negotiation and preparation of this Agreement and in any divorce, dissolution of marriage, legal separation or annulment action which might ever be brought by either party.

Article 16. BINDING ON PERSONAL REPRESENTATIVES

Except as otherwise provided, all of the covenants, promises, stipulations, agreements and provisions contained herein shall apply to, bind and be obligatory upon the heirs, executors, administrators, personal representatives and assigns of the parties hereto, whether so expressed or not.

Article 17. NO REPRESENTATIONS

Each party hereto agrees that no representations of any kind whatsoever have been made to him or her as an inducement to enter into this Agreement, other than the representations set forth herein, and that this Agreement contains all of the terms of the contract between the parties hereto.

Article 18. ENTIRE AGREEMENT

Both the legal and practical effect of this Agreement in each and every respect and the financial status of the parties have been fully explained to both parties by their respective counsel, and they both acknowledge that it is a fair Agreement, and is not the result of any fraud, duress or undue influence exercised by either party upon the other or by any other person or persons upon either, and they further agree that this Agreement contains the entire understanding of the parties. Each party affirms that they have had ample time to consider the terms and conditions of this Agreement and were not hurried or coerced in any manner whatsoever.

The parties agree that the preamble contained as Page 1 is an integral and essential part of this Agreement and hereby incorporated fully as part of the entire Agreement.

Article 19. AFTER-DOCUMENTS

Each of the parties hereby agrees to sign and deliver free of cost and expense, any documents which may be necessary or desirable to effectuate or implement any of the provisions of this Agreement on the request of the other party.

Article 20. ORIGINAL COPY

This Agreement may be executed in any number of counterparts, any one of which executed by both parties, shall be deemed to be the original, although the others are not produced.

Article 21. HEADINGS

The paragraph headings herein are for convenience only and shall not be construed to limit or affect any provisions of this Agreement.

IN WITNESS WHEREOF, the parties have hereunto set their hands and seals as of the day and year first above written.

"With all this practice, I'm getting good at this negotiating thing!"

CHAPTER 9

Negotiating Additional Practice Problems

In this chapter, you will continue to practice a variety of negotiating problems using the TABLE method. As in Chapters 7 and 8, this chapter begins with an overview of legal principles, followed by three problems in which you will negotiate a dog bite lawsuit, a security deposit dispute, and a plea bargain in an embezzlement case. The TABLE method provides a path to resolve these matters effectively and efficiently.

Instructions

After reading the legal principles in this chapter, you will be ready to apply those principles to the practice problems below using the TABLE method. As noted throughout this book, the limited legal information you are given should not be interpreted as a primer on those areas of the law. Rather, the information is included here solely to use as a basis for negotiating the various problems. As an alternative or in addition to negotiating these problems with the limited information about the law provided here, you may wish to research the law in your state, or another state, and negotiate the problem using that research.

The format for negotiating these problems is the same format as provided in Chapters 7 and 8. Because you are by now experienced with the TABLE method, you should feel comfortable applying the method to the various problems in this chapter.

After completing a Tactical Planning Worksheet for each problem, you and your counterpart are ready to conduct a negotiation in which you attempt to reach an agreement. While there is no time limit set for each problem, you should be able to complete the initial negotiations for each problem within 30 minutes.

After you complete each negotiation, you and your negotiating counterpart should exchange your Tactical Planning Worksheet so that you can analyze the bargaining positions you and your counterpart planned for the negotiation. Finally, you should complete the Post Negotiation Self-Reflection Worksheet (found in Appendix B).

For further explanation of the methodology for negotiating the problems, please refer to the Authors' notes in Chapter 1, Introduction.

Laws Relevant to Dog Bites

Dog ownership is on the rise in the United States. In 2024, there were approximately 89.6 million dogs living in households throughout the United States.[1] However, as dog ownership increases, so do dog bite incidents. According to the Center for Disease Control, approximately 4.5 million dog bites occur in the United States every year.[2] Given these alarming statistics, states have grappled with enacting laws that will protect and compensate people bitten by dogs, while recognizing that dogs are considered members of the family for many people.

The majority of states have stringent laws that hold dog owners responsible for their dogs' biting with limited exceptions.[3] In fact, most states impose strict liability on owners whose dog has bitten and caused injury. This standard provides compensation for the victim and relieves the victim of the need to offer proof that the owner had knowledge of the prior viciousness of the dog, or that the owner acted negligently in handling his dog. The dog bite that results in injury to the victim is the only proof needed to state a cause of action under strict liability laws.

Florida is an example of a state that has recognized strict liability for dog bites. The statute states in part:

> **§767.04 Dog owner's liability for damages to persons bitten.** The owner of any dog that bites any person while such person is on or in a public place, or lawfully on or in a private place, including the property of the owner of the dog, is liable for damages suffered by persons bitten, regardless of the former viciousness of the dog or the owners' knowledge of such viciousness. However, any negligence on the part of the person bitten that is a proximate cause of the biting incident reduces the liability of the owner of the dog by the percentage that the bitten person's negligence contributed to the biting incident.[4]

Note that although the Florida statute holds the dog owner strictly liable for the dog bite, the dog owner's liability may be reduced if the victim acted negligently. For example, if the victim had stepped on the dog's foot prior to the dog biting him, the jury may determine that the victim's act of stepping on the dog's foot provoked the dog and thus, the victim is partially liable for being bitten. In this case, the jury would reduce the amount of damages by the percentage of fault attributable to the victim.

A minority of states do not apply the strict liability standard, but instead rely on what is known as the "one bite rule."[5] The "one bite rule" holds a dog owner liable for a bite only if the owner had scienter, a standard which requires the dog owner to have known, or should have known, that the dog had dangerous propensities to bite prior to the dog biting the victim. The one bite rule is often referred to the one free bite rule, in that an owner can often escape liability for the first time a dog bites, since the owner can claim that he did not have knowledge of the dog's dangerous propensities prior to the bite. However, once the dog has bitten, the owner is now on notice that the dog has a propensity to bite and will be liable for any subsequent bites. However, the one bite rule is a bit of a misnomer. The dog owner may also be on notice of his dog's dangerous propensities even if his dog has not bitten before. If, for example, the dog was trained as an attack dog, the owner should be well aware of the dog's dangerous propensities. Further, if the dog has frequently growled or barred its teeth at people previously, this conduct may be enough to prove the required notice to the owner of the dog's dangerous propensities.

One bite rule states typically do not have statutes that address the liability of dog owners for dog bites, but instead the law is derived from common law. For example, in Kansas, a dog bite victim must prove that the dog owner either had scienter or was negligent before they can recover.[6] Therefore, if the victim is unable to prove scienter, which requires that the owner knew (or should have known) that the dog had a dangerous propensity to bite, the dog victim may be able to recover under a negligence standard.

Further, many cities and counties have leash laws, requiring that a dog owner walk his dog on a leash. For example, Palm Beach County, Florida has an ordinance that provides in part:

> It shall be unlawful for any dog to be off the owner's property (which property is exclusive to the owner) unless the dog is under the restraint or control of a person by means of a leash or other device such as a cage, crate or vehicle in accordance with section 4-24, Animal care; manner of keeping.[7]

If the owner does not leash his dog, he not only is in violation of local law, but if his dog bites, there may be a cause of action for negligence per se.[8] Negligence per se provides a cause of action when a person violates a statute that was enacted for an intended purpose.[9] One of the intended purposes of leash laws is to prevent a dog from causing harm to others. Therefore, in cities or counties with leash laws, a violation of the leash laws will likely result in a claim under negligence per se.

Due to the popularity of dogs residing in households, it is likely that you have already or will encounter a situation involving a dog bite. Many dog bites do not rise to the level of a serious injury resulting in a lawsuit, but for those that do, it is probable that the parties and their attorneys will engage in settlement negotiations. Given the adversarial nature of litigation, it may be difficult for the parties to approach negotiations in a calm and efficient manner. Nevertheless, just as in any negotiation, using the TABLE approach may help diffuse the emotion and find mutually acceptable solutions.

PROBLEM 9-1 is a two-person negotiation in which a woman was bitten by a dog while jogging around a park area. She has filed a lawsuit against the dog owner for her injuries resulting from the bite. In this problem, the attorneys, on behalf of their clients, are attempting to negotiate a settlement before trial. Each of you will play the role of an attorney. Since this problem involves litigation, the attorneys have taken depositions of the parties. Summaries of those depositions are included as part of the general information.

PROBLEM 9-1: DOG BITE

GENERAL INFORMATION: *Assume for purposes of this negotiation that the dog bite incident took place in Palm Beach County, Florida and that the Florida laws discussed above apply.*

Maria Carlson is a 19-year-old single woman. She just graduated from high school and will attend college in September. Andy Tipton is a 35-year-old male, who is employed as a nurse at the local hospital. This case involves a dog bite incident, in which Tipton's dog, Mickey, bit Carlson.

As a result of this incident, Carlson hired an attorney, who filed a lawsuit on behalf of Carlson against Tipton, asking for damages in excess of $25,000. Tipton subsequently hired an attorney to defend him in the lawsuit. The parties' attorneys' have agreed to meet to negotiate and hopefully resolve this matter before going to trial.

The following information is a summary of statements from the parties and a witness.

DEPOSITION SUMMARY OF PLAINTIFF MARIA CARLSON

I was jogging on the sidewalk that surrounds Pine Tree Park at 5:00 PM on February 23. I wear headphones and play music when I jog but keep the volume low, so I can hear my surroundings. The sidewalk is outside the park and close to the street. I jog often on the sidewalk and I'm very familiar with the area. The sidewalk is about five feet in width. I was jogging for about ten minutes when I noticed the Defendant and his dog walking about 15 feet in front of me. The Defendant's back was to me. As I approached him from about 10 feet away, I called out "excuse me," and I prepared to pass him on the left side of the sidewalk. I did not want to leave the sidewalk because even though there was a small area of grass to the left and right of the sidewalk, the grass was uneven. Of course, I didn't want to pass by Defendant on the street because of the traffic. After I said, "excuse me," the Defendant appeared to move to the right a little and his dog was on the right side on a leash. As the sidewalk is narrow, when I was about 5 feet from him, I again said, "excuse me." Defendant did not respond but as I passed him, I noticed he seemed to be talking to his watch on his left wrist.

As I jogged past him, I did not bump into Defendant and his dog, but his dog made a sudden move towards me and Defendant dropped the leash. Then the dog began to chase me, so I stopped jogging and reached down to pet the dog. I figured since this was a cute 25-pound dog, the dog was friendly, and I wanted to calm the dog down because he seemed very crazy. However, as I reached to pet him, the dog jumped at me and bit my finger before the Defendant was able to retrieve the dog. I never stepped on the dog's foot. I didn't do anything to the dog except reach out to pet him. I was in excruciating pain from the bite. The defendant called an ambulance and I was taken to the hospital. I had a bite wound on my finger that was bleeding profusely. I received five stitches at the hospital for my finger. The stitches were removed 10 days later.

Currently, my finger is still somewhat stiff and painful. I am not receiving any more medical treatment at this point. I play the trombone in my high school marching band and was planning on becoming a member of the marching band in college, but at this point, my finger is too painful for me to even practice playing the trombone. Tryouts for the marching band are in August so I may have to pass up the opportunity if my finger isn't healed by that time. My doctor has told me that my finger looks good and should not be stiff or sore by the time of the tryout, but honestly, he doesn't understand how it feels or how much you have to use your index finger to play the trombone. I will be so bummed if I can't try out for the marching band. I'm sure I would've made the marching band even though my college's marching band is one of the best in the state. But I was the third best trombone player at my high school and we came in fourth in the district marching band competition.

DEPOSITION SUMMARY OF DEFENDANT ANDY TIPTON

I was walking my dog Mickey on February 23. Mickey is a 25-pound Maltese/Terrier mix that I rescued from the animal shelter. He was five years old at the time of the incident. I often walked Mickey on the sidewalk surrounding the park, but usually around 4:00 pm. However, on this date, I returned late from the dentist, so it was around 5:00 pm. I was always very careful about staying clear of other individuals on the sidewalk, and always kept Mickey on a leash. On that day, I was talking on the phone, using my watch phone on my left wrist to talk. I was not wearing headphones, so I could hear my surroundings.

On the day of the incident, I did hear Ms. Carlson's footsteps behind me, but I assumed Ms. Carlson would simply pass me by leaving the sidewalk and passing by me on the grassy part of the embankment on the left. However, Ms. Carlson decided to remain on the sidewalk and pass me. The sidewalk is so narrow that when she passed me, she bumped into me and Mickey. She was running fast, and she bumped into me and Mickey so forcefully that I dropped the leash. Mickey was confused and did start to run after Plaintiff, but not in a threatening way. However, once Plaintiff stopped and Mickey came to her, I saw Plaintiff step on Mickey's foot. I did not see her trying to pet him. Mickey did bite her finger but only because she stepped on his foot. Mickey had never bitten anyone before, and he was very obedient. Luckily, Plaintiff did not injure Mickey by stepping on his foot. By the way, I never heard her say "excuse me" or make any statements to me before she passed me. I have excellent hearing.

At the time of the incident, Mickey was a healthy dog and up to date on all of his shots. Unfortunately, two weeks after the incident, Mickey died in his sleep, apparently from a heart attack. I think it was due to all the stress he felt from the incident. He was never the same. Plaintiff was reckless. I'm sorry she was hurt, but she did provoke Mickey by stepping on his foot. By the way, her finger bite is very minor. She only required 5 stitches and it did not get infected. I'm a nurse and I've seen so many severe dog bites. This was very minor. Also, since Mickey had all his shots, she was in no danger of getting rabies or any other disease from him. She also doesn't appear to be such a great trombone player so it's doubtful she can even make her college marching band.

DEPOSITION SUMMARY OF WITNESS— FRANCINE PARKER

I was walking about 20 feet from where the incident took place. I was directly facing Mr. Tipton and Ms. Carlson. I saw Ms. Carlson pass Mr. Tipton and his dog. I could not see if Ms. Carlson bumped into Mr. Tipton but I did see Mr. Tipton jump as if startled by her passing him, and he dropped the leash. It all happened so quickly that I couldn't tell if Ms. Tipton stepped on the dog's foot or if she was petting the dog when she was bitten. Everyone knows you shouldn't pass on the sidewalk so close to dogs or try and pet strange dogs. But Mr. Tipton should have been more careful with his dog and not dropped the leash.

Summary of Damages

Past medicals: $10,000 (unpaid)—**not in dispute as to amount**

Pain and Suffering: $20,000 (Plaintiff's demand)—**disputed as to amount**

No future anticipated medical bills—**not in dispute**

No psychological damages—**not in dispute**

Please Note. Assume also that neither party has insurance so do not discuss insurance coverage.

CONFIDENTIAL INFORMATION

Recall that the parties will prepare Tactical Planning Worksheets for the upcoming negotiation. Each party's Tactical Planning Worksheet is to be kept confidential. This information should not be shared with the other party prior to the negotiation. For purposes of this problem, your planning worksheet should include your confidential bargaining position on these issues:

A. For Carlson (Dog bite victim/Plaintiff): The minimum amount she will accept as settlement. Include the maximum percentage of comparative fault she would accept.

B. For Tipton (Dog Owner/Defendant): The maximum he will pay as settlement. Include the percentage of comparative fault, if any, he would accept.

TACTICAL PLANNING WORKSHEET REVEAL

After concluding the negotiations, you and your counterpart should exchange your individual Tactical Planning Worksheets so that you both can see the bargaining positions you had planned to use during the negotiation. You should compare the two worksheets and see how far apart you were initially. Also, you should analyze whether and why you strayed from your worksheet, especially in the areas of offers and counteroffers. What positive aspects from your counterpart's worksheet do you wish you had included in yours?

POST-NEGOTIATION SELF-REFLECTION WORKSHEET

At the conclusion of the reveal session for this dog bite problem, be sure to complete the Post-Negotiation Self-Reflection Worksheet (found in Appendix B). Your Post-Negotiation Self-Reflection Worksheet should be completed individually and optimally within a short period of time after the Tactical Planning Worksheet reveal, while the negotiation session is fresh in your mind.

Laws Relevant to Security Deposit Disputes

Moving into an apartment is for many people a positive experience. Renters may have searched long and hard for their new apartments, and once they find it, they look forward to their new residences. Due to their optimism, they often give the lease a quick once over, and as is required by most leases, give the landlord the first and last month's rent and a security deposit. In an optimum setting, the renter lives quietly and comfortably in his apartment for the duration of the lease.

However, while moving into an apartment may be exciting, moving out is usually devoid of any entertaining value. Often, moving out of an apartment is a chaotic and exhausting experience. Packing up your belongings, cleaning the apartment, arranging for a moving company or a good friend to help you move, and cancelling cable service are some of the many mundane tasks associated with moving out. One task that should be mundane and standard is the landlord returning the security deposit. However, for many tenants, getting back their security deposit becomes a tug of war with the landlord which can quickly escalate to a stressful situation. By knowing how to effectively negotiate for return of a security deposit, both tenant and landlord can de-escalate the situation and amicably resolve their dispute.

Security deposits have been used by landlords for more than a century in order to monetarily compensate the landlord for damage done to his property by a tenant. In essence, the deposit secures the tenant's performance under the lease.[10] However, even though the security deposit has been used for over a century, courts have struggled to delineate the rights of the landlord and the tenant with respect to the deposited funds. In response to this struggle, most states have enacted specific statutes to provide clear guidance and authority on the issues involving security deposits.

State laws encompass a wide variety of issues that may arise concerning security deposits. While some states have unique provisions, most state laws uniformly address the following major issues.

Maximum-Security Deposit Permitted by Law

Security deposit limits are generally established by state statutes.[11] Some states statutes do not set limits on the amount a landlord may charge as a security deposit. Many of the state statutes that impose limits set the security deposit at the price of one month's rent. However, even in those states in which there is no maximum-security deposit limit, city or county ordinances may impose a limitation on the amount a landlord can hold as a security deposit.

Charges Landlord May Claim Against the Security Deposit

Tenants assume that the security deposit is for the purpose of repairing damage to the apartment caused by the tenant. In fact, the security deposit is often called the damage deposit. Yet the tenant is not responsible for all damage to the apartment. Conditions caused by normal wear and tear are the responsibility of the landlord, not the tenant. For example, faded paint and frayed carpet are examples of conditions caused by normal wear and tear. However, broken windows, holes in the wall, even an excessively dirty bathroom is likely to be classified as damage and the responsibility of the tenant. The key distinction between normal wear and tear and damage is the reasonable use of the apartment. Tenants are expected to maintain their unit, but not expected, for example, to pay to replace a rug that has faded due to normal use. In contrast, broken tiles or gaping holes in the walls go beyond normal wear and tear and the tenant's security deposit may be properly used by the landlord to pay for the repair or replacement of those items.[12]

While most people consider damage to the apartment as the only legitimate deduction from their security deposit, states permit landlords to use the security deposit for other purposes. In most states, the security deposit may be used for unpaid rent. It may also be used in some states to replace or restore personal property that has been damaged or lost, such as keys. Cleaning costs, unpaid utilities, and costs associated with an early termination of the lease are other purposes for which some states permit use of the security deposit. The purposes for which the security deposit may be used must comply with state law.

Time Frame for Landlord to Return Deposit or Provide Accounting to Tenant

State laws set forth the procedure for the landlord to return the security deposit or to give notice to the tenant that there will be no return, or a partial return, of the security deposit. States vary widely in the number of days required to return or give notice of no return. For example, Arizona allows landlords fourteen days to return the deposit, while Arkansas gives landlords sixty days to return the deposit.[13] State laws strictly hold landlords to the time requirements under the principle that security deposit funds belong to the tenant, and any further delay past the time allotment is depriving that tenant of the right to his money. Of course, proper notification of the landlord's intent to retain all or part of the security deposit will forestall the tenant from receiving his money, until there is a proper resolution of the dispute. There are time requirements for notifying the tenant that the money will not be returned, which sometimes differ from the time requirement for returning the deposit.

Requirement of a Walk-through Inspection of Apartment Prior to Tenant Vacating

The majority of states do not require the landlord to conduct a walkthrough of the apartment. However, Michigan not only requires a walkthrough, but also requires that the landlord make inventory lists both before the tenant takes occupancy and again at termination of occupancy. At the end of the lease, the landlord's inventory checklist must list all the damages the landlord claims are chargeable to the tenant against the security deposit.[14] Similarly, Kentucky also requires inventory lists at the beginning and end of the tenancy, with the landlord listing damages at the end of the tenancy chargeable against the security deposit.[15] Also, in Kentucky, both the landlord and tenant must sign off to the inventory list, and if the tenant disputes the damage assessment by the landlord, the tenant must sign a separate statement listing his objections to the landlord's assessment.[16]

Landlord Placing Security Deposit in a Separate and/or Interest-Bearing Account

When a tenant pays a security deposit, that money remains the property of the tenant unless and until the time that the landlord establishes a right to retain the deposit under applicable law. As such, the landlord has a duty to safe keep the deposit on behalf of the tenant. Most states' laws require landlords to keep tenants' security deposits in a separate account from any funds of the landlord. While the landlord may be permitted to place all tenants' security deposits in the same account, he must keep his own funds in a separate account.

State law also determines whether a landlord must pay interest on a security deposit. Most states do not require a landlord to place a tenant's security deposit in an interest-bearing account for the benefit of the tenant.17 A handful of states, however, do have that requirement. For example, North Dakota requires the landlord to deposit a tenant's security deposit in a federally insured interest-bearing account for the benefit of the tenant. Upon termination of the lease, the security deposit and interest must be paid to the tenant unless the landlord follows the procedure to make a claim against the security deposit for the reasons set forth under the statute.18

States are very specific as to the methodology for retaining security deposits and include numerous penalties for failure of the landlord to comply with the procedures for taking possession and retuning the security deposit. While some tenants may feel that seeking return of the deposit is not worth their time and potential court costs, familiarizing themselves with the law can go a long way in negotiating a successful return of the deposit. For example, Illinois law provides that a landlord who acts in bad faith in failing to return the security deposit is liable to the tenant for an amount equal to twice the security deposit, along with court costs and fees.19 Therefore, as in any negotiation, it is in the best interest of tenants to research their state law in order to prepare for negotiations with the landlord concerning return of the security deposit. Furthermore, the landlord and tenant should attempt to resolve the security deposit matter before turning to the courts to settle their dispute. In fact, Florida law provides that if the landlord requires a security deposit, the lease must contain a notice that the parties try to resolve any dispute regarding security deposits informally before filing a lawsuit.20 Hopefully, the landlord and tenant will negotiate and come to an amical resolution.

PROBLEM 9-2 is a two-person negotiation in which a landlord is withholding a tenant's security deposit. In this problem, the landlord and tenant are attempting to negotiate a resolution before taking the matter to court. You will play the role of either the landlord or the tenant.

PROBLEM 9-2: SECURITY DEPOSIT

GENERAL INFORMATION: *Assume for purposes of this negotiation that the security deposit dispute is governed by the laws as described above.*

Riley entered into a one-year lease at the Ridge Apartments. The lease required a security deposit of $2,300, which was the equivalent of one month's rent. At the time he signed the lease, Riley gave Mertz, the landlord, a check for the first and last month's rent, and the additional $2,300 for the security deposit.

Throughout the course of the year, Riley had some parties at his apartment. One of the neighbors, Mrs. Flanders, who lived across the hall complained to Mertz about the noise. Mertz told Riley that his parties were disturbing the neighbors, and Riley had better tone it down or he would be asked to leave the apartment. Riley told Mertz that Mrs. Flanders, the complaining neighbor, was being unreasonable, and his parties were low key and ended by midnight, in line with the city's noise ordinance. After speaking with Mertz, Riley continued to have several parties. In fact, Mrs. Flanders recorded the noise coming from Riley's apartment during one of the parties, and turned the recording over to Mertz. Mertz wrote an email to Riley, informing him that if he received any more complaints about Riley, he would be evicted, as was permitted in the lease. Riley emailed Mertz back and said he would not have future parties and there would be no more problems with the noise. He also asked Mertz if he could renew his lease, which was due to expire in two months. Mertz told him he would not renew his lease. At that point, Riley emailed Mertz and told him he believed he was being discriminated against because he is Native American. Riley, who is Native American, suspected this because the young family that lived in the apartment below him had told Riley that they had overheard Mertz saying that Riley should "go back and live on the reservation." Mertz denied any discrimination and told Riley he was unaware that Riley was Native American.

The week before Riley was to vacate the apartment, Mertz contacted Riley and told him he would like to do a walkthrough inspection with Riley to determine if there was any damage to the apartment. Riley agreed to meet with Mertz on Wednesday at 3:00 PM for the walkthrough. However, at 12:00 PM on that date, Mertz emailed Riley and told him he had an emergency and had to re-schedule the walkthrough to Friday, which was the last day of Riley's lease. Riley was annoyed at the cancellation, because he had left work early Wednesday to make the appointment. Riley told Mertz he was moving out a day early on Thursday, and Mertz could inspect the apartment whenever he wanted to on Friday without Riley, since Riley could not take another day off work. Riley also told Mertz to send his security deposit to him as soon as possible, since the apartment is in great condition, better than when he moved in.

Twenty-eight days after Riley moved out, he received a letter from Mertz stating that Mertz was keeping the security deposit due to the fact that Riley had damaged the apartment, and that it was necessary for Mertz to make repairs and cleaning beyond normal wear and tear. Mertz said it was necessary to make the repair and cleaning immediately after Riley moved out, since a new tenant moved in a few days after Riley vacated the apartment. Mertz sent an itemized list to Riley, detailing the following repair and cleaning costs:

1) $400.00 for rug cleaning.

   The rugs were stained, apparently with dog stains and food stains. Riley did not disclose on the lease that he had a pet and paid no extra deposit for a pet. Mertz hired a carpet cleaner, who cleaned the rug but was unable to get all the stains out of the rug. Mertz believes he may have to replace the rug due to the stains sooner than he had planned.

2) $1,200 for wall repair.

   There was a hole in the wall near the patio, and it appeared to be caused by a hammer or a portable piece of furniture, like a bartender's cart, crashing into it. The wall needed drywall and a new coat of paint to repair the damage.

3) $300.00 for bathroom cleaning.

   The bathroom shower and toilet were filthy and appeared as if they had not been cleaned during the lease period. Mertz hired a cleaning crew who needed to spend several hours beyond a routine apartment cleaning to clean the bathroom.

Riley responded to Mertz that he had the apartment professionally cleaned once a month and that he also personally cleaned the bathrooms. Riley also said the stains were on the rug prior to his moving in. However, neither Riley nor Mertz took pictures of the rugs before Riley moved in. Mertz did admit that the prior owner had a dog, but that he had the rugs cleaned before Riley moved in so there were no stains. Further, Mertz told Riley that a neighbor had informed him that Riley had a frequent visitor who brought her dog with her to the apartment, and that visitor often stayed overnight. Riley told Mertz that the neighbor's account was inaccurate. While he had a friend who brought her dog over one time to visit him, he did not have a frequent overnight guest, and any overnight guests he had did not have pets. As for the hole in the wall, Riley claims the hole was a result of him trying to hang a picture when the wall collapsed, due to no fault of his. Riley also claims the bathroom was not dirty beyond normal wear and tear. There are no pictures of the wall or bathroom's condition prior to Riley moving in or when Riley moved out.

Riley told Mertz again that he felt Mertz was discriminating against him, and that Riley was probably going to go to small claims court to get his money back. Mertz told him that they should try and work this out before going to court, and Mertz suggested they meet and try and come to a solution. Riley agreed to meet and negotiate a resolution.

Assume for purposes of this negotiation that the rental apartment is located in a state with the following laws concerning security deposits.

1. A Landlord shall not demand or receive as a security deposit an amount or value in excess of two months' rent.
2. Security deposits shall not be commingled with the personal funds of the Landlord. All security deposits may, but are not required, to be held in an interest-bearing account. Any interest earned on a rental deposit during the first five years of a tenancy shall be the property of the Landlord.
3. A Landlord shall, within thirty days from the date of termination of the tenancy and receipt of the Tenant's mailing address or delivery instructions, return the security deposit to the Tenant or furnish to the tenant a written statement showing the specific reason for withholding of the rental deposit or any portion thereof.
4. A Landlord may withhold from the security deposit only such amounts as are reasonably necessary for the following reasons: (1) to remedy a Tenant's default in the payment of rent or of other funds due to the landlord pursuant to the rental agreement; (2) to remedy damage caused by Tenant, ordinary wear and tear excepted. Ordinary wear and tear is defined as the expected decline in the condition of the property due to normal everyday use. The Tenant is responsible for maintaining and cleaning the property on a regular basis during the course of the tenancy.
5. A Landlord who fails to provide a written statement within thirty days of termination of the tenancy and receipt of the Tenant's mailing address or delivery instructions shall forfeit all rights to withhold any portion of the rental deposit. If no mailing address or instructions are provided to the Landlord within one year from the termination of the tenancy, the rental deposit shall revert to the Landlord and the Tenant will be deemed to have forfeited all rights to the rental deposit.
6. Landlord and Tenant must meet and attempt to resolve all matters concerning return of the security deposit before seeking a remedy in court.
7. The bad-faith retention of a security deposit by a Landlord, or any portion of the rental deposit, in violation of this section shall subject the Landlord to punitive damages not to exceed twice the monthly rental payment in addition to actual damages. In an action concerning the security deposit, the burden of

proving, by a preponderance of the evidence, the reason for withholding all or any portion of the rental deposit shall be on the Landlord.

8. The court may, in any action on a rental agreement, award reasonable attorney fees to the prevailing party.

CONFIDENTIAL INFORMATION

Recall that the parties will prepare Tactical Planning Worksheets for the upcoming negotiation. Each party's Tactical Planning Worksheet is to be kept confidential. This information should not be shared with the other party prior to the negotiation.

For purposes of this problem, your planning worksheet should include your confidential bargaining position on these issues:

A. For Mertz (Landlord): The maximum amount of the security deposit he would return to Riley.

B. For Riley (Tenant): The minimum amount he would accept as a return of his security deposit.

TACTICAL PLANNING WORKSHEET REVEAL

After concluding the negotiations, you and your counterpart should exchange your individual Tactical Planning Worksheet so that you both can see the bargaining positions you had planned to use during the negotiation. You should compare the two worksheets and see how far apart you were initially. Also, you should analyze whether and why you strayed from your worksheet, especially in the areas of offers and counteroffers. What positive aspects from your counterpart's worksheet do you wish you had included in yours?

POST-NEGOTIATION SELF-REFLECTION WORKSHEET

At the conclusion of the reveal session for this problem, be sure to complete the Post-Negotiation Self-Reflection Worksheet (found in Appendix B). Your Post-Negotiation Self-Reflection Worksheet should be completed individually and optimally within a short period of time after the Tactical Planning Worksheet reveal, while the negotiation session is fresh in your mind.

Laws Relevant to Plea Bargaining and Embezzlement

Throughout this book, the problems you have been asked to role-play have all focused on negotiating civil cases or transactions. However, negotiating is also very common in criminal cases through a plea-bargaining process. Negotiating in a civil case to resolve a civil matter and plea bargaining in a criminal case to resolve a criminal matter have similarities as well as differences in approach and outcome. However, just as in negotiating a civil matter, using the TABLE method is still optimal for preparing and conducting a plea bargaining session.

Below is a summary of the plea bargaining process followed by a legal discussion of the crime of embezzlement. Following the legal analysis, for the final problem in the book, you are given a role-playing problem in which a defendant is charged with embezzlement. The defendant's attorney has scheduled a plea bargaining session with the prosecutor in hopes of resolving the case.

Plea Bargaining

A plea bargain is a negotiated agreement between a prosecutor and a criminal defendant where most often a defendant agrees to plead guilty to a charge in exchange for a concession from the prosecutor, such as a reduced charge or a recommendation for a lighter sentence.[21] Plea bargains are used in both misdemeanor and felony criminal cases, including drug offenses, theft, assault, and white-collar crimes such as insider trading and embezzlement. Studies have shown that an overwhelming majority (90 to 95 percent) of cases result in plea bargaining.[22] Plea bargaining is often endorsed by prosecutors for allowing the efficient resolution of cases and the conservation of judicial resources.

Generally, prosecutors have wide discretion in offering plea deals. In deciding whether to offer a plea deal prosecutors consider the strength of the evidence, the seriousness of the offense, and the defendant's prior record, among other factors. Defendants may accept a plea bargain to avoid the risk of harsher penalties if convicted at trial. The plea bargaining process is not without controversy, as concerns persist regarding the potential for coercion by the prosecution, disparate treatment among defendants, and the possibility that innocent defendants may plead guilty to avoid the risk of adverse trial outcomes.[23] Nevertheless, the efficient and quick resolution of a case through plea bargaining versus going to trial makes the process appealing to both the prosecutor and defendant. Furthermore, having the final plea bargaining deal subject to judicial approval adds a safeguard to the process.[24]

There are many similarities between civil negotiation and criminal plea bargaining. First, both involve an attempt to resolve a matter without a trial. Second, both are voluntary in nature, as parties in civil negotiations and criminal plea bargains are not required to settle. Third, parties in civil negotiations and criminal plea bargains both attempt to avoid the uncertainty of a jury's verdict by reaching a mutually acceptable resolution before trial. In both contexts, parties weigh the strengths and weaknesses of their positions and the likely outcomes.

However, civil negotiations and plea bargaining also differ in several ways. Civil negotiations typically involve private parties seeking to resolve disputes over money and other remedies, while plea bargaining seeks to resolve criminal charges brought by the government. Furthermore, parties in civil negotiations who reach an agreement enter into a settlement agreement, which is a binding contract. In contrast, the prosecutor who enters into a plea bargain agreement with a defendant agrees to drop the criminal charge in exchange for the defendant agreeing to certain conditions and requirements, such as accepting a guilty plea to a lesser crime, probation, or testimony against other defendants. Additionally, plea agreements require judicial approval to ensure fair administration of justice.

Embezzlement

Generally, to secure a conviction for embezzlement, prosecutors must establish four essential elements: (1) the existence of a trust or fiduciary relationship between the defendant and the victim; (2) the property came into the defendant's possession by virtue of their employment or position; (3) the defendant fraudulently converted the property for their own use; and (4) the defendant acted with specific intent to deprive the owner of the property's use, either permanently or temporarily.[25]

Defendants facing embezzlement charges usually assert various defenses. A typical defense is a lack of intent on the part of the defendant, more specifically that the defendant lacked the requisite knowledge and willful purpose to commit the crime, usually by claiming the appropriation of the property was a mistake or a misunderstanding. Alternatively or in addition, the defendant may claim as a defense that he had actual consent or authorization from the property owner to use the funds in the manner alleged. Other frequent defenses challenge the sufficiency of the prosecution's evidence or assert that the defendant acted under duress or coercion from third parties. Notably, the defendant's intent to return or restore the property is not a defense to the crime of embezzlement.

Like many white collar cases, embezzlement cases present significant opportunities for plea bargaining, because they are often complicated and documentary evidence alone is generally not as engaging for a jury as live witnesses. Even if documentary evidence is strong, prosecutors often prefer to have live witnesses describe the crime, and thus may enter into pleas in exchange for testimony. Furthermore, prosecutors often lack evidence and need testimony from lower-level participants to pursue higher-ranking participants, making plea agreements with lower-level participants especially appealing to prosecutors to ensure conviction of higher-ranking high profile participants. However, plea bargains may fail when defendants refuse to testify against their fellow alleged participants for fear of their own safety. Also, prosecutors may be reluctant to offer a plea deal in cases where the evidence would most likely lead to convictions for all of the wrongdoers.

PROBLEM 9-3 is a plea bargaining problem between a prosecutor and one of the defendants in an embezzlement case. You will play the role of either the prosecutor or the attorney for the defendant.

PROBLEM 9-3: PLEA BARGAINING IN AN EMBEZZLEMENT CASE

GENERAL INFORMATION: *For purposes of this plea bargaining problem use the current laws for embezzlement in the state where you reside.*

Xander Franklin, a 28-year-old junior accountant at Coast Shipping, stands accused of felony embezzlement, along with fellow employees Malia Fisher and Peter Crane. Franklin is represented by Attorney Klein. Coast Shipping is a supply chain management company specializing in domestic shipping, warehousing, and freight solutions. The company arranges transportation for a wide variety of cargo, including perishable and hazardous materials, and serves clients ranging from manufacturers and importers/exporters to retailers and distributors.

Over the course of sixteen months, Franklin allegedly participated in an elaborate scheme that siphoned a total of $550,000 from his employer. The prosecution, led by Kendra Matluck, asserts that Franklin was not the mastermind but was recruited by two senior employees, Malia Fisher, who was the company's Chief Financial Officer, and Peter Crane, the company's former Payroll Manager. According to the prosecution's theory, Fisher and Crane created shell companies with names nearly identical to legitimate vendors, such as "WW Shipping" rather than the actual "WWW Shipping." Payments meant for legitimate business partners were instead diverted to accounts controlled by Fisher and Crane. They carefully timed and staggered fraudulent payments so that they did not immediately disrupt the company's ability to pay actual vendors. Invoices from the actual companies were still processed and paid, but they would insert fake invoices into the payment cycle, often inflating the total disbursements for a given period. Sometimes, the shell companies would even mimic the invoice numbers and payment schedules of real vendors, making detection more difficult.

Franklin's specific role allegedly involved approving fraudulent invoices and making ledger changes to conceal the discrepancies, thereby enabling their conduct to continue undetected. Franklin has no prior criminal record and claims any involvement by him was under duress. He has turned over to the prosecutor text messages from Fisher, sent before the embezzlement began, threatening to frame Franklin for unrelated financial discrepancies and have him fired if he refused to participate. Franklin has also stated that his motive was to help his mother, who suffers from a terminal illness, and had lost her health insurance. She was unable to work, leaving Franklin as her financial provider and caregiver. The prosecution has traced $125,000 of the embezzled funds to Franklin, and Franklin has produced bank records and medical bills to show that $110,000 of the embezzled funds went directly to pay for his mother's expenses, treatments, and care. The prosecution has of yet been unable to trace the rest of the embezzled funds as evidence suggests that Fisher and Crane kept the remaining money and moved the stolen funds into offshore accounts in Grand Cayman, making asset recovery difficult to trace.

Prosecutor Matluck decided to initiate plea bargaining with Franklin. Her initial offer was to reduce Franklin's embezzlement felony charge to a misdemeanor if Franklin pleads guilty, pays full restitution of $550,000, and agrees to testify at trial against Fisher and Crane. The offer includes 12 months of probation, 400 hours of community service, and no jail time. Attorney Klein, however, argues that Franklin is financially unable to make full restitution and that he should not be held responsible for the entire $550,000 of the embezzled funds, since he only obtained $125,000 and the remainder was retained by Fisher and Crane. Klein also insists that Franklin's participation was under duress. Franklin's primary concern is continuing to work to financially support his terminally ill mother and making him perform 400 hours of community service would not allow him time to earn enough money for her care. Since fired from his job at Coast, he has taken multiple odd jobs to earn money to care for his mother. Further, Franklin refuses to testify against Fisher and Crane for fear of retaliation.

Prosecutor Matluck's case against Franklin is strong. She has evidence of digital audit trails that tie Franklin's login credentials to nearly 80% of the fraudulent transactions. These records show Franklin's involvement in approving fake invoices and overriding system alerts that flagged duplicate vendor names and paved the way for payments to the shell companies. However, the fact that nearly all his embezzled money went for his mother's care, while not a legal defense, humanizes Franklin and is likely to garner much sympathy from the jury.

Although Matluck has a solid case against Franklin, her case against Fisher and Crane is weaker. Matluck is under pressure to secure convictions against them as they are the true ringleaders, as their status in the company allowed them to control and manipulate company protocols and pressure subordinates, including Franklin, to carry out their illegal plan. Further, they profited most from the embezzlement. Other employees have agreed to testify that Fisher allegedly pressured them to pre-sign blank authorization forms, bypassing the company's dual-signature requirement for payments over $10,000. Despite this evidence, Matluck believes Franklin's testimony against Crane and Fisher at trial would provide much needed additional evidence and help secure their convictions.

Negotiations have become deadlocked. Prosecutor Matluck still insists Franklin pay the full $550,000 as restitution to satisfy the company's demands and send a message to the public as an example. Attorney Klein continues to argue that Franklin should only be responsible for the $125,000 he personally retained, with Fisher and Crane liable for the rest. Also, considering Franklin's dire financial situation, Klien has conveyed to the prosecutor that the agreement would need to include a repayment plan over many years. Franklin is also unwilling to testify publicly against his co-conspirators. However, he has offered to try to obtain records that could help prosecutors trace the stolen funds, which is appealing to Matluck, as she knows with Fisher and Crane's assets hidden offshore, the likelihood of recovering the full amount is slim without more evidence.

Franklin's situation with caring for his mother also makes this plea bargain more difficult. Since his mother has less than a year to live, Franklin's ability to care for her is a priority. The defense is pushing for probation terms that would exempt or defer him from community service so that he can earn money to support her care. Matluck, aware of the public and internal pressure to resolve the high-profile case quickly, is considering allowing Franklin to postpone his community service for two years and is offering a reduced restitution if Franklin's cooperation leads to the recovery of a significant amount of the stolen funds. Nonetheless, both sides recognize the risks. Franklin faces the possibility of a felony conviction and prison time if the case goes to trial, while the prosecution risks losing a conviction against Crane and Fisher if Franklin refuses to cooperate in any way. In this plea bargaining session, both attorneys will attempt to seek a balance between Franklin's restitution, cooperation against his co-defendants, and Matluck's probationary and other terms.

CONFIDENTIAL INFORMATION

Before beginning the plea bargaining session, Prosecutor Matluck and Attorney Klein should each prepare a Tactical Planning Worksheet (found in Appendix A). Each party's Tactical Planning Worksheet is to be kept confidential. This information should not be shared with the other party prior to the negotiation.

For purposes of this problem, your planning worksheet should include your confidential bargaining position for either Prosecutor Matlock or Attorney Klein on the following issues:

A) the amount of restitution, if any, to be paid by Franklin.

B) the probationary terms of the plea agreement, and

C) the parameters of Franklin's cooperation on the issues of testifying and providing evidence against Fisher and Crane.

TACTICAL PLANNING WORKSHEET REVEAL

After concluding the plea bargaining session, you and your counterpart should exchange your individual Tactical Planning Worksheets so that you both can see the bargaining positions you had planned to use during the session. You should compare the two worksheets and see how far apart you were initially. Also, you should analyze whether and why you strayed from your worksheet, especially in the areas of offers and counteroffers. What positive aspects from your counterpart's worksheet do you wish you had included in yours?

POST-NEGOTIATION SELF-REFLECTION WORKSHEET

At the conclusion of the reveal session for this problem, be sure to complete the Post-Negotiation Self-Reflection Worksheet (found in Appendix B). Your Post-Negotiation Self-Reflection Worksheet should be completed individually and optimally within a short period of time after the Tactical Planning Worksheet reveal, while the plea bargaining session is fresh in your mind.

CHAPTER 10

Conclusion

Now that you have learned to apply the TABLE method to negotiate a variety of practice problems, you are ready to tackle some real negotiations. Here are some of our final thoughts.

First, whether you are negotiating in the boardroom or the living room, remember always to be professional and courteous. In the heat of a negotiation, we often lose sight of niceties and resort to anger and personal attacks, especially when we feel cornered. While anger may initially work for you in some instances and get you a quick concession, this bullying tactic, in the long run, will not be effective. Those negotiating with you will soon come to know your reputation as a bully and will either respond similarly or just choose not to negotiate with you at all.

Second, be willing to make concessions. A good deal does not mean you get everything you want. In a true negotiation, you make concessions and counteroffers and arrive at a mutually beneficial resolution. If you truly are not willing to give up anything, you are not negotiating, you are demanding. You do not need to wait until you are sitting down to negotiate to realize you are not willing to give up anything. If you cannot list what you will concede, then you are not invested in negotiating. In that case, realize that you have, in effect, chosen your alternative (BATNA) instead of negotiating for something better.

Third, understand that the term "discuss" often means negotiate. We used the word discuss in many of our problems because, especially in arms-open negotiations, people often say they want to discuss something with you. For example, "I'd like to discuss our living arrangements," or "I'd like to discuss our finances," or I'd like to discuss selling our family business." These statements are really invitations to negotiations. Therefore, you should be prepared for the opportunity to make a deal. Take the offer to "discuss" and head to the negotiating table.

Fourth, remember that planning is key. You should always plan for a negotiation. Whether you have ten minutes or ten days, have a plan before you start a negotiation. If you have time, use the Tactical Planning Worksheet and map out your negotiation strategy. However, if time is short, you should at least plan your optimal realistic goal, your minimal acceptable level, and analyze your alternatives. You should also write these down, or at least text them to yourself so you can refer to them during the negotiation.

Fifth, recognize that artificial intelligence (AI) can be a useful tool in preparing for negotiations and assisting during negotiations. AI tools can find and analyze relevant market information, historical contract data, and even help you role-play for an upcoming negotiation. However, it is crucial not to delegate your preparation to AI and overly rely on its results. AI-generated information must always be thoroughly fact-checked and verified with trusted sources. While AI can enhance your preparation and performance in negotiations, human judgment remains the essential component for successful outcomes.

Sixth, make sure your decision to accept a final offer is based on the offer itself and not on extraneous factors. For example, you may be feeling tired and just want to be done with the negotiation, or feeling angry and not want to meet ever again with the other side, or you may want to go on vacation next month instead of going to trial if the case does not settle. If you make a decision based on these reasons instead of purely based on the benefits of the offer, you may regret that you did not make the best decision for yourself and, if you are an attorney representing a client, you may not have made a decision in your client's best interest and could face legal or professional ramifications. Therefore, before accepting a final offer to settle, take a minute and honestly assess whether you are experiencing any extraneous emotions. This self-check can prevent regrettable outcomes and help ensure you are making decisions based on the facts in front of you.

Finally, remember that if you are an ethical and egalitarian negotiator, you will be more successful and will be welcome to sit at any negotiating table.

Appendices

APPENDIX A

Tactical Planning Worksheet

1. Identify the Relationship

   Describe whether your relationship with the other side is arms-open or arms-length.

2. Conducting Research

   A. List the research you plan to use as objective criteria to support your goals.

   B. List the important facts you plan to rely on to support your goals.

3. Optimal Realistic Goals and Minimum Acceptable Level

   A. What are your optimal realistic goal(s)?

   B. What is your minimum acceptable level?

   C. What do you think is the other side's optimal, realistic goal(s) and minimum acceptable level?

4. Alternative Options If Negotiation Fails

   A. What is your best alternative(s) if there is no agreement (BATNA)?

   B. What do you think is the other side's best alternative(s) if there is no agreement (BATNA)?

5. Opening Offers, Concessions, and Counteroffers

   A. What is your opening offer? Does it match your optimal realistic goal?

   B. What concessions are you willing to make? In what order will you make these concessions?

   C. List a minimum of three anticipated offers you intend to make after your opening offer. Explain why you would make these offers. Your last offer should be your minimum acceptable level.

6. Questions and Anticipated Responses to Questions
    A. What information do you wish to obtain from the other side?
    B. List the questions you plan to ask the other side to obtain this information.
    C. What questions do you anticipate you may be asked by the other side?
    D. How do you plan to respond to questions you may be asked? What information do you not want to reveal (*e.g.*, confidential)? Why? What diversionary responses will you give if asked these questions?

APPENDIX A-1

Multi-party Tactical Planning Worksheet

1. Identify the Relationship

   Describe whether your relationship with the other side is arms-open or arms-length. Consider how these relationships might differ among the various parties and how this may affect the negotiation dynamics.

2. Conducting Research

   A. List the research you plan to use as objective criteria to support your goals.

   B. List the important facts you plan to rely on to support your goals. Note how these facts might have different significance to different parties.

3. Identifying and Forming Alliances

   A. Identify the primary interests of all parties involved in the negotiation.

   B. Which parties have interests that likely align most closely with yours?

   C. Would your party benefit from forming an alliance with one of these parties? Why might an alliance be beneficial or harmful in reaching an agreement?

   D. What might be the benefits and drawbacks of remaining independent versus forming an alliance?

   E. How will you prevent or respond to alliances that form against your interests?

4. Optimal Realistic Goals and Minimum Acceptable Level

   A. What are your optimal realistic goal(s)?

   B. What is your minimum acceptable level?

   C. What do you think are each of the other parties' optimal, realistic goal(s) and minimum acceptable levels?

5. Alternative Options If Negotiation Fails

   A. What is your best alternative(s) if there is no agreement (BATNA)?

   B. What do you think are each of the other parties' best alternative(s) if there is no agreement (BATNA)? How might the BATNAs of other parties strengthen or weaken potential coalitions?

6. Opening Offers, Concessions, and Counteroffers

   A. What is your opening offer? Does it match your optimal realistic goal? Consider how your opening offer might position you with each of the other parties.

   B. What concessions are you willing to make? In what order will you make these concessions? Consider how concessions to one party might affect your relationships with other parties.

   C. List a minimum of three anticipated offers you intend to make after your opening offer. Explain why you would make these offers and how they might appeal differently to different parties. Your last offer should be your minimum acceptable level.

7. Questions and Anticipated Responses to Questions

   A. What information do you wish to obtain from each of the other parties?

   B. List the questions you plan to ask each party to obtain this information.

   C. What questions do you anticipate you may be asked by each of the other parties?

   D. How do you plan to respond to questions you may be asked, considering that your answers may be heard by all parties? What information do you not want to reveal (*e.g.* confidential)? Why? What diversionary responses will you give if asked these questions?

APPENDIX B

Post-Negotiation Self-Reflection Worksheet

Answer the questions below and provide brief explanations with your answers.

1. Tactical Planning:
   A. What were the strengths and weaknesses of your Tactical Planning Worksheet?
   B. When did you refer to your worksheet during the negotiation?
   C. How would you change your worksheet for future negotiations?
2. Arranging:
   A. Was the forum for your negotiation optimal?
   B. What other forums might have been conducive to this negotiation?
   C. If the negotiation were to continue, would it be beneficial to change forums?
3. Bargaining:
   A. Were your offers, counteroffers, and concessions well-timed and responsive to the other side?
   B. Did you effectively communicate objective criteria to support your offers?
   C. Did you ask the questions you had planned?
   D. Did you respond adequately to questions you were asked?
   E. Were there any tricks or tactics used by the other side? If so, how did you respond?
4. Letting Go or Resolving:
   A. If you did not reach an agreement, what were the main reasons for not resolving the matter? What might you have done differently to reach an agreement?
   B. If you did reach an agreement, do you believe the agreement was fair from

everyone's perspective? Did you memorialize key provisions of the agreement before leaving the negotiating table? Did you determine if you or the other side will prepare the initial draft of the agreement? Did you and the other side agree on a time schedule for completion of the agreement?

5. Ethics and Equity:
   A. Were there any ethical issues that arose during the negotiation? If so, how did you respond to those issues?
   B. Were you treated equitably by the other side? If not, how did you handle the situation?

Notes

Chapter 2

1. Charles B. Craver, Effective Legal Negotiation and Settlement §2.02 (8th Ed. 2016).
2. *See id.* §2.02(1).
3. *Id.* §2.02(2)(d).
4. *Id.* at 258.
5. *See* Roger Fisher & William Ury, *Getting to Yes: Negotiating Agreements Without Giving In*, 43 2d Ed. 1991).
6. *Talent Representation Agreements & Legal Considerations*, Justia (July 2023), http://www.justia.com/entertainment-law/talent-representation-agreements/.
7. *See* Bob Gibson, *What Are the Best Negotiation Strategies?*, Vistage (Oct. 2023), http://www.vistage.com/research-center/business-growth-strategy/six-successful-strategies-for-negotiation/.
8. *See* Pon Staff, *How to Avoid the Negative Impact of Goal Setting: Setting Realisitc Objectives in Negotiations*, Daily Blog (June 27, 2016), http://www.pon.harvard.edu/daily/negotiation-skills-daily/how-to-avoid-the-negative-impact-of-goal-setting-setting-realistic-objectives-in-negotiations/.
9. *See id.*
10. Michael Corkery, *Wells Fargo Fined $185 Million for Fraudulently Opening Accounts*, The NY Times (Sept. 8, 2016), http://www.nytimes.com/2016/09/09/business/dealbook/wells-fargo-fined-for-years-of-harm-to-customers.html
11. *See What is a BATNA?*, The Program on Negot., http://www.pon.harvard.edu/about/welcome/ (last visited June 21, 2024).
12. *See* G. Richard Shell, Bargaining for Advantage: Negotiation Strategies for Reasonable People, 30 (Penguin, Second Edition 2006).
13. *Id.*
14. Hugging Face, HUGGING FACE, https://huggingface.co (last visited Apr. 8, 2025).
15. *See* Pon Staff, *Ask Better Negotiation Questions*, Daily Blog (June 20, 2024), http://www.pon.harvard.edu/daily/negotiation-skills-daily/ask-better-questions-in-negotiation-nb/.
16. *See* Model Rules of Pro. Conduct r. 1.6 (Am. Bar Ass'n 2024).
17. *See id.*

18. *See* Karen Wells Roby, *Ethics in Settlement: The Effect of Material Misrepresentation*, Fed. Bar Ass'n (Aug. 2012*)*, http://www.fedbar.org/Resources_1/Federal-Lawyer-Magazine/2012/August/Features/Ethics-in-Settlement-The-Effects-of-Material-Misrepresentation.aspx?FT=.pdf.
19. *See generally* Douglas Richmond, *Lawyer's Professional Responsibilities and Liabilities in Negotiations*, 22 Geo. J. Legal Ethics 249, 262 (2009).

Chapter 3

1. Pon Staff, *Why First Impressions Matter in Negotiation*, Daily Blog (Jan. 3, 2023), http://www.pon.harvard.edu/daily/negotiation-skills-daily/why-first-impressions-matter/.
2. *Id.*
3. *See* Lynn A. Epstein, *Cyber E-Mail Negotiation vs. Traditional Negotiation: Will Cyber Technology Supplant Traditional Means of Settling Litigation,* 36 Tulsa L.J. 839, 845 (Summer 2001).
4. *See* Pon Staff, *Using Body Language in Negotiation*, Daily Blog (May 30, 2024), http://www.pon.harvard.edu/daily/negotiation-skills-daily/negotiation-techniques-and-body-language-body-language-negotiation-examples-in-real-life/.
5. Zhaleh Semnani-Azad & Wendi L. Adair, *Nonverbal Cues Associated with Negotiation "Styles" across Cultures*, presented at the 2011 International Association for Conflict Management Conference, Istanbul (June 2011), available at Strategy+Business, https://www.strategy-business.com/article/re00159.
6. Max H. Bazerman, *Negotiation: The Game Has Changed* 119 (Princeton Univ. Press 2025).
7. *Id.*
8. *See e.g.*, Samantha Whitehorne, *When Face-to-Face Falls Short*, AssociationsNow.com (April 19, 2013), https://associationsnow.com/2013/04/when-face-to-face-falls-short/.
9. Gabriella Ziccarelli & Eric Goldman, *How a Chipmunk Emoji Cost an Israeli Texter $2,200*, Tech. & Mktg. L. Blog (May 25, 2017), http://blog.ericgoldman.org/archives/2017/05/how-a-chipmunk-emoji-cost-an-israeli-texter-2200.htm.
10. Carolyn Thompson, *Police Add Texting to Crisis Negotiation Arsenal*, The Associated Press (May 11, 2014), http://apnews.com/general-news-989aa06f08434fec906b879bc827655b.

Chapter 4

1. Katie Shonk, *Negotiation Advice: When to Make the First Offer in Negotiation*, Daily Blog (May 27, 2024), http://www.pon.harvard.edu/daily/negotiation-skills-daily/when-to-make-the-first-offer-in-negotiation/.
2. Katie Shonk, *What is Anchoring in Negotiation?*, Daily Blog (Feb. 6, 2024), http://www.pon.harvard.edu/daily/negotiation-skills-daily/what-is-anchoring-in-negotiation/.
3. *Id.*

4. *See generally*, Greg Northcraft & Margaret Neale, *Experts, Amateurs, and Real Estate: An Anchoring-and Adjustment Perspective on Property Pricing Decisions*, 39 ORGANIZATIONAL BEHAVIOR AND HUMAN DECISION PROCESSES 84, 94–96 (1986).
5. Pon Staff, *The Anchoring Effect and How it Can Impact Your Negotiation*, DAILY BLOG (Mar. 12, 2024), http://www.pon.harvard.edu/daily/negotiation-skills-daily/the-drawbacks-of-goals/.
6. Barrie Blake-Coleman, *The Man Who Lit Up the World*, IVENTRICITY.COM, http://www.inventricity.com/edison-the-man-who-lit-up-the-world-1 (last visited June 5, 2024).
7. Katie Shonk, *Principled Negotiation: Focus on Interests to Create Value*, DAILY BLOG (June 4, 2024), http://www.pon.harvard.edu/daily/negotiation-skills-daily/principled-negotiation-focus-interests-create-value/.
8. *See* Richard G. Halpern, *Negotiation Bracketing: How to Use It and When to Avoid It*, NEGOT. EXPERTS, http://www.negotiations.com/articles/negotiation-blunder/ (last visited June 8, 2024).
9. *See* Pon Staff, *Four Strategies for Making Concessions in Negotiation*, DAILY BLOG (May 20, 2024), http//www.pon.harvard.edu/daily/negotiation-skills-daily/four-strategies-for-making-concessions/.
10. *See id.*
11. Pon Staff, *Negotiating Tips: Listening Skills for Dealing with Difficult People*, DAILY BLOG (Feb. 19, 2024), http://www.pon.harvard.edu/daily/dealing-with-difficult-people-daily/negotiation-tips-listening-skills-for-dealing-with-difficult-people/.
12. *What are Negotiation Tactics*, THE PROGRAM ON NEGOT., http://www.pon.harvard.edu/tag/negotiation-tactics/ (last visited June 8, 2024).
13. *See* Gerben A. Van Kleef, Carsten De Dreu & Anthony Manstead, *The Interpersonal Effects of Emotions in Negotiations: A Motivated Information Processing Approach*, 87 J. PERSONALITY & SOC. PSYCH. 510 (2004).

Chapter 5

1. *See* Pon Staff, *Asking Better Negotiation Questions*, DAILY BLOG (Feb. 19, 2023), http://www.pon.harvard.edu/daily/negotiation-skills-daily/ask-better-questions-in-negotiation-nb/.
2. *See* Matt Gavin, *Business Insights*, HARV. BUS. SCH. (May 18, 2023), http://online.hbs.edu/blog/post/emotion-in-business-negotiation.
3. Kwame Christian, *Splitting the Difference In Negotiation: A Double-Edged Sword*, FORBES (Mar. 26, 2023), http://www.forbes.com/sites/kwamechristian/2023/03/26/splitting-the-difference-in-negotiation-a-double-edged-sword/?sh=279252352db5.
4. *See* Roger Dawson, *Why It's a Mistake to Offer to Split the Difference*, REICLUB, http://www.reiclub.com/articles/mistake-split-difference (last visited June 5, 2024).
5. *See generally* Pon Staff, The Right Negotiation Environment: Your Place or Mine?, DAILY BLOG (Apr. 25, 2024), http://www.pon.harvard.edu/daily/negotiation-skills-daily/your-place-or-mine/.

6. *See* Clay Halton, *Oral Contract: Definition, Example, How to Prove and Enforce*, Investopedia (May 31, 2024), http://www.investopedia.com/terms/o/oral-contract.asp.
7. *See* Katie Shonk, *In Contract Negotiations, Agree on How You'll Disagree*, Daily Blog (May 30, 2024), http://www.pon.harvard.edu/daily/dispute-resolution/in-contract-negotiations-agree-on-how-youll-disagree/.
8. *See id.*

Chapter 6

1. *See* Roy J. Lewicki & Robert J. Robinson, *Ethical and Unethical Bargaining Tactics: An Empirical Study*, 17 J. of Bus. Ethics 665, 666 (1998).
2. Model Rules of Professional Conduct r. 4.1. (Am. Bar Ass'n 2025).
3. *Id.* at cmt 2.
4. *Id.*
5. *See* James K.L. Lawrence, *Lying, Misrepresentation, Puffing, and Bluffing: Legal Ethical and Professional Standards for Negotiators and Mediation Advocates*, 29 Ohio State J. on Disp. Resol. 35, 36 (2014).
6. *Id.* at 37.
7. *See id.*
8. Leigh Thompson, *Negotiation Tips: Lies, Damned Lies, and Negotiations*, Northwestern Kellog, http://www.kellogg.northwestern.edu/news_articles/2014/05122014-negotiation_lies.aspx (last visited May 24, 2024).
9. *See* G. Richard Shell, *When Is It Legal to Lie in Negotiations?* MIT Sloan Management Rev. (April 15, 1991), https://sloanreview.mit.edu/article/when-is-it-legal-to-lie-in-negotiations/.
10. *See id.*
11. Shell *supra* note 9.
12. John Duffley, *Rethinking How Investigators Detect Lies and Deceit*, Fraud Conf. News (June 12, 2023), http://www.fraudconferencenews.com/home/dr-david-lieberman-rethinking-how-investigators-detect-lies-and-deceit.
13. *See id.*
14. *See* Brianna Steinhilber, *How to Tell If Someone Is Lying to You, According to Behavioral Experts*, NBC News (Aug. 15 2017), http://www.nbcnews.com/better/health/how-tell-if-someone-lying-according-behavioral-experts-ncna786326.
15. Kelly Capatosto, *et al,, State of the Science: Implicit Bias Review 2016,* Candid (July 13, 2016), http://search.issuelab.org/resource/state-of-the-science-implicit-bias-review-2016.html.
16. L. Song Richardson and Nicole Van Cleve, *Systemic Triage: Implicit Racial Bias in the Criminal Courtroom Crook County: Racism and Injustice in America's Largest Criminal Court*, 126 Yale L.J. 862, 865 (2017).
17. *See e.g.*, L. Song Richardson, *Arrest Efficiency and the Fourth Amendment*, 95 Minn. L. Rev. 2035 (2011).
18. *See generally* Ian Ayres, *Fair Driving: Gender and Race Discrimination in Retail Car Negotiations*, 104 Harv. L. Rev. 817, 856 (1991); Ian Ayres and Peter Siegelman,

Race and Gender Discrimination in Bargaining for a New Car, 85 Econ. Rev. 304, 312–13 (1995) (Demonstrating how Professor Ayers' studies on racial and gender bias found overwhelming evidence that in a variety of markets—retail car sales, bail bonding, and kidney transplantation – racial minorities are consistently at a disadvantage).

19. *See generally* Michael Z. Green, *Negotiating While Black* 17 Texas A&M Univ. School of L., *Legal Studies Research Paper* available at https://papers.ssrn.com/sol3/papers.cfm?abstract_id=2694160.
20. *See generally* Hernandez, Morela & Derek R. Avery, *Getting the Short End of the Stick: Racial Bias in Salary Negotiations*, MIT Sloan Management Rev., (June 15, 2016), sloanreview.mit.edu/article/getting-the-short-end-of-the-stick-racial-bias-in-salary-negotiations.
21. *See* Turetsky, *et al.*, *Explaining the Gender Gap in Negotiation Performance: Social Network Ties Outweigh Internal Barriers,* 79 J. Soc. Issues, 50, 54–55 (2023).
22. *See general* Linda Babcock, Hannah Riley Bowles, & Lei Lai , *Social Incentives For Gender Differences In The Propensity To Initiate Negotiations: Sometimes It Does Hurt To Ask*, Organizational Behavior and Human Decision Processes 84 (Jun. 25, 2005), *available at* https://wappp.hks.harvard.edu/files/wappp/files/social_incentives_for_gender_differences_in_the_propensity_to_initiate_negotiations_sometimes_it_does_hurt_to_ask_0.pdf.
23. *See e.g.*, Hannah Bowles, *Psychological Perspectives on Gender in Negotiation.* HKS Faculty Research Working Paper Series RWP12-046, John F. Kennedy Sch. of Government, Harv. Univ. (2012), https://dash.harvard.edu/bitstream/handle/1/9830358/RWP12-046_Bowles.pdf?sequence=1 (Referencing studies by Rubin and Brown 1975). *See also*, Mary Sharp Emerson, *Women Negotiation Skills: How Women Can Get What They Want in Negotiation*, Pro. & Exec. Dev. Blog (July 28, 2022), http://professional.dce.harvard.edu/blog/women-negotiation-skills-how-women-can-get-what-they-want-in-a-negotiation/.
24. *See* Art Hinshaw & Jess K. Alberts, *Gender and Attorney Negotiation Ethics*, 39 Wash. U. J. L. & Pol'y 145 (2012), http:// openscholarship.wustl.edu/ law_journal_law_policy/ vol39/ iss1/ 6.
25. *Id.* At 146.
26. *Id.*
27. Jens Mazei, *et al. A Meta-Analysis on Gender Differences in Negotiation Outcomes and Their Moderators*, 141 Psych. Bull. 94, 95 (2014), http://www.apa.org/pubs/journals/releases/bul-a0038184.pdf.
28. *Id.*
29. *Id. See generally,* Ashleigh Shelby Rosette, *When Women May Be Better Negotiators Than Men*, Duke Univ. Sch. of Bus. (Nov. 8, 2023), http://www.fuqua.duke.edu/duke-fuqua-insights/when-women-may-be-better-negotiators-men.
30. *See* Leslie Cooney, *Surfing to Success as a Mindful Negotiator*, 17 Pepperdine Dispute Resolution L. J. (2017), available at https://nsuworks.nova.edu/law_facarticles/327. See also, Kaitlyn M. Murphy, *Using Meditation Techniques to Succeed During Stressful Negotiations*, Am. Bar Ass'n. (Sept. 8 2016), *available at* http://apps.americanbar.org/litigation/committees/womanadvocate/articles/summer2016-0916-using-mediation-techniques-succeed-during-stressful-negotiations.html.

31. ABA Comm. on Ethics & Prof'l Responsibility, Formal Op. 512 (2024).
32. *See* Heidi Grant, *A Second Chance to Make the Right Impression*, HARV. BUS. REV. (Jan. 2015), *available at* https://hbr.org/2015/01/a-second-chance-to-make-the-right-impression.

Chapter 7

1. 42 U.S.C. § 2000e-2(e) (2024).
2. Lilly Ledbetter Fair Pay Act of 2009, Pub. L. No. 111-2, 123 Stat. 5 (2009).
3. 490 U.S. 228, 251–253 (1989).
4. *See Zarda v. Altitude Express, Inc.*, 883 F.3d 100, 132 (2d Cir. 2018) (holding that plaintiffs are "entitled to bring a Title VII claim for discrimination based on sexual orientation") and *See Hively v. Ivy Tech Cmty. College*, 853 F.3d 339, 351–52 (7th Cir. 2017) (holding that "a person who alleges that she experienced employment discrimination on the basis of her sexual orientation has put forth a case of sex discrimination for Title VII purposes").
5. *Age Discrimination*, U.S DEP'T OF LAB., http://www.dol.gov/general/topic/discrimination/agedisc (last visited June 12, 2025).
6. *Small Business Requirements*, US EQUAL OPPORTUNITY COMM'N., http://www.eeoc.gov/employers/smallbusiness/requirements.cfm (last visited June 12, 2025).
7. *Id.*
8. 29 U.S.C. § 206(d)(1) (2024).
9. *Id.*
10. Iris Hentze and Rebecca Tyus, *Discrimination and Harassment in the Workplace*, NAT'L CONF. OF STATE LEGIS., http://www.ncsl.org/labor-and-employment/discrimination-and-harassment-in-the-workplace (Aug. 12, 2021).
11. *See* ALA. ADMIN. CODE § 25-1-20 (2024).
12. *See* GA. CODE ANN. §34-6a-1 (2024); *but see* GA. CODE ANN. § 31-4-2 (2024); GA. CODE ANN. § 34-5-1 (2024); GA. CODE ANN. § 45-19-20 (2024) (demonstrating how there is no state law prohibiting discrimination of private Georgia employees).
13. CONN. GEN. STAT. ANN. § 46a-60 (2024).
14. *Id.*; CONN. GEN. STAT. ANN. § 21a-408p (2024).
15. OR. REV. STAT. § 659A.001 (2024); OR. REV. STAT. § 174.100 (2024).
16. *See Employment Discrimination Laws*, JUSTIA, https://www.justia.com/employment/employment-laws-50-state-surveys/employment-discrimination-laws-50-state-survey/ (last visited June 12, 2025).
17. Richard Fry & Carolina Aragão, *Gender Pay Gap in U.S. Has Narrowed Slightly Over 2 Decades*, Pew Research Center (June 10, 2025), *Gender pay gap remained stable over past 20 years in US*, Pew Research Center.
18. *Institute for Women's Policy Research, National Gender Wage Gap Widens Significantly in 2023 for the First Time in 20 Years (Sept. 12, 2024)*, https://iwpr.org/national-gender-wage-gap-widens-significantly-in-2023-for-the-first-time-in-20-years/
19. *Id.*

20. *Anwesha Majumder & Jessica Mason, The Wage Gap #IRL (In Real Life) for Women of Color(Nat'l P'ship for Women & Families, Mar. 2025),* https://nationalpartnership.org/wp-content/uploads/2023/02/quantifying-americas-gender-wage-gap.pdf.
21. Elise Gould & Katherine deCourcy, Gender Pay Gap Hits Historic Low in 2024—But Remains Too Large, Econ. Pol'y Inst. Blog (Mar. 25, 2025), https://www.epi.org/blog/gender-pay-gap-2024/.
22. *Id.*
23. Seth Rosenberg, Washington State Greatly Expands Equal Pay Protections on July 1, 2025, Seattle Litig. Grp. (Dec. 9, 2024), https://www.seattlelitigation.com/blogs/washington-state-greatly-expands-equal-pay-protections-on-july-1-2025.
24. Diana J. Nehro, *Puerto Rico Equal Pay Act Aims to Close Gener Pay Gap*, OGLETREE DEAKINS (Mar. 20, 2017), http://ogletree.com/insights-resources/blog-posts/puerto-rico-equal-pay-act-aims-to-close-gender-pay-gap/.
25. Puerto Rico Enacts Equal Pay Law, Prohibits Employers from Inquiring about Past Salary History, PAY EQUITY ADVISOR BLOG.
26. https://ago.vermont.gov/sites/ago/files/2024-12/Final%20Version%20of%20H%20704%20Guidance%20(12-31-24).pdf
27. *Id.*
28. Cal.Lab.Code §11975 (West 2024) code §432.3 (West 2024)
29. Duane Morris, *Delaware Enacts Pay History Ban*, SHRM (Jun. 28, 2018), http://www.shrm.org/topics-tools/employment-law-compliance/delaware-enacts-pay-history-ban.
30. *Introduction to the Basics of the Massachusetts Equal Pay Act*, MASS.GOV, http://www.mass.gov/info-details/introduction-to-the-basics-of-the-massachusetts-equal-pay-act (last visited May 21, 2024).
31. *Equal Pay Law,* OR. BUREAU OF LAB. & INDUS., http://www.oregon.gov/boli/TA/Pages/Equal%20Pay%20Law.aspx (last visited May 21, 2024).
32. *Asking About Salary History During the Hiring Process Is Illegal in NYC*, N.Y.C. COMM'N ON HUM. RTS., http://www1.nyc.gov/assets/cchr/downloads/pdf/materials/SalaryHistory_KYO.pdf (last visited May 21, 2024).
33. Joseph N. DiStefano, *Court: Philly Salary-History Ban Violates Free Speech, But Firms Can't Use Data to Underpay*, THE PHILA. INQUIRER (May 1, 2018), http://www.inquirer.com/philly/blogs/inq-phillydeals/phillys-job-applicant-salary-history-ban-federal-judge-20180501.html .
34. *Conversation Starter: More Than Half of Professionals Did Not Negotiate Salary for Most Recent Job*, GLASSDOOR (Sept. 19, 2023) http://www.glassdoor.com/research/conversation-starter-more-than-half-of-professionals-did-not-negotiate-salary-for-most-recent-job.
35. *See 10 Salary Negotiation Strategies for Employers*, INDEED FOR EMP., http://www.indeed.com/hire/c/info/employer-salary-negotiation-tactics (last visited May 23, 2024); *10 Salary Negotiation Strategies for Employers*, FACTOHR HR SOL. FOR GROWTH, http://factohr.com/salary-negotiation-strategies-for-employers/.
36. *See Career Planning*, THE FARWELLGRP., INC., http://www.farwellgroup.com/services-career-salary-negotiation.asp.

37. *Supporting Market Accountability, Workplace Equity, and Fair Competition by Reining in Non-Disclosure Agreements*, Federation of American Scientists (Mar. 2024), https://fas.org/publication/supporting-market-accountability-workplace-equity-and-fair-competition-by-reining-in-non-disclosure-agreements/.
38. 18 U.S.C. § 1839(3) (2024).
39. *Speak Out Act & FTC Ban: Exploring Work Agreements in 2024*, Tulane University Online (Aug. 2024), https://online.law.tulane.edu/blog/speak-out-act-and-non-disclosure-agreements.
40. *See, Caudill Seed & Warehouse Co. v. Jarrow Formulas, Inc.*, 53 F.4th 368, 380–81 (6th Cir. 2022).
41. *Zenimax Media Inc et al v. Oculus VR Inc et al*, No. 3:2014cv01849 - Document 1117 (N.D. Tex. 2018).
42. Alexandria Sage, Dan Levine & Heather Somerville, *Waymo Accepts $245 Million and Uber's 'Regret' to Settle Self-Driving Car Dispute*, Reuters (Feb. 9, 2018, 8:07 PM), https://www.reuters.com/article/us-alphabet-uber-trial/waymo-accepts-245-million-and-ubers-regret-to-settle-self-driving-car-dispute-idUSKBN1FT2F1.
43. U.S. Small Bus. Admin., Apply for Licenses and Permits, https://www.sba.gov/business-guide/launch-your-business/apply-licenses-permits (last visited May 6, 2025).
44. Apply for an Employer Identification Number (EIN) Online, IRS, https://www.irs.gov/businesses/small-businesses-self-employed/apply-for-an-employer-identification-number-ein-online (last visited May 6, 2025).
45. U.S. Food & Drug Admin., Food Service Establishment Guidelines, https://www.fda.gov/food (last visited May 6, 2025).
46. U.S. Food & Drug Admin., Food Service Establishment Guidelines, https://www.fda.gov/food (last visited May 6, 2025).
47. Int'l Code Council, Certificate of Occupancy Guidelines, https://www.iccsafe.org (last visited May 6, 2025).
48. *See, e.g.*, Cal. Dep't of Tax & Fee Admin., Seller's Permit Requirements, https://www.cdtfa.ca.gov/services/#Register-Renewals (last visited May 6, 2025).
49. U.S. Small Bus. Admin., Apply for Licenses and Permits, https://www.sba.gov/business-guide/launch/apply-licenses-permits (last visited May 6, 2025).
50. Food Safety Modernization Act (FSMA), 21 U.S.C. § 2201 et seq. (2011).
51. Cal. Assemb. B. 418, 2023–2024 Reg. Sess. (Cal. 2024) (to be codified at Cal. Health & Safety Code §§ 110423–110424)
52. Fla. Dep't of Bus. & Prof'l Regulation, Division of Hotels and Restaurants Licensing Portal, https://www.myfloridalicense.com/dbpr/hr/ (last visited May 6, 2025).
53. Md. State Dep't of Assessments & Taxation, Business Licensing Resources, https://dat.maryland.gov (last visited May 6, 2025).
54. Foundation for Community Association Research, 2023–2024 U.S. National and State Statistical Review (2024), https://foundation.caionline.org/publications/factbook/statistical-review/.
55. See *Restatement (Third) of Property: Servitudes* § 6.19 (Am. Law Inst. 2000) ("Common-interest communities commonly require that all owners within the community be

members of the association and that the obligations of membership be binding on successors.")

56. James Chen, *What Is a Homeowners Association (HOA), and How Does It Work?*, Investopedia (July 27, 2024), https://www.investopedia.com/terms/h/homeowners-association-fee-hoa.asp.
57. *Id.*
58. *See* Justia, Homeowners' Association Liens Leading to Foreclosure & Other Legal Concerns, https://www.justia.com/foreclosure/foreclosures-based-on-hoa-liens/ (last visited May 8, 2025)
59. Florida's Homeowners' Association Act, codified in Chapter 720 of the Florida Statutes, provides a comprehensive legal framework governing HOAs, detailing aspects such as governance, member rights, and dispute resolution.
60. 42 U.S.C. §§ 3601–3619.

Chapter 8

1. *See generally* Mary Cushing Doherty & Stephanie M. Shortall, Drafting Prenup Agreements, §X Negotiating Prenuptial Agreements (2d. Aspen Pub. 2017-2 Supplement).
2. *See* Margret Ryznar & Anna Stepien-Sporek, *To Have and to Hold, for Richer or Richer: Premarital Agreements in the Comparative Context*, 13 Chap. L. Rev. 27, 31 (2009).
3. Puerto Rico also uses the community property regime. Alaska has a voluntary (opt-in) system of community property allowing spouses in Alaska to create community property by entering into a community property agreement or by creating a community property trust. See Alaska Stat. §§ 34.77.020–34.77.995.
4. Mark Patton, *Quasi-Community Property in Arizona: Why Just at Divorce and Not Death?*, 47 Ariz. L. Rev. 167, 168 (2005).
5. *See* Kenneth W. Kingma, *Property Division at Divorce or Death for Married Couples Migrating Between Common Law and Community Property States*, 35 ACTEC J. 74 (2009).
6. *See* Steven Sheinwald & Jennifer Kirschenbaum, *Your Medical License as Marital Property*, Kirschenbaum & Kirschenbaum, http://www.kirschenbaumesq.com/article/your-medical-license-as-marital-property-jennifer-kirschenbaum (last visited June 17, 2025) (stating that some states "consider a professional degree or license to be 'marital property,' which upon the dissolution of a marriage would be divisible as property between the parties . . . while "remaining states have recognized a medical license to represent the 'potential for significant future earnings, which cannot be assigned, sold, transferred, conveyed or pledged'").
7. Dawn D. Nichols & Sean K. Ahmed, *Nonmarital Real Estate: Is the Appreciation Marital, Nonmarital or a Combination of Both?* 81 Fla. Bar. J. 75 (2007).
8. *See* Jeff Landers, *Why Divorcing Women Need to Pay Careful Attention to the Date of Separation*, Forbes, (Sep. 28, 2011), http://www.forbes.com/sites/jefflanders/2011/09/28/why-divorcing-women-need-to-pay-careful-attention-to-the-date-of-separation/#5992af03b227; *See also*, Joseph Pandolfi, *Florida Divorce: Dividing Property*,

DivorceNet, http://www.divorcenet.com/resources/divorce/marital-property-division/florida-divorce-dividing-prope (last visited July 29, 2024) (demonstrating that marital property is cut-off in Florida when the couple signs a valid separation agreement, when one of the spouses files for divorce, or another date the spouse chooses in an agreement).

9. *See e.g.*, Cathy Meyer, *What Is Marital Property and How Is It Divided at Divorce?*, Liveabout.com (July 14, 2017).
10. *See generally* Kingma, *supra* note 5.
11. *See* Ryznar *supra* note 2 at 38.
12. Of course, valuing property to divide the community property in half may be quite complex, especially if some of the assets are not easily marketable).
13. *See* Katherine D. Black et. al., *Community Property for Non-Community Property States*, 24 Quinnipiac Prob. L. J. 260, 267 (2011).
14. *Id.* at 264.
15. *See* Kingma, *supra* note 5.
16. *See* LexisNexis, *Classification of Gifts, Inheritance, and Life Insurance in the Context of Divorce*, Lexis Legal Newsroom (Feb. 5, 2009).
17. *See* Margaret Ryznar & Anna Stepien-Sporek, *To Have and to Hold, for Richer or Richer: Premarital Agreements in the Comparative Context*, 13 Chap. L. Rev. 27, 32 (2009).
18. *See generally* Thomas M. Featherston, et. al., *Handbook for Texas Martial Property Law for Estate Administration and Planning*, Baylor Univ. (2016), available at https://www.baylor.edu/law/facultystaff/doc.php/268848.pdf; *See also, Community Property: General Considerations (Portfolio 802)*, http://pro.bloombergtax.com/portfolios/community-property-general-considerations-portfolio-802/ (last visited Aug. 5, 2024).
19. Cynthia Lee Starnes, *One More Time: Alimony, Intuition, and the Remarriage-Termination Rule*, 81 Ind. L.J. 971, 999 (2006).
20. *See* Jeff Landers, *Five Reasons Your Prenup May Be Invalid*, Forbes (Apr. 2, 2013), http://www.forbes.com/sites/jefflanders/2013/04/02/five-reasons-your-prenup-might-be-invalid/#346f9da419a5
21. In some states, an agreement to waive death-type benefits (such as spousal elective share or intestacy) would be valid even without disclosure as long as the agreement, contract, or waiver was executed before marriage. *See, e.g.*, FL Stat. §732.702. Even in those states, however, disclosure would be required for the agreement to serve to waive rights upon divorce.
22. *See* Christopher J. Roman, *Protecting Your Clients' Assets from Their Future Son-in-Law and Daughters-in-Law: The Impact of Evolving Trust Laws on Alimony Awards*, 39 ACTEC L.J. 157 (2013); *See also*, Lisa Brown, *Worried About Your Child's Inheritance If They Divorce? A Trust Can Be Your Answer*, Kiplinger (Apr. 16, 2021), http://www.kiplinger.com/retirement/estate-planning/602612/worried-about-your-childs-inheritance-if-they-divorce-a-trust-can.
23. *See* Roman, *supra* note 22.
24. Trusts provide protection against creditors of trust beneficiaries only while the assets are held in the trust. Once trust assets are distributed to the beneficiary, the assets lose their protected status.

25. *See e.g.*, Berlinger v. Casselberry, 133 So. 3d 961 (Fla. 2d Dist. Ct. App. 2013).
26. Uniform Premarital and Marital Agreements Act, Prefatory Note (Nat'l Conf. of Comm'rs on Unif. State Laws 2012).
27. Jeff Landers, *Can A Prenup Or A Postnup With An Infidelity Clause Deter A Husband From Cheating?*, FORBES.COM (Mar. 13, 2014), http://www.forbes.com/sites/jefflanders/2014/03/13/can-a-prenup-or-a-postnup-with-an-infidelity-clause-deter-a-husband-from-cheating/#20f293e97328.
28. Bill Hoffmann, *Zeta Wins if Michael Sins—Douglas to Pay $5M if Unfaithful: Report*, N.Y. POST (Jan. 10, 2001), http://nypost.com/2001/01/10/zeta-win-if-michael-sins-douglas-to-pay-5m-if-unfaithful-report/.
29. *See* Elisabeth R. Feeny, *Lifestyle Clauses and Prenuptial Agreements*, MAVRRIDESLAW.COM (Feb. 19, 2015), http://mavrideslaw.com/lifestyle-clauses-prenuptial-agreements/.
30. Rachel Gillet, *The Surprising 'Prenups' of America's Richest Couples*, BUS. INSIDER (Nov. 30, 2017), http://www.businessinsider.com/surprising-prenups-americas-richest-couples-2017-11.
31. *See* Jill Brooke, *No-Child Clauses More Frequent in Prenuptial Pacts*, CHIC. TRIB. (Oct. 23, 2002), *available at* http://articles.chicagotribune.com/2002-10-23/features/0210230012_1_prenuptial-pacts-prenuptial-agreements-younger.
32. *See* Brad Reid, *Common Prenuptial Agreement Legal Issues,* HUFF POST (Feb. 18, 2018), https://www.huffingtonpost.com/brad-reid/common-prenuptial-agreeme_b_6706898.html.
33. *See* Zummo v. Zummo, 574 A.2d 1130 (Pa. Super. Ct. 1990).
34. Pon Staff, *What Are the Three Basic Types of Dispute Resolution? What to Do About Mediation, Arbitration, and Litigation*, DAILY BLOG (Apr. 25, 2024), http://www.pon.harvard.edu/daily/dispute-resolution/what-are-the-three-basic-types-of-dispute-resolution-what-to-know-about-mediation-arbitration-and-litigation/.
35. *See* Julia Marsh and Priscilla DeGregory, *Chris Rock's Wife Seeking Huge Payout in Divorce*, PAGE SIX, (June 15, 2015, 12:30 AM) http://pagesix.com/2015/06/15/chris-rocks-estranged-wife-seeking-huge-payout-in-divorce/; *See also*, Deborah Hope Wayne, *Should My Prenup Include a Sunset Clause*, FAM. L. MATTERS BLOG (Mar. 30, 2024), http://www.familylawmatters-blog.com/should-my-prenup-include-a-sunset-clause/ (explaining that a sunset clause is "one that specifies a date or trigger event in which certain terms in the prenuptial agreement would expire").
36. *See* Johnathan E. Fields, *Forbidden Provisions in Prenuptial Agreements: Legal And Practical Considerations For The Matrimonial Lawyer*, 21 J. OF THE AM. ACAD. OF MATRIM. LAW., 413, 415 (2008); *See also*, Daniel Liberto, *What Is an Escalator Clause? Definition, How It Works and Example*, INVESTOPEDIA, http://www.investopedia.com/terms/e/escalatorclause.asp (Apr. 30, 2023).
37. *See generally* Christopher J. Roman, *Protecting your Clients' Assets from their Future Son-in-Law and Daughters-in-Law: The Impact of Evolving Trust Laws on Alimony Awards*, 39 ACTEC L. J. 157, 159–60 (2013).
38. *See* Jeffrey Pennell, *Third Party Trusts in Divorce*, CENT. ARIZ. EST. PLAN. COUNCIL, http://www.caepc.org/assets/Councils/CentralArizona-AZ/library/Trusts%20in%20Divorce.pdf.

39. Karl Pillemer et al., *Mothers' Differentiation and Depressive Symptoms Among Adult Children*, 72 J. Marriage & Fam. 333 (2010), https://doi.org/10.1111/j.1741-3737.2010.00703.x.
40. *Knives Out* (Lionsgate 2019) (film dramatizing a fictional dispute among siblings following the death of a wealthy patriarch and a contested will).
41. Marty-Nelson, Gilmore, and Rodriguez-Dod, 824-3rd T.M., *Testamentary Capacity, Undue Influence, and Validity of Wills*, A-58.
42. *Id.*
43. *Id.*
44. *Id.*
45. *In re Carpenter's Estate*, 253 So. 2d 697, 702 (Fla. 1971).
46. Fla. Stat. Ann. § 733.107 (West 2024).
47. *See e.g.*, Fla. Stat. Ann. § 732.505 and § 732.506 (West 2024).

Chapter 9

1. Michelle Megna, *Pet Ownership Statistics 2025*, Forbes Advisor, http://www.forbes.com/advisor/pet-insurance/pet-ownership-statistics/ (May 22, 2025).
2. https://www.dogsbite.org/dog-bite-statistics-quick-statistics.php
3. Lynn A. Epstein, *There Are No Bad Dogs, Only Bad Owners: Replacing Strict Liability with a Negligence Standard in Dog Bite Cases*, 13 Animal L. 129, 131 (2006).
4. Fla. Stat. Ann. § 767.04 (West 2024).
5. Epstein, *supra*, note 3.
6. *Hahn v. Kordula*, 5 Kan. App. 142, 48 P. 896, 896 (1897).
7. Palm Beach County Ordinance 98-22 §4-4(a).
8. *See Butler v. Frieden*, 208 Va. 352, 353, 158 S.E.2d 121, 122 (1967).
9. *Id.*
10. Sheldon F. Kurtz & Alice Noble-Allgire, *The Revised Uniform Residential Landlord and Tenant Act: A Perspective from the Reporters*, 52 Real Prop. Tr. & Est. L.J. 417, 507 (2018).
11. *See* Kaycee Miller, *Security Deposit Laws, Limits & Deadlines—State Guide for Rentals*, RentecDirect.com (Mar. 16, 2018), https://www.rentecdirect.com/blog/security-deposit-state-guide/.
12. *See* Laura Agadoni, *The Ultimate Guide to "Normal Wear and Tear*, Landlordology.com (Nov. 1 2017), available at https://www.landlordology.com/normal-wear-and-tear/.
13. Ariz. Rev. Stat. Ann. § 33-1321; Ark. Code § 18-16-305.
14. Mich. Comp. Laws § 554.608.
15. Ky. Rev. Stat. § 383.580.
16. *Id.*
17. Kurtz *supra* note 10 at 524.
18. N.D. Cent. Cod. § 47-16-07.1.
19. 765 Ill. Comp. Stat. Ann. 710/1.
20. Fla. Stat. § 83.49.

21. Plea Bargain, CORNELL L. SCH. LEGAL INFO. INST., https://www.law.cornell.edu/wex/plea_bargain (last visited May 27, 2025).
22. Lindsey Devers, *Plea and Charge Bargaining: Research Summary*, Bureau of Justice Assistance, U.S. Dep't of Justice (Jan. 24, 2011), https://bja.ojp.gov/sites/g/files/xyckuh186/files/media/document/pleabargainingresearchsummary.pdf
23. In the Shadows: A Review of the Research on Plea Bargaining, VERA INST. OF JUSTICE 2 (2020).
24. *See generally* Fed. R. Crim. P. 11(c).
25. *See generally United States v. Stockton,* 788 F.2d 210, 217 (4th Cir. 1986).

Index

A

Alternative Options, 11, 23, 64, 111, 203, 206
Anchor, 47, 48
Anchoring Bias, 47, 48
Anger in Negotiations, 36, 55, 59, 60, 199
Anticipated Questions, 11, 28, 29, 31
Arbitration, 68, 138, 139, 219
Arms-length Negotiation, 12, 16, 24, 33, 42, 60
Arms-open Negotiation, 12, 16, 24, 33, 42, 60, 121, 144
Arranging the Negotiation, 5, 33, 99, 106, 111, 117, 143, 147, 148
Artificial Intelligence (AI), 3, 18, 26, 69, 70, 83, 84, 93, 96, 200
Authority
  Lack of Authority, 58
  Limited Authority, 58

B

Balance of Power, 12, 14, 15, 48, 92, 99, 117
Bargaining Tactics, 39, 56, 212
BATNA (Best Alternative to a Negotiated Agreement), 23 24, 64, 199, 203, 206, 209
Behavior, 6, 36, 71–73, 75–78, 80, 81, 83, 101, 135, 144, 211, 213
Bias, 6, 47, 48, 56, 80, 81, 83, 84, 212, 213
Body Language, 35, 37, 210
Bracket, 49, 50
Business Acquisition, 4, 23, 87, 88, 101, 107
Business Relationship, 87–118

C

Capacity, 30, 119, 120, 149, 151, 152, 154, 172, 220
Changes in Behavior, 76
Closed Ended Questions, 28, 29, 31
Common Law States, 122–125, 127, 128, 130
Community Property, 122, 123, 126–130, 134, 146, 160, 164, 173, 217, 218
Competitive Negotiator, 16
Complimentary Questions, 29
Concessions, 4, 5, 11, 13–15, 18, 24–27, 47, 50–53, 61–65, 72, 74, 106, 144, 149, 199, 203, 206, 207, 211
Confidential Information, 7, 30, 88, 99, 101–106, 110, 111, 116, 117, 120, 141, 143, 147, 154, 156, 159, 186, 193, 198
Confidentiality, 7, 35, 70, 101–103, 109, 149
Confidentiality Agreements, 4, 70, 101–106, 109
Confrontational Questions, 29, 31
Contingent Concessions, 52
Cooperative Negotiator, 16
Counteroffers, 5, 11, 24, 26, 27, 41, 46, 47, 49–52, 63, 65, 72, 74, 99, 101, 106, 111, 117, 144, 146, 149, 150, 159, 186, 193, 198, 199, 203, 206, 207
Covid-19 Pandemic, 3, 34, 37–38
Cream Puff Negotiators, 75

D

Deception, 35, 72
Demands, 4, 13, 14, 16, 17, 28, 46, 56, 73, 94, 155, 160, 197
Discriminatory Conduct, 101
Distributive Bargaining, 17, 82
Divorce, 20, 121–124, 127, 128, 130, 132–140, 142, 146, 149, 158, 160, 161, 167, 174–176, 178, 217–220
Dog Bites, 182, 183, 185
Drafting the Agreement, 68, 69

E

Email Negotiation, 36, 37
Embezzlement, 181, 193–197
Emotions, 36, 60, 62, 83, 200, 211
Equitable Distribution, 123, 124, 130, 133, 140, 142, 146, 160
Equity, 6, 30, 56, 71, 80, 91, 100, 103–106, 111, 118, 124, 134, 145, 150, 208, 215, 216
Ethics, 6, 7, 30, 56, 71–73, 75, 78, 80, 100, 106, 111, 118, 145, 150, 208, 210, 212–214
Executing the Agreement, 67, 70, 100, 106, 111, 117, 144, 149
Extreme Opening Demand, 16, 56
Extreme Opening Offer, 56

F

Fairness, 6, 65, 84, 124
Family Relationship, 12, 62, 97, 110, 119–179
First Impressions, 210
First Offer, 24, 25, 47, 48, 50, 51, 65, 210
    Anchor, effect of, 47–48
Fraud, 30, 75, 150, 178, 212

G

Gender, 81–83, 89–92, 101, 212–215
Gendered Expectations, 91
Goal, 4, 11, 12, 17, 19–22, 24, 49, 50, 96, 119, 136, 143, 200, 203, 205, 206, 209
    Highest Realistic, 24, 48, 96, 100

H

Highest Realistic Goal, 24, 48, 96, 100
Homeowners' Association, 87, 112–116, 217

I

Ice-breaking, 34, 45–47, 49, 55, 63, 99, 106, 117, 143, 148
Identifying the Relationship, 11–13
    Arms-length, 12
    Arms-open, 12, 13, 145
    Balance of Power, 12, 14, 15, 48, 92, 99, 117
    Personality Styles, 12, 15, 16
Identity, 81–83, 91
Inconsistent Statements, 76
Information, 21–31
    Asking and answering questions, 29, 55, 62, 65, 77, 94
    Gathering, 29
Initial offer, 47, 50, 97, 196
In-person Negotiation, 33, 34, 36, 37, 39, 43
Integrative Bargaining, 16, 17, 81

L

Lack of Authority, 58
Letting Go or Resolving, 5, 60, 61, 100, 106, 111, 117, 144, 149, 207
Lies, 4, 73–75, 78, 212
    Physical Signs, 77
    Responses, 71, 77–78
    Uncovering, 75
    Unethical Behavior, 6, 71, 72, 75, 101
Lifestyle provisions in a Prenup, 135, 138, 139
Listening, 53, 54, 211

M

Mediation, 68, 114, 138, 139, 156, 212, 219
Mentors, 84
Mindfulness, 83
Minimum Acceptable Level, 11, 19, 21, 22, 95, 96, 203, 205, 206

Misrepresentation, 30, 75, 78, 210, 212
Model Rules of Professional Conduct, 73, 212
Multi-party, 4, 35, 88, 116–118, 154, 155, 157, 159, 205

N

Negotiation Bracket, 49
Negotiation Planning, 17, 24, 28
Negotiation Relationship Arms-length, 12
Negotiation Relationship Arms-open, 12, 13, 145
Non-disclosure, 87, 88, 101–104, 106, 146, 216

O

Objective Criteria, 17–19, 24, 46, 48–51, 55–57, 64, 65, 69, 93, 96, 144, 149, 203, 205, 207
Offer, 3, 4, 7, 12, 17, 24–27, 29, 34, 36, 41–43, 45, 47–53, 55–59, 63–66, 72–74, 81, 87, 88, 90, 92–100, 103, 104, 106, 117, 139, 144, 145, 149, 150, 158, 182, 194–196, 199, 200, 203, 206, 210, 211
  Counteroffer, 25–27, 36, 47, 49–51, 64
  Extreme Opening, 56
  First Offer, 24, 25, 47, 48, 50, 51, 65, 210
  Opening Offer, 24, 25, 27, 45, 47, 48, 56, 65, 99, 203, 206
  Unreciprocated Offer, 51
Optimal Realistic Goal, 11, 19, 20, 22, 24, 50, 200, 203, 205, 206

P

Paltering, 73, 74, 77–79
Personality Styles, 12, 15, 16
Personality Traits, 59
  Anger, 36, 55, 59, 60, 199
  Sadness, 59
Phone Negotiations, 35, 36, 38
Physical Signs of Lying, 77
Platforms for Negotiation, 34, 38–39, 42–43, 45–46
Plea Bargaining, 4, 193–196, 198, 221
Post Negotiation Self-Reflection Worksheet, 88, 120, 141, 154, 181
Power, 4, 12, 14, 15, 23, 39, 48, 52, 72, 92, 99, 113, 117, 120, 121, 124
  Balance of, 12, 14, 15, 48, 92, 99, 117
Prenuptial Agreements, 119–121, 130, 131, 134–137, 139, 141, 150, 217, 219

Q

Questions, 7, 11, 13, 21, 28–31, 42, 43, 53–57, 62, 64, 65, 77–79, 90, 94, 99, 111, 117, 124, 143–145, 155, 204, 206, 207, 209, 211
  Closed-ended, 31
  Complimentary, 29
  Confrontational, 29, 31
  Interspersed, 29, 53, 54, 99
  Open-ended, 28, 29, 31, 54, 64

R

Reciprocal Concessions, 46, 51–52
Relationships, 3, 4, 12, 66, 81, 87, 105, 111, 116–118, 119, 120, 132, 142, 153, 205, 206
  Arms-length, 12–14
  Arms-open, 12–14
  Business, 87
  Family, 3, 12, 22, 31, 62, 63, 94, 97, 110, 119, 120, 125–127, 132–134, 136, 137, 140, 151, 154, 156–158, 161, 162, 173, 182, 190, 199
  Friends, 3, 13, 15, 40, 136
Reputation, 16, 23, 57, 72, 75, 97, 98, 116, 117, 199
Research, 7, 11, 14–19, 22–24, 26, 35, 39, 43, 46–48, 51, 52, 63, 65, 69, 81, 88, 89, 93, 96, 108, 141, 149, 181, 189, 203, 205, 213–216, 221
Resolving, 5, 60, 61, 62, 75, 100, 106, 111, 117, 144, 145, 149, 151, 194, 207
Responses to Anticipated Questions, 11, 28, 29, 31

S

Salary Negotiation, 14, 48, 92, 93, 95, 97, 99, 215
  Expectation relating to, 93
  Federal Law, 90, 101
  Local Law, 183
  Previous pay relating to, 92
  State Law, 90, 114, 122, 125, 126, 133, 138, 161, 172, 188, 189, 214
  Wages and gender, 89, 90, 91–92
Salary Offers, 87–90, 93, 94, 96, 100
Scheduling, 34, 64, 66
  Follow up, 28, 35, 53, 54, 77, 79
  Initial negotiation, 33–35, 42, 45–50, 63, 88, 120, 131, 141, 143, 145, 146, 148, 150, 154, 181
Security Deposits, 187, 189, 190, 192
Settlement, 4, 20, 25, 30, 49, 50, 55, 57, 58, 64, 67–70, 73, 100, 116, 117, 156, 162, 174, 175, 183, 186, 194, 209, 210
Social Networks, 84
Splitting the Difference, 64–66, 211
Strategies for Employees, 95
Strategies for Employers, 92, 215
Sunset or Escalator provisions in a prenup, 139, 142, 143

T

TABLE Method, 5–8, 9, 71, 85, 87, 88, 119–121, 141, 154, 181, 193, 199
Tactics, 5, 18, 37, 39, 55, 56, 60, 72, 107, 207, 211, 212
Tactical Planning, 5, 7, 11, 15, 17, 19, 23, 25, 33, 47, 51–55, 63, 65, 72, 81, 83, 88, 94, 99, 101, 106, 107, 110, 111, 116–118, 120, 141, 143, 146, 147, 149–151, 154, 156, 157, 159, 181, 186, 187, 193, 198, 199, 203, 205, 207
Tactical Planning Worksheet, 5, 7, 11, 51, 52, 54, 55, 63, 65, 88, 99, 101, 106, 107, 110, 111, 116–118, 120, 141, 143, 146, 147, 150, 151, 154, 156, 157, 159, 181, 186, 187, 193, 198, 199, 203, 205, 207
Take it or Leave it, 14, 56–57
Testamentary Capacity, 120, 151, 152, 154, 220
Text Messaging, 5, 39–41
Threats, 16, 57, 118
Time Constraints, 59, 62, 64, 68, 110, 148
Trade Secrets, 101–104, 106
Trusts, 20, 133, 140, 167, 219, 220
Truth Emphasizers, 77

U

Unconscious Bias, 80
Undue Influence, 119, 120, 151–154, 178, 220
Unequal Balance of Power, 48

V

Videoconference, 5, 33–35, 37–40, 66, 106, 148

W

Wages, 89–92, 114, 116, 126
  Salary Negotiation, 14, 48, 92, 93, 95, 97, 99, 215
Wills, 132, 141, 151, 155, 220